Cambridge Elementary Classics

XENOPHON

ANABASIS BOOK III

The Route is shewn thus ————

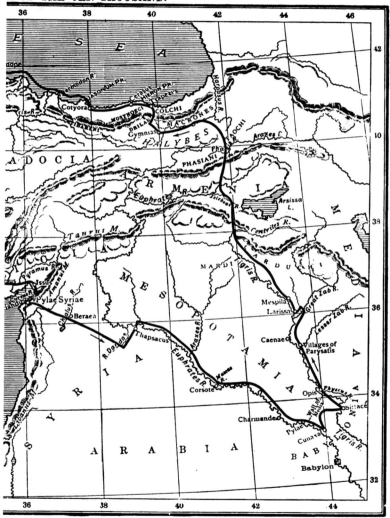

XENOPHON

ANABASIS BOOK III

Edited by

G. M. EDWARDS

Cambridge:
at the University Press
1953

CAMBRIDGE
UNIVERSITY PRESS

University Printing House, Cambridge CB2 8BS, United Kingdom

Published in the United States of America by Cambridge University Press, New York

Cambridge University Press is part of the University of Cambridge.

It furthers the University's mission by disseminating knowledge in the pursuit of education, learning and research at the highest international levels of excellence.

www.cambridge.org
Information on this title: www.cambridge.org/9781107655058

© Cambridge University Press 1897

First edition 1897
First published 1897
Reprinted 1913, 1933, 1953
First paperback edition 2014

A catalogue record for this publication is available from the British Library

ISBN 978-1-107-65505-8 Paperback

PREFACE.

PORTIONS of Layard's *Nineveh and Babylon* provide us with an excellent commentary on the topography of the Third Book of the *Anabasis*. Some of his most useful passages are quoted in my notes. I am also indebted to the works of Grote, Mure, E. Curtius, Kühner, Rehdantz, Macmichael, R. W. Taylor, Pretor, and Nall. Mr Nall's book contains much useful information, especially on military matters. In the text I have adopted only a few of the alterations proposed by the new school of Xenophontean critics. These scholars appear to me to be far too much enamoured of the drastic methods of Cobet. Arnold Hug's edition is of great value; but I cannot think that he has given us a final text, as some English editors of the Anabasis appear to believe.

The student is advised to read sections 2–5 of the Introduction before beginning the Greek text of the Third Book.

G. M. E.

CAMBRIDGE,
 May, 1897.

CONTENTS.

INTRODUCTION.

§ 1. EARLY LIFE OF XENOPHON.

XENOPHON was the son of Gryllus an Athenian of the deme of Ercheia. Our information about his early life is extremely meagre and uncertain. The date of · his birth is entirely a matter of conjecture ; the slender evidence available seems to point to the year 435 B.C. The date usually given, 444 B.C., is unquestionably incorrect.

In his boyhood he made the acquaintance of Socrates, who, it is said, one day met the young Xenophon in the street and proceeded to catechise him after his fashion, enquiring of him where different articles could be obtained. He then asked him where men were made good and noble ; and, the boy being unable to answer his question, Socrates bade him follow him and see. Henceforth Xenophon became the devoted disciple of the philosopher, whose *Memorabilia* (*Memoirs*) he afterwards wrote. When still a boy, he was present with his master at the banquet given by Callias in honour of Autolycus, 'Victor among the boys' at the Panathenaic games. The story of his preservation from death by Socrates at the battle of Delium in 424 B.C. is evidently a fiction, like many other stories in Greek literary biography.

When Xenophon reached the age for military service, Athens was suffering severely from the stress of the Peloponnesian War ; and he doubtless took part in the defence of the city down to its capture by Sparta in 404 B.C. He seems to have belonged to the 'Knights.' Several of his books manifest a keen interest in horses and horsemanship. Any one familiar with Aristophanes' picture of the 'Thousand good Knights' and their aristocratic contempt for the demagogue will to some extent appreciate that strange feature in the life of Xenophon, his antipathy to the Athenian democracy and his enthusiastic admiration for Sparta and all things Spartan. Still it is very remarkable that one who evidently owed his success in life mainly to his training in democratic Athens should display a marked preference for the Spartan system of education and government.

Before Xenophon left Athens in 401 B.C. he had probably completed the first two books of his *Hellenica* or *History of Greece*, a continuation of the unfinished work of Thucydides. These books describe the closing scenes of the great war, the tyranny of the Thirty and the restoration of the democracy by Thrasybulus in 403 B.C. The extremely interesting essay *on the Athenian Constitution*, ascribed to Xenophon, is the earliest remaining specimen of Attic Prose ; it must have been written when Xenophon was quite a boy, and cannot be his work. It is now generally thought to have been an anonymous publication ; and different critics have suggested Alcibiades, Critias, and even Thucydides as possible authors of the treatise.

§ 2. CYRUS AND THE GREEKS.

Cyrus, the younger and abler of the two surviving sons of Darius II King of Persia and his queen Parysatis, came into prominence in 408 B.C., when at the early age of seventeen he was appointed Satrap, or Viceroy, of Lydia, Phrygia and Cappadocia and Commander-in-chief of the royal troops in those parts. He was thus practically supreme in Asia Minor. In 404 B.C. Darius died before the Queen could obtain from him a declaration in favour of Cyrus on the ground that the elder son Artaxerxes was born before his father's accession,—an argument which in old days Atossa had advanced on behalf of Xerxes. Cyrus had hastened to his father's deathbed at Susa only to find himself completely disappointed in his expectation of succeeding to the throne, and to witness the accession of his brother Artaxerxes II. Further, Cyrus nearly lost his life on a charge of treason preferred against him by his enemy Tissaphernes, who had accompanied him to Susa. Tissaphernes was Satrap of Caria and had rights of sovereignty over a number of Greek towns in Ionia ; and Cyrus had provoked his hostility by scheming to bring these under his own control. So now on the evidence of a priest, the prince's spiritual director, Tissaphernes accused Cyrus of conspiring to assassinate the King on the occasion of his accession. Cyrus barely escaped death on the intercession of his mother Parysatis, who threw herself between the royal guards and her favourite son. Eventually he was allowed to return with undiminished powers to his government in Asia Minor ; Artaxerxes hoping to conquer his brother by this generous treatment.

Meanwhile Cyrus, nursing the bitterest feelings of hatred and revenge, conceived the brilliant idea of collecting a Greek force, in addition to his large Asiatic army, to fight Artaxerxes for the throne. The circumstances of the time were highly favourable to this policy ; for at the end of the Peloponnesian War began the rise of mercenary troops in the Hellenic world. During the long years of that war many Greeks had become professional soldiers, and, being unwilling to return to the quiet life of citizens, were ready to hire themselves out as mercenaries. The tyranny of the oligarchies established, under the Spartan Empire, in the Greek cities had driven many from their homes ; while the general demoralisation caused by a long period of war and the dissolution of family ties hastened the decay of patriotism and kindled the passion for a roving life of profit and adventure.

Cyrus saw his opportunity ; despatching his agents in all directions, he drew together to his court at Sardis many Greeks of ruined fortunes. A born leader of men, he dazzled the Greek imagination by his brilliant personality, his youthful

enthusiasm and his open-handed generosity. Hellenic patriotism was practically dead ; and here, apparently at the dawn
of a new era, was a prince with a great future, having at his dis-
posal 'the gold of Asia and the men of Hellas.' He demanded
no sacrifices,—so ran his magnificent invitation to Sparta,—
without ample rewards. The soldier who came on foot should
receive a horse; he who came on horse-back, a chariot and
pair. Owners of fields should be made masters of villages ; and
masters of villages lords of cities. So successful was this policy
that early in 401 B.C. Cyrus had concentrated at Sardis a force
of 8000 men, whom his Greek officers had collected in the
Peloponnese, Thessaly, Ionia and elsewhere.

§ 3. XENOPHON, PROXENUS AND CYRUS.

Among the Greek officers whom Cyrus had attracted to
Sardis was the Theban Proxenus, an old friend of Xenophon,
who in the Second Book gives a sympathetic account of his
noble and ambitious nature. From his description of Proxenus
as a disciple of the rhetorician Gorgias, and as one who recognised the importance of culture as an element of distinction
in public life, we may infer that the bond which united the two
friends was of a literary character. Moreover we are told
elsewhere that Xenophon, who was a few years older than
Proxenus, had acted as his tutor. Hence it appears probable
that Cyrus wished to secure, through Proxenus, the services of
Xenophon as a *civil* officer to aid him in his ambitious schemes.
Xenophon expressly tells us that he joined the expedition *neither*
as general nor captain nor soldier.

Early in 401 B.C. Xenophon, as he tells us at the beginning
of the Third Book, received from Proxenus a letter, in which
he undertook to introduce him to Cyrus, adding the cynical
remark that he considered the friendship of such a patron
was *worth more to himself than his native city*,—a striking
illustration of the decay of patriotism during this period.
He communicated the proposal of Proxenus to his master
Socrates, who feared that his young friend might provoke

the hostility of the democracy, if he threw in his lot with one who had been the bitter enemy of Athens and had actually furnished Sparta with the means of crushing her. He accordingly advised him to consult the oracle at Delphi. Thither Xenophon repaired. But, instead of asking the God, 'Shall I go to Sardis or shall I forbear?' he put the narrower question : 'Having a journey in view, to which of the gods must I offer prayers and sacrifices in order to make it propitious?' The oracle indicated to him the proper deities. Socrates, however, was displeased with his disciple because he had not submitted the question with perfect frankness. 'Nevertheless,' he added, 'since you have elected to put the question in your own way, you must act on the answer vouchsafed.' So Xenophon set sail after duly performing the necessary rites. Probably he was not sorry to leave his native city; for Athens under the restored democracy cannot have been an agreeable residence for a member of the Knights, the class which had been the chief support of the atrocious tyranny of the Thirty.

He reached Sardis in the spring of 401 B.C., and found Cyrus and Proxenus preparing to set out on an expedition directed, so it was alleged, against the Pisidians, a refractory robber tribe in a distant part of the prince's satrapy. They both expressed a strong wish that Xenophon should accompany them. He was deceived by their statements, for which, he adds, Proxenus was not responsible ; for neither Proxenus nor any other Greek officer except .learchus, the intimate friend of Cyrus, had at present any suspicion that the expedition was really directed against the King of Persia.

§ 4. THE ANABASIS. CYRUS THE HERO OF BOOK I. HE MARCHES FROM SARDIS TO CUNAXA WHERE HE IS KILLED IN BATTLE.

The title Κύρου ’Ανάβασις can in strictness be applied to the First Book only, which describes the march *up country* from the west of Asia Minor into Babylonia. This occupied about six months. The Second Book begins the account of the Κατάβασις or the journey *down* to the Euxine Sea.

In March 401 B.C. Cyrus had completed his preparations. The 8000 Greek troops now concentrated at Sardis he placed under the command of his Spartan general Clearchus, an outlaw from his native city, having been condemned to death by the Lacedaemonian authorities for disobedience to their orders. The Asiatic troops of Cyrus, numbering 100,000, were commanded by his friend Ariaeus the Persian. Cyrus still told the Greeks that the object of his enterprise was merely to secure the frontiers of his province against the Pisidian free-booters ; and, in order to deceive Artaxerxes, he gave out that the Greek force which he had collected was designed for service against his jealous rival, Tissaphernes, Satrap of Caria. But Tissaphernes suspected the real designs of Cyrus, and, when he heard of the magnitude of the prince's army, started with all speed to inform the Great King, who at once began his preparations.

The route of Cyrus from Sardis to Cunaxa can be easily seen upon the Map. The chief events of the march may be briefly mentioned here. At Colossae Cyrus was overtaken by one of his Greek generals, Menon the Thessalian, at the head of 1500 troops. At Celaenae he halted for thirty days, waiting for further reinforcements which were brought by Clearchus and Sophaenetus. After their arrival a review was held, the Greek force now amounting to over 13,000 men. At Caystri Campus we have the interesting meeting of Cyrus with Epyaxa, wife of Syennesis, prince of Cilicia and a vassal of Persia. She provided Cyrus with a large sum of money for the payment of his troops, and accompanied him for some way on his march. At Tyriaeum a grand review was held in her honour. The almost impregnable pass, called the Cilician Gates, was occupied by Syennesis ; but his resistance was a mere sham, and at Tarsus he furnished Cyrus with troops. It was at Tarsus that the difficulties of Cyrus with his Greeks first arose. Suspecting the real object of the expedition, they refused to advance. After much discussion they agreed to send to Cyrus a deputation including Clearchus, who was not known to be in the secrets of the prince. Cyrus replied that he was really marching against Abrocomas, Satrap of Syria, who was encamped on the Euphrates, and promised the Greeks additional pay. With these assurances they were satisfied.

At the port of Issus Cyrus received further reinforcements brought by his fleet, amongst them 700 Spartan hoplites under the command of Cheirisophus, sent, it was said, by the Lacedaemonian government. The number of his Greek force now reached 14,000. Abrocomas, who was in command of 300,000 men, seems to have been alarmed by the rapid progress of the invader and fled from the Syrian coast into the interior, abandoning three defensible positions in succession:—(1) the Syrian Gates, (2) the pass of Beilan over Mount Amanus, and (3) the passage of the Euphrates. At Thapsacus, just before crossing the Euphrates, Cyrus at last publicly informed the Greeks that he was leading them to Babylon to fight against the Great King. The announcement was received with loud murmurs; but the soldiers were appeased by the promise of a liberal donation to be given to each man on arrival at Babylon. At Charmandé a serious dispute arose between Clearchus and Menon, in which the troops of the two generals joined. The intervention of Proxenus as peacemaker was unsuccessful; and the gravity of the situation was only allayed by an appeal from Cyrus himself.

Hitherto Cyrus had been advancing with overweening self-confidence; for he had been allowed to pass without resistance all the natural obstacles of which the Persians might have taken advantage to bar his progress, and now he seemed to think that victory would be his without a struggle. This feeling was only increased when, three days after leaving Pylae, he found quite undefended the great trench which Artaxerxes had caused to be dug across the plain for a length of 40 miles. It had been abandoned from some unaccountable panic. Cyrus now imagined that the Persians would never face him in the plains of Babylonia. And when one day early in September his troops were about to halt for their morning meal at the village of Cunaxa, it was announced that a vast Persian host of 900,000 men was approaching in order of battle over the open plain. Cyrus, quite taken by surprise, arranged his forces with all speed. The Greeks under Clearchus were on the right wing resting on the Euphrates; Ariaeus with his Asiatic troops was on the left; and Cyrus surrounded by a body-guard of 600 Persian cavalry was in the centre. So great was the superiority of Artaxerxes in numbers that his centre extended beyond the left wing of the Cyreians.

Just before the battle began, Cyrus ordered Clearchus to attack the Persian centre, because the King was there. But Clearchus, afraid of withdrawing his right from the river and exposing himself to an attack in flank and rear, simply answered that he was taking care that all should be well. He charged the Persian left and routed it almost without a blow; Tissaphernes alone, with his body of horse, not taking part in the general flight. Meanwhile the Persian centre under Artaxerxes began to surround the left wing of Cyrus. Then the reckless prince cried out, 'I see the man'; and rode forward with a mere handful of companions to attack the King who was protected by a body-guard of 6000 horse. Cyrus broke their ranks and hurling his javelin wounded his brother slightly in the breast; but he was immediately surrounded and slain. Next Ariaeus and all the Asiatic troops of Cyrus fled in confusion, and their camp was plundered by the enemy. The Persians were thus victorious both here and in the centre; and Artaxerxes drew up his troops to attack the Greeks, who were unaware of the death of Cyrus. Clearchus gained a second victory; for the Persians fled without awaiting his onset. Thus relieved of all enemies he remained on the field in hopes of hearing tidings of Cyrus. He then returned to his camp, which he found completely plundered. So the Greeks retired supperless to rest; most of them had had no morning meal owing to the early hour at which the battle had begun.

§ 5. THE ANABASIS CONTINUED. CLEARCHUS THE HERO
OF BOOK II. THE GREEKS BEGIN THEIR RETREAT.
THE TREACHEROUS SEIZURE OF THEIR GENERALS BY
TISSAPHERNES.

Early in the morning of the day after the battle of Cunaxa
Clearchus and the other Greek generals decided to march out
and meet Cyrus, whom they supposed to be still alive. On learning the disastrous news the Greeks were deeply grieved. Cyrus,
the one hope of the expedition, was gone, and here they were in
the heart of the Persian empire entirely destitute of resources
and surrounded by treacherous foes. Still, with splendid self-
confidence, as conquerors in the battle of Cunaxa, they proceeded to offer their prize of victory, the Persian throne, to
Ariaeus, who had commanded the Asiatic troops of Cyrus.
He politely declined their invitation ; probably he had already
made up his mind to seek the favour of Artaxerxes and to betray
his brothers in arms. Clearchus seems at first to have placed a
blind confidence in Ariaeus, who undertook to conduct the
Greeks to the sea by a route different from that by which they
had come. Accordingly it was resolved to begin the retreat in
his company.

'This strategy,' says Xenophon, 'was no better than running
away.' 'But Fortune,' he adds, 'proved a nobler strategist';
for they had not proceeded far when they suddenly found
themselves close to the camp of the Persians, who at once
retreated in a panic. This led the Greeks to adopt a bolder
policy. The King, they saw, was evidently alarmed. On
the previous day he had claimed the victory on the ground
that Cyrus was dead, and he had demanded that the Greeks
should surrender their arms; and now he sent envoys to
negotiate a truce. To overawe the Persians who came on this
mission Clearchus arranged a grand display of his forces. It
must be borne in mind that the two great difficulties of the
Greeks now were (1) lack of supplies and (2) ignorance of
routes. This will explain the course of the negotiations which
Xenophon describes.

Tissaphernes next appeared on the scene with another set of envoys. In three days a treaty was concluded, by which arrangements were made for provisioning the Greek force, and the Persians agreed to facilitate their progress with Tissaphernes as guide. Tissaphernes took his departure, the Greeks promising to await his return. Then ensued a fatal delay of twenty days, during which he was absent at the Persian court. Meanwhile, as we learn elsewhere, (1) the Great King had returned to Babylon to celebrate his supposed victory at Cunaxa; (2) he gave to Tissaphernes his daughter's hand and the provinces previously held by Cyrus; and (3) he received from the satrap a promise that the Greeks should be destroyed. At last Tissaphernes returned. The Greeks had already begun to suspect that Ariaeus was playing them false. When the retreat was resumed, there was great distrust between the Greeks and the Persian portion of the Cyreian army; and they kept clear of one another both on the march and in their encampments. They soon approached the so-called 'Median Wall,' and marched on, keeping to the south of it. Then, after crossing two canals connected with the Tigris, they arrived at Sittacé, where the Greeks encamped. But the Persians crossed the river and attempted to alarm the Greeks by intimating that Tissaphernes intended to entrap them by breaking down the bridge. They were evidently afraid that the Greeks might conceive the idea of settling in Babylonia. The Greeks, however, crossed the Tigris and marching along the other bank reached the river Physcus and the town of Opis. Then they continued their march and, after plundering the villages of Queen Parysatis, they arrived at Caenae.

In a few days they reached a river called the Greater Zab. While encamping on its banks, Clearchus attempted to put an end to the constant jealousy and distrust between the Greek and Asiatic troops. Accordingly he consented to a conference with Tissaphernes, who promised that, if the Greek generals would come to his tent, he would give them the name of the treacherous person who was causing all the trouble. On the next day Clearchus went to Tissaphernes accompanied by four

generals, twenty captains and two hundred soldiers. On their
arrival the generals were seized and their companions massacred. Four of the generals, Clearchus, Proxenus, Agias and
Socrates, were taken to the Persian court and soon afterwards
beheaded. The other general Menon, who was the reputed
traitor, was kept alive under torture for a year and then put to
death. After the seizure of the generals, Ariaeus summoned
the Greeks to surrender; but in an indignant and contemptuous
message they declined.

§ 6. The Anabasis continued. Xenophon the hero
of books iii—vii. The journey of the Greeks to
Trapezus. Their subsequent troubles.

Book III.

The situation of the Greeks now seemed more desperate
than ever; Xenophon speaks of it in most pathetic language.
Their spirits were however speedily revived by his own energetic
action. During the night after the disaster he awoke from a
remarkable dream and at once aroused the captains who had
served under Proxenus. In a midnight council of war he urged
them with simple and stirring eloquence to take measures for
the common safety. They at once recognised his fitness for
command and called upon him to fill the place of his friend.
At Xenophon's suggestion, the captains of the other divisions
were convened, and they nominated four other generals. At
daybreak the new generals summoned the soldiers, who met
after the fashion of a Greek Ecclesia and proceeded to discuss
the future conduct of the expedition and to confirm the appoint-
ment of the generals proposed. They had soon risen from
the paralysis of despair to a sense of their national greatness.
The meetings of the Ten Thousand are an exact reproduction
of the citizen-assemblies at home. The army is a wandering
political community; and the national characteristics of the
race are wonderfully brought out in the narrative of the
Retreat.

It is very remarkable that an Athenian should have exercised a commanding influence over the Ten Thousand. For Athens was now unpopular in Greece, especially in the Peloponnese ; and a large majority of the soldiers were Peloponnesians, more than half being Arcadians or Achaeans. Xenophon was almost the only Athenian taking part in the expedition, and he had come 'neither as general nor captain nor soldier.' His extraordinary rise to power is doubtless due to the Athenian democratic training, which had given him flexibility and resource and, above all, persuasive eloquence. He displays throughout a marvellous faculty of tactful dealing with mixed multitudes and embarrassing circumstances ; and possesses in Athenian perfection the threefold power of thought and speech and action. 'The Athenian alone,' says Dr Curtius, 'possessed that superiority of culture which was necessary for giving order and self-control to the band of warriors barbarised by their selfish life, and for enabling him to serve them in the greatest variety of situations as spokesman, as general and as negotiator. And to him it was essentially due that, in spite of their unspeakable trials, through hostile tribes and desolate snow-ranges, 8000 Greeks in the end reached the coast.'

The Greeks began their march in a hollow square designed to protect the light-armed troops, camp-followers and baggage. They crossed the Great Zab River, strangely enough without any molestation from the enemy. Their route lay over the plain to the east of the Tigris, in a course, roughly speaking, parallel with that river. Soon they began to suffer severely from the attacks of the Persian cavalry under Mithradates, who continually harassed their rear, so that the Greeks spent the greater part of one day in marching three miles. In order to repel these embarrassing attacks, the generals organised a small force of cavalry, slingers and javelin-men. On the morrow these light troops distinguished themselves by an effective attack on the Persian cavalry, who fled in dismay. During the next two days the Greeks reached the ruins of two cities, called by Xenophon Larissa and Mespila, which Sir Austen Layard has identified as portions of the once colossal Nineveh.

Tissaphernes now came up with a large army, which enveloped the Greeks in flank and rear. In spite of courageous efforts on the part of the newly-organised light troops, for the next four days the Greeks suffered considerably in many skirmishes during their marches over the open plain.

After this they reached hilly ground, where they found marching in a hollow square to be very inconvenient ; so they decided to give up this formation in favour of a new order of march, which Xenophon describes at length, though he fails to make the details as clear as we could wish. The Greeks soon reached some villages well supplied with provisions, near the modern town of Zakhu. Here they rested for three days ; after which they descended again into the plain. When Tissaphernes proceeded to harass them once more, they halted and repelled the Persian cavalry with ease. During the following night they made such rapid progress that the enemy were unable to overtake them for the next two days. After this the Persians, who had made a forced march by night, suddenly appeared in advance of the Greeks on a mountain-spur commanding their route. Then ensued a long and exciting engagement on the hills, in which the Greeks gained the victory and Xenophon shewed great prowess. After the battle the Greeks encamped in some well-stocked villages on the bank of the Tigris ; and they suffered but little from the desultory attacks which the enemy still continued to make upon them.

The Greeks, who were now in the neighbourhood of Jezireh, had reached a very critical point in their journey. On their left was the Tigris, which they had no means of crossing, especially in face of a Persian army on the western bank ; and in front rose the Carduchian mountains, which, coming close down to the river's edge, rendered further progress along the eastern bank quite impracticable. The generals saw that their only possible course was to enter the inhospitable region of northern Kurdistan and to fight their way across the mountains into Armenia.

Dr Adolf Holm, the most recent historian of Greece, states

that the Spartan Cheirisophus was commander-in-chief at this time, Xenophon acting as his adviser. This is an error, doubtless due to a misinterpretation of chapter ii, § 37 (see note). The Greeks evidently had no commander-in-chief at present. All arrangements were made by the board of generals in consultation ; 'it seemed good to the generals' is a frequent phrase. Later on at Harmené (VI. i. 32) Cheirisophus was appointed commander-in-chief ; but he held office for less than a week (VI. ii. 12).

The events recorded in the Third Book occupied about three weeks, probably in the months of October and November, 401 B.C.

Books IV—VII.

'The sea ! The sea !' was the triumphant cry of the Greeks, when the Euxine burst upon their view early in March 400 B.C. after five months of weary marching and fighting. In two days they reached the Greek colony of Trapezus, where they rested for a month, fondly imagining that all their troubles were over and that they could easily return to their homes by sea. They were bitterly disappointed. Sparta was supreme in the Grecian world, and her officials on the Euxine refused to provide the Cyreians with means for their return. After great difficulties they at last reached Byzantium. There, owing to their cruel treatment by the Spartan admiral Anaxibius, they resumed their profession of mercenaries, accepting the offer of the Theban Coeratidas, who promised them ample rewards if they would undertake a campaign in Thrace under his leadership. This agreement soon fell to the ground ; and in 399 B.C. we find them in the service of the Thracian prince Seuthes, assisting him to subdue some rebel tribes. They fought for two months ; but met with cruel injustice as their reward.

Now, however, came a complete change in the policy of Sparta, which determined to support the Greek cities in Asia Minor against the satraps Tissaphernes and Pharnabazus. This meant war with Persia. Thimbron, the Spartan general,

who was sent into Ionia, finding himself in want of rein-
forcements, invited to his aid Xenophon and the remnant of the
Cyreians, whose numbers had now dwindled away to 6000.
Smarting under the treatment they had just received from
Seuthes, they obeyed the summons with alacrity. Xenophon
crossed over into Asia and conducted his troops over Mount
Ida to Pergamus. 'Then,' he says in the last words of the
Anabasis, 'Thimbron took over the army and incorporated it
with the rest of his Greek force, and fought against Tissaphernes and Pharnabazus.' So Tissaphernes, to quote again
from Curtius, 'saw before him once more the hated men whom
he had assumed on the day of Cunaxa to be doomed to perish
hopelessly under the swords of the Carduchi or amid the snow-
fields of Armenia.'

§ 7. LATER LIFE OF XENOPHON.

Before Xenophon handed over his troops to Thimbron in
the spring of 399 B.C., he was, he tells us, *preparing* to return
home ; for, he adds, the decree of banishment had *not yet* been
passed against him at Athens. These words have an important
bearing on the vexed question of the date of his banishment.
They certainly support the view that the blow came *soon*. He
seems to have expected such a disaster for some time past ; for
he speaks of hoping for an asylum with Seuthes the Thracian
prince, and his project of founding a colony of his own on the
Euxine was probably due to the same fear. The decree of
banishment was passed on the proposition of the orator
Eubulus. His alleged offence is differently stated by two
authorities. He was banished either (1) 'because he had taken
part with Cyrus, the greatest enemy of the Athenian democracy,
in an expedition against the Great King their well-wisher,' or
(2) 'for Laconism,' *i.e.* for favouring Sparta. But these two
statements may be looked upon as practically identical ; for
taking part with Cyrus, who had shewn his friendship for
Sparta by providing her with the 'sinews of war' against

Athens, might well be looked upon as 'Laconism.' This view is strongly supported by the anxiety of Socrates on the subject (see above, § 3). Grote, however, owing to an apparent misunderstanding of a passage in the *Anabasis* (v. iii. 7), places Xenophon's banishment in 394 B.C. after the battle of Coroneia, when he actually fought for Sparta against his native city.

Xenophon was 'preparing to return.' Whether he actually did return to Greece in 399 B.C. is uncertain. The trial and death of his master Socrates took place in the summer of this year ; and the Athenians would not have been inclined to shew any tenderness to one of the Socratic brethren. The decree of banishment was probably passed very soon afterwards. Anyhow, in a few months we find him again in command of his old Cyreian troops in Asia Minor, serving first under Dercyllidas, who succeeded Thimbron in 398 B.C., and then under King Agesilaus, who went out in 396. For Agesilaus he entertained the warmest admiration and became his intimate friend. But the King was not allowed to remain long in Asia Minor; for, on the formation of the confederacy of Athens, Thebes and Corinth against Sparta, he was summoned to fight for his country in Greece. Xenophon and his troops accompanied him into Boeotia and took part in his victory at Coroneia.

When Xenophon's service under Agesilaus was over, the Spartans gave him a house and grounds at Scillus, near Olympia. Soon after Xenophon had settled there he met Megabyzus, High-priest of the Ephesian Artemis, who chanced to have come to the Olympic Games. He paid over to Xenophon a sum of money, which represented a part of the tithe of plunder devoted by the Cyreian army to Artemis and deposited with her priest. With this money Xenophon purchased an estate near his own residence, which he consecrated to the goddess, and built thereon a chapel containing a statue, a copy in miniature of the great Ephesian temple. He appointed himself Conservator of the demesne of Artemis, which consisted largely of wild ground well stocked with game. He was an ardent sportsman ; every year he held a hunting festival on a large scale, to which he invited his neighbours and entertained them lavishly at the expense of the Huntress Queen, who, he says, 'provided the fare.' At Scillus Xenophon was joined by his wife Philesia and his sons Gryllus and Diodorus ; and there he lived a happy country life for twenty years, spending his time not only in sport, but in great literary labours, one of which was the composition of the *Anabasis.* From the fact that Xenophon is spoken of throughout the *Anabasis* in the third person, it has been thought by some that the writer was Themistogenes of Syracuse, whom Xenophon mentions elsewhere as the author of a history of the Retreat. Others hold that Xenophon published the *Anabasis* under the name of Themistogenes.

At Scillus he probably wrote the *Memorabilia* of his master Socrates, 'whose loss,' he says, 'men even now continue to mourn'; and its appendix, the *Apology of Socrates,* if that work is really Xenophon's. The last five books of the *Hellenica* (see above, § 1), carrying the history of Greece down to the battle of Mantineia, 362 B.C., belong to a later time ; so also does the *Cyropaedeia* or *Education of Cyrus the Great,* a political romance in eight books, 'not historically accurate nor a true picture of Persian thought and manners, but rather an encomium on Socratic principles and Spartan practice, in which Cyrus himself, drawn with some touches from the young Cyrus whom Xenophon had known, is half a Socrates and half an Agesilaus' (Jebb, *Primer of Greek Literature,* p. 113). Two Socratic dialogues by Xenophon are extant, the *Oeconomicus* and the *Symposium* ; also another dialogue called *Hiero* and a treatise on the *Spartan Constitution.* The *Panegyric on Agesilaus,* ascribed to Xenophon, is probably a rhetorical exercise of later date. Three essays on horses and horsemanship are assigned to the time of his residence at Scillus:—(1) the *Cavalry Officer's Manual,* (2) *on Horsemanship,* in which he specially inculcates the duty of kindness to horses, (3) *on Hunting,* the work of a keen sportsman and lover of dogs, treating chiefly of hare-hunting. The hare, in the eyes of Xenophon, is a 'charming creature to hunt.'

In 371 B.C. after the battle of Leuctra, by which the power of

Sparta was finally broken, the Eleians expelled Xenophon from Scillus. He then settled at Corinth. When Sparta became the ally of Athens against Thebes, this sentence of banishment was revoked on the motion of the same Eubulus who had proposed it. Xenophon's two sons, who had been educated at Sparta under the oversight of Agesilaus, fought on the Spartan side against Epameinondas at Mantineia, 362 B.C. The elder son, Gryllus, fell fighting with great bravery in the cavalry engagement at the gates just before the general battle began. From some passages in the essay *on the Athenian Revenues* (if it is Xenophon's work) it appears probable that towards the end of his life he spent some time at Athens. He died at Corinth. The date of his death is not known ; but it cannot have been earlier than 355 B.C.

ΞΕΝΟΦΩΝΤΟΣ
ΚΥΡΟΥ ΑΝΑΒΑΣΙΣ.
Γ.

___

I.

Despair of the Greeks after the seizure of their generals.

Ὅσα μὲν δὴ ἐν τῇ Κύρου ἀναβάσει οἱ Ἕλληνες 1
ἔπραξαν μέχρι τῆς μάχης, καὶ ὅσα ἐπεὶ Κῦρος ἐτελεύ-
τησεν ἐγένετο ἀπιόντων τῶν Ἑλλήνων σὺν Τισσαφέρνει
ἐν ταῖς σπονδαῖς, ἐν τῷ πρόσθεν λόγῳ δεδήλωται. ἐπεὶ 2
δὲ οἱ στρατηγοὶ συνειλημμένοι ἦσαν καὶ τῶν λοχαγῶν
καὶ τῶν στρατιωτῶν οἱ συνεπισπόμενοι ἀπωλώλεσαν,
ἐν πολλῇ δὴ ἀπορίᾳ ἦσαν οἱ Ἕλληνες, ἐννοούμενοι μὲν
ὅτι ἐπὶ ταῖς βασιλέως θύραις ἦσαν, κύκλῳ δὲ αὐτοῖς
πάντῃ πολλὰ καὶ ἔθνη καὶ πόλεις πολέμιαι ἦσαν,
ἀγορὰν δὲ οὐδεὶς ἔτι παρέξειν ἔμελλεν, ἀπεῖχον δὲ τῆς
Ἑλλάδος οὐ μεῖον ἢ μύρια στάδια, ἡγεμὼν δ' οὐδεὶς τῆς
ὁδοῦ ἦν, ποταμοὶ δὲ διεῖργον ἀδιάβατοι ἐν μέσῳ τῆς
οἴκαδε ὁδοῦ, προυδεδώκεσαν δὲ αὐτοὺς καὶ οἱ σὺν Κύρῳ
ἀναβάντες βάρβαροι, μόνοι δὲ καταλελειμμένοι ἦσαν

οὐδὲ ἱππέα οὐδένα σύμμαχον ἔχοντες, ὥστε εὔδηλον ἦν
ὅτι νικῶντες μὲν οὐδένα ἂν κατακάνοιεν, ἡττηθέντων δὲ
3 αὐτῶν οὐδεὶς ἂν λειϕθείη· ταῦτ' ἐννοούμενοι καὶ ἀθύμως
ἔχοντες ὀλίγοι μὲν αὐτῶν εἰς τὴν ἑσπέραν σίτου ἐγεύ-
σαντο, ὀλίγοι δὲ πῦρ ἀνέκαυσαν, ἐπὶ δὲ τὰ ὅπλα πολλοὶ
οὐκ ἦλθον ταύτην τὴν νύκτα, ἀνεπαύοντο δὲ ὅπου ἐτύγχανεν ἕκαστος, οὐ δυνάμειοι καθεύδειν ὑπὸ λύπης καὶ
πόθου πατρίδων, γονέων, γυναικῶν, παίδων, οὓς οὔποτ'
ἐνόμιζον ἔτι ὄψεσθαι. οὕτω μὲν δὴ διακείμενοι πάντες
ἀνεπαύοντο.

*Xenophon explains how he came to take part in the
expedition of Cyrus.*

4   ἦν δέ τις ἐν τῇ στρατιᾷ Ξενοφῶν Ἀθηναῖος, ὃς οὔτε
στρατηγὸς οὔτε λοχαγὸς οὔτε στρατιώτης ὢν συνηκο-
λούθει, ἀλλὰ Πρόξενος αὐτὸν μετεπέμψατο οἴκοθεν
ξένος ὢν ἀρχαῖος· ὑπισχνεῖτο δὲ αὐτῷ, εἰ ἔλθοι, φίλον
αὐτὸν Κύρῳ ποιήσειν, ὃν αὐτὸς ἔφη κρείττω ἑαυτῷ
5 νομίζειν τῆς πατρίδος. ὁ μέντοι Ξενοφῶν ἀναγνοὺς
τὴν ἐπιστολὴν ἀνακοινοῦται Σωκράτει τῷ Ἀθηναίῳ
περὶ τῆς πορείας. καὶ ὁ Σωκράτης ὑποπτεύσας μή τι
πρὸς τῆς πόλεως ὑπαίτιον εἴη Κύρῳ φίλον γενέσθαι, ὅτι
ἐδόκει ὁ Κῦρος προθύμως τοῖς Λακεδαιμονίοις ἐπὶ τὰς
Ἀθήνας συμπολεμῆσαι, συμβουλεύει τῷ ·Ξενοφῶντι
ἐλθόντα εἰς Δελφοὺς ἀνακοινῶσαι τῷ θεῷ περὶ τῆς
6 πορείας. ἐλθὼν δ' ὁ Ξενοφῶν ἐπήρετο τὸν Ἀπόλλω
τίνι ἂν θεῶν θύων καὶ εὐχόμενος κάλλιστ' ἂν καὶ ἄριστα
ἔλθοι τὴν ὁδὸν ἣν ἐπινοεῖ καὶ καλῶς πράξας σωθείη.
καὶ ἀνεῖλεν αὐτῷ ὁ Ἀπόλλων θεοῖς οἷς ἔδει θύειν. ἐπεὶ
7 δὲ πάλιν ἦλθε, λέγει τὴν μαντείαν τῷ Σωκράτει. ὁ δ'
ἀκούσας ᾐτιᾶτο αὐτὸν ὅτι οὐ τοῦτο πρῶτον ἠρώτα,

πότερον λῷον εἴη αὐτῷ πορεύεσθαι ἢ μένειν, ἀλλ᾽ αὐτὸς
κρίνας ἰτέον εἶναι τοῦτ᾽ ἐπυνθάνετο, ὅπως ἂν κάλλιστα
πορευθείη. "ἐπεὶ μέντοι οὕτως ἤρου, ταῦτ᾽," ἔφη, "χρὴ
ποιεῖν ὅσα ὁ θεὸς ἐκέλευσεν." ὁ μὲν δὴ Ξενοφῶν οὕτω 8
θυσάμενος οἷς ἀνεῖλεν ὁ θεὸς ἐξέπλει, καὶ καταλαμβάνει
ἐν Σάρδεσι Πρόξενον καὶ Κῦρον μέλλοντας ἤδη ὁρμᾶν
τὴν ἄνω ὁδόν, καὶ συνεστάθη Κύρῳ. προθυμουμένου 9
δὲ τοῦ Προξένου καὶ ὁ Κῦρος συμπρουθυμεῖτο μεῖναι
αὐτόν, εἶπε δὲ ὅτι, ἐπειδὰν τάχιστα ἡ στρατεία λήξῃ,
εὐθὺς ἀποπέμψει αὐτόν. ἐλέγετο δὲ ὁ στόλος εἶναι
εἰς Πισίδας. ἐστρατεύετο μὲν δὴ οὕτως ἐξαπατηθεὶς 10
οὐχ ὑπὸ Προξένου· οὐ γὰρ ᾔδει τὴν ἐπὶ βασιλέα
ὁρμὴν οὐδὲ ἄλλος οὐδεὶς τῶν Ἑλλήνων πλὴν Κλεάρ-
χου· ἐπεὶ μέντοι εἰς Κιλικίαν ἦλθον, σαφὲς πᾶσιν ἤδη
ἐδόκει εἶναι ὅτι ὁ στόλος εἴη ἐπὶ βασιλέα. φοβούμενοι
δὲ τὴν ὁδὸν καὶ ἄκοντες ὅμως οἱ πολλοὶ δι᾽ αἰσχύνην
καὶ ἀλλήλων καὶ Κύρου συνηκολούθησαν· ὧν εἷς καὶ
Ξενοφῶν ἦν.

Xenophon's dream and his reflections thereon.

ἐπεὶ δὲ ἀπορία ἦν, ἐλυπεῖτο μὲν σὺν τοῖς ἄλλοις καὶ 11
οὐκ ἐδύνατο καθεύδειν· μικρὸν δ᾽ ὕπνου λαχὼν εἶδεν
ὄναρ. ἔδοξεν αὐτῷ βροντῆς γενομένης σκηπτὸς πεσεῖν
εἰς τὴν πατρῴαν οἰκίαν, καὶ ἐκ τούτου λάμπεσθαι πᾶσαν.
περίφοβος δ᾽ εὐθὺς ἀνηγέρθη, καὶ τὸ ὄναρ τῇ μὲν ἔκρινεν 12
ἀγαθόν, ὅτι ἐν πόνοις ὢν καὶ κινδύνοις φῶς μέγα ἐκ Διὸς
ἰδεῖν ἔδοξε· τῇ δὲ καὶ ἐφοβεῖτο, ὅτι ἀπὸ Διὸς μὲν βασιλέως τὸ ὄναρ ἐδόκει αὐτῷ εἶναι, κύκλῳ δὲ ἐδόκει λάμπεσθαι τὸ πῦρ, μὴ οὐ δύναιτο ἐκ τῆς χώρας ἐξελθεῖν τῆς
βασιλέως, ἀλλ᾽ εἴργοιτο πάντοθεν ὑπό τινων ἀποριῶν.
ὁποῖόν τι μὲν δὴ ἐστὶ τὸ τοιοῦτον ὄναρ ἰδεῖν ἔξεστι 13

σκοπεῖν ἐκ τῶν συμβάντων μετὰ τὸ ὄναρ. γίγνεται γὰρ
τάδε. εὐθὺς ἐπειδὴ ἀνηγέρθη, πρῶτον μὲν ἔννοια αὐτῷ
ἐμπίπτει· "τί κατάκειμαι; ἡ δὲ νὺξ προβαίνει· ἅμα δὲ
τῇ ἡμέρᾳ εἰκὸς τοὺς πολεμίους ἥξειν. εἰ δὲ γενησόμεθα
ἐπὶ βασιλεῖ, τί ἐμποδὼν μὴ οὐχὶ πάντα μὲν τὰ χαλε-
πώτατα ἐπιδόντας, πάντα δὲ τὰ δεινότατα παθόντας
14 ὑβριζομένους ἀποθανεῖν; ὅπως δ' ἀμυνούμεθα οὐδεὶς
παρασκευάζεται οὐδὲ ἐπιμελεῖται, ἀλλὰ κατακείμεθα
ὥσπερ ἐξὸν ἡσυχίαν ἄγειν. ἐγὼ οὖν τὸν ἐκ ποίας
πόλεως στρατηγὸν προσδοκῶ ταῦτα πράξειν; ποίαν
δ' ἡλικίαν ἐμαυτῷ ἐλθεῖν ἀναμένω; οὐ γὰρ ἔγωγ' ἔτι
πρεσβύτερος ἔσομαι, ἐὰν τήμερον προδῶ ἐμαυτὸν τοῖς
πολεμίοις."

*Xenophon calls together the captains of the division of
Proxenus and addresses them in a stirring speech.*

15   ἐκ τούτου ἀνίσταται καὶ συγκαλεῖ τοὺς Προξένου
πρῶτον λοχαγούς. ἐπεὶ δὲ συνῆλθον, ἔλεξεν· "ἐγώ, ὦ
ἄνδρες λοχαγοί, οὔτε καθεύδειν δύναμαι, ὥσπερ οἶμαι
οὐδ' ὑμεῖς, οὔτε κατακεῖσθαι ἔτι, ὁρῶν ἐν οἷος ἐσμέν.
16 οἱ μὲν γὰρ πολέμιοι δῆλον ὅτι οὐ πρότερον πρὸς ἡμᾶς
τὸν πόλεμον ἐξέφηναν πρὶν ἐνόμισαν καλῶς τὰ ἑαυτῶν
παρασκευάσασθαι, ἡμῶν δ' οὐδεὶς οὐδὲν ἀντεπιμελεῖται
17 ὅπως ὡς κάλλιστα ἀγωνιούμεθα. καὶ μὴν εἰ ὑφησόμεθα
καὶ ἐπὶ βασιλεῖ γενησόμεθα, τί οἰόμεθα πείσεσθαι; ὃς
καὶ τοῦ ὁμομητρίου ἀδελφοῦ καὶ τεθνηκότος ἤδη ἀπο-
τεμὼν τὴν κεφαλὴν καὶ τὴν χεῖρα ἀνεσταύρωσεν· ἡμᾶς
δέ, οἷς κηδεμὼν μὲν οὐδεὶς πάρεστιν, ἐστρατεύσαμεν δὲ
ἐπ' αὐτὸν ὡς δοῦλον ἀντὶ βασιλέως ποιήσοντες καὶ ἀπο-
18 κτενοῦντες εἰ δυναίμεθα, τί ἂν οἰόμεθα παθεῖν; ἆρ' οὐκ ἂν
ἐπὶ πᾶν ἔλθοι ὡς ἡμᾶς τὰ ἔσχατα αἰκισάμενος πᾶσιν

ἀνθρώποις φόβον παράσχοι τοῦ στρατεῦσαί ποτε ἐπ'
αὐτόν; ἀλλ' ὅπως τοι μὴ ἐπ' ἐκείνῳ γενησόμεθα πάντα
ποιητέον. ἐγὼ μὲν οὖν, ἔστε μὲν αἱ σπονδαὶ ἦσαν, οὔποτε 19
ἐπαυόμην ἡμᾶς μὲν οἰκτείρων, βασιλέα δὲ καὶ τοὺς σὺν
αὐτῷ μακαρίζων, διαθεώμενος αὐτῶν ὅσην μὲν χώραν
καὶ οἵαν ἔχοιεν, ὡς δὲ ἄφθονα τὰ ἐπιτήδεια, ὅσους δὲ
θεράποντας, ὅσα δὲ κτήνη, χρυσὸν δέ, ἐσθῆτα δέ· τὰ 20
δ' αὖ τῶν στρατιωτῶν ὁπότε ἐνθυμοίμην, ὅτι τῶν μὲν
ἀγαθῶν τούτων οὐδενὸς ἡμῖν μετείη, εἰ μὴ πριαίμεθα,
(ὅτου δ' ὠνησόμεθα ᾔδειν ἔτι ὀλίγους ἔχοντας, ἄλλως
δέ πως πορίζεσθαι τὰ ἐπιτήδεια ἢ ὠνουμένους ὅρκους
ἤδη κατέχοντας ἡμᾶς)—ταῦτ' οὖν λογιζόμενος ἐνίοτε
τὰς σπονδὰς μᾶλλον ἐφοβούμην ἢ νῦν τὸν πόλεμον.
ἐπεὶ μέντοι ἐκεῖνοι ἔλυσαν τὰς σπονδάς, λελύσθαι μοι 21
δοκεῖ καὶ ἡ ἐκείνων ὕβρις καὶ ἡ ἡμετέρα ἀσάφεια. ἐν
μέσῳ γὰρ ἤδη κεῖται ταῦτα, ἃ ἀγαθὰ ἆθλα ὁπότεροι
ἂν ἡμῶν ἄνδρες ἀμείνονες ὦσιν, ἀγωνοθέται δ' οἱ
θεοί εἰσιν, οἳ σὺν ἡμῖν, ὡς τὸ εἰκός, ἔσονται. οὗτοι 22
μὲν γὰρ αὐτοὺς ἐπιωρκήκασιν· ἡμεῖς δὲ πολλὰ ὁρῶν-
τες ἀγαθὰ στερρῶς αὐτῶν ἀπειχόμεθα διὰ τοὺς τῶν
θεῶν ὅρκους· ὥστε ἐξεῖναί μοι δοκεῖ ἰέναι ἐπὶ τὸν
ἀγῶνα πολὺ σὺν φρονήματι μείζονι ἢ τούτοις. ἔτι 23
δ' ἔχομεν σώματα ἱκανώτερα τούτων καὶ ψύχη καὶ
θάλπη καὶ πόνους φέρειν· ἔχομεν δὲ καὶ ψυχὰς σὺν
τοῖς θεοῖς ἀμείνονας· οἱ δὲ ἄνδρες καὶ τρωτοὶ καὶ
θνητοὶ μᾶλλον ἡμῶν, ἢν οἱ θεοί, ὥσπερ τὸ πρόσθεν,
νίκην ἡμῖν διδῶσιν. ἀλλ' (ἴσως γὰρ καὶ ἄλλοι ταὐτὰ 24
ἐνθυμοῦνται) πρὸς τῶν θεῶν μὴ ἀναμένωμεν ἄλλους
ἐφ' ἡμᾶς ἐλθεῖν παρακαλοῦντας ἐπὶ τὰ κάλλιστα ἔργα,
ἀλλ' ἡμεῖς ἄρξωμεν τοῦ ἐξορμῆσαι καὶ τοὺς ἄλλους
ἐπὶ τὴν ἀρετήν· φάνητε τῶν λοχαγῶν ἄριστοι καὶ τῶν

25 στρατηγῶν ἀξιοστρατηγότεροι. κἀγὼ δέ, εἰ μὲν ὑμεῖς
ἐθέλετε ἐξορμᾶν ἐπὶ ταῦτα, ἕπεσθαι ὑμῖν βούλομαι,
εἰ δ᾽ ὑμεῖς τάττετ᾽ αὐτόν με ἡγεῖσθαι, οὐδὲν προφασίζομαι τὴν ἡλικίαν, ἀλλὰ καὶ ἀκμάζειν ἡγοῦμαι ἐρύκειν
ἀπ᾽ ἐμαυτοῦ τὰ κακά."

The captains call upon Xenophon to take the command.
An objector is silenced.

26   ὁ μὲν ταῦτ᾽ ἔλεξεν· οἱ δὲ λοχαγοὶ ἀκούσαντες
ἡγεῖσθαι ἐκέλευον πάντες, πλὴν Ἀπολλωνίδης τις ἦν
βοιωτιάζων τῇ φωνῇ· οὗτος δ᾽ εἶπεν ὅτι φλυαροίη
ὅστις λέγοι ἄλλως πως σωτηρίας ἂν τυχεῖν ἢ βασιλέα
πείσας, εἰ δύναιτο, καὶ ἅμα ἤρχετο λέγειν τὰς ἀπορίας.
27 ὁ μέντοι Ξενοφῶν μεταξὺ ὑπολαβὼν ἔλεξεν ὧδε· "ὦ
θαυμασιώτατε ἄνθρωπε, σύ γε οὐδὲ ὁρῶν γιγνώσκεις
οὐδὲ ἀκούων μέμνησαι. ἐν ταὐτῷ γε μέντοι ἦσθα τούτοις ὅτε βασιλεύς, ἐπεὶ Κῦρος ἀπέθανε, καταφρονήσας
28 ἐπὶ τούτῳ πέμπων ἐκέλευε παραδιδόναι τὰ ὅπλα. ἐπεὶ
δὲ ἡμεῖς οὐ παραδόντες, ἀλλ᾽ ἐξοπλισάμενοι ἐλθόντες
παρεσκηνήσαμεν αὐτῷ, τί οὐκ ἐποίησε πρέσβεις πέμπων
καὶ σπονδὰς αἰτῶν καὶ παρέχων τὰ ἐπιτήδεια, ἔστε
29 σπονδῶν ἔτυχεν; ἐπεὶ δ᾽ αὖ οἱ στρατηγοὶ καὶ λοχαγοί,
ὥσπερ δὴ σὺ κελεύεις, εἰς λόγους αὐτοῖς ἄνευ ὅπλων
ἦλθον πιστεύσαντες ταῖς σπονδαῖς, οὐ νῦν ἐκεῖνοι
παιόμενοι, κεντούμενοι, ὑβριζόμενοι οὐδὲ ἀποθανεῖν
οἱ τλήμονες δύνανται, καὶ μάλ᾽, οἶμαι, ἐρῶντες τούτου;
ἃ σὺ πάντα εἰδὼς τοὺς μὲν ἀμύνεσθαι κελεύοντας
30 φλυαρεῖν φής, πείθειν δὲ πάλιν κελεύεις ἰόντας; ἐμοί,
ὦ ἄνδρες, δοκεῖ τὸν ἄνθρωπον τοῦτον μήτε προσ-
ίεσθαι εἰς ταὐτὸν ἡμῖν αὐτοῖς ἀφελομένους τε τὴν
λοχαγίαν σκεύη ἀναθέντας ὡς τοιούτῳ χρῆσθαι. οὗτος

γὰρ καὶ τὴν πατρίδα καταισχύνει καὶ πᾶσαν τὴν
Ἑλλάδα, ὅτι Ἕλλην ὢν τοιοῦτός ἐστιν." ἐντεῦθεν ὑπο- 31
λαβὼν Ἀγασίας Στυμφάλιος εἶπεν· "ἀλλὰ τούτῳ γε
οὔτε τῆς Βοιωτίας προσήκει οὐδὲν οὔτε τῆς Ἑλλάδος
παντάπασιν, ἐπεὶ ἐγὼ αὐτὸν εἶδον ὥσπερ Λυδὸν ἀμφότερα τὰ ὦτα τετρυπημένον." καὶ εἶχεν οὕτως. τοῦτον 32
μὲν οὖν ἀπήλασαν.

The officers of the other divisions are summoned.

οἱ δὲ ἄλλοι παρὰ τὰς τάξεις ἰόντες, ὅπου μὲν στρατηγὸς σῶς εἴη, τὸν στρατηγὸν παρεκάλουν, ὁπόθεν δὲ
οἴχοιτο τὸν ὑποστράτηγον, ὅπου δ' αὖ λοχαγὸς σῶς
εἴη τὸν λοχαγόν. ἐπεὶ δὲ πάντες συνῆλθον, εἰς τὸ 33
πρόσθεν τῶν ὅπλων ἐκαθέζοντο· καὶ ἐγένοντο οἱ συνελ-
θόντες στρατηγοὶ καὶ λοχαγοὶ ἀμφὶ τοὺς ἑκατόν. ὅτε
δὲ ταῦτα ἦν, σχεδὸν μέσαι ἦσαν νύκτες. ἐνταῦθα Ἱερώ- 34
νυμος Ἠλεῖος πρεσβύτατος ὢν τῶν Προξένου λοχαγῶν
ἤρχετο λέγειν ὧδε· "ἡμῖν, ὦ ἄνδρες στρατηγοὶ καὶ
λοχαγοί, ὁρῶσι τὰ παρόντα ἔδοξε καὶ αὐτοῖς συνελθεῖν
καὶ ὑμᾶς παρακαλέσαι, ὅπως βουλευσαίμεθα εἴ τι
δυναίμεθα ἀγαθόν. λέξον δ'," ἔφη, " καὶ σύ, ὦ Ξενοφῶν,
ἅπερ καὶ πρὸς ἡμᾶς."

Second speech of Xenophon.

ἐκ τούτου λέγει τάδε Ξενοφῶν· " ἀλλὰ ταῦτα μὲν δὴ 35
πάντες ἐπιστάμεθα ὅτι βασιλεὺς καὶ Τισσαφέρνης οὓς
μὲν ἐδυνήθησαν συνειλήφασιν ἡμῶν, τοῖς δ' ἄλλοις δῆλον
ὅτι ἐπιβουλεύουσιν, ὡς ἢν δύνωνται ἀπολέσωσιν. ἡμῖν
δέ γε οἶμαι πάντα ποιητέα ὡς μήποτε ἐπὶ τοῖς βαρβάροις
γενώμεθα, ἀλλὰ μᾶλλον ἐκεῖνοι ἐφ' ἡμῖν. εὖ τοίνυν 36

8 ΞΕΝΟΦΩΝΤΟΣ [I.

ἐπίστασθε ὅτι ὑμεῖς, τοσοῦτοι ὄντες ὅσοι νῦν συνεληλύ-
θατε, μέγιστον ἔχετε καιρόν. οἱ γὰρ στρατιῶται οὗτοι
πάντες πρὸς ὑμᾶς βλέπουσι, κἂν μὲν ὑμᾶς ὁρῶσιν ἀθυ-
μοῦντας, πάντες κακοὶ ἔσονται, ἢν δὲ ὑμεῖς αὐτοί τε
παρασκευαζόμενοι φανεροὶ ἦτε ἐπὶ τοὺς πολεμίους καὶ
τοὺς ἄλλους παρακαλῆτε, εὖ ἴστε ὅτι ἔψονται ὑμῖν καὶ
37 πειράσονται μιμεῖσθαι. ἴσως δέ τοι καὶ δίκαιόν ἐστιν
ὑμᾶς διαφέρειν τι τούτων. ὑμεῖς γάρ ἐστε στρατηγοί,
ὑμεῖς ταξίαρχοι καὶ λοχαγοί· καί, ὅτε εἰρήνη ἦν, ὑμεῖς
καὶ χρήμασι καὶ τιμαῖς τούτων ἐπλεονεκτεῖτε· καὶ νῦν
τοίνυν, ἐπεὶ πόλεμός ἐστιν, ἀξιοῦν δεῖ ὑμᾶς αὐτοὺς
ἀμείνους τε τοῦ πλήθους εἶναι καὶ προβουλεύειν τού-
38 των καὶ προπονεῖν, ἤν που δέῃ. καὶ νῦν πρῶτον μὲν
οἶμαι ἂν ὑμᾶς μέγα ὠφελῆσαι τὸ στράτευμα, εἰ ἐπι-
μεληθείητε ὅπως ἀντὶ τῶν ἀπολωλότων ὡς τάχιστα
στρατηγοὶ καὶ λοχαγοὶ ἀντικατασταθῶσιν. ἄνευ γὰρ
ἀρχόντων οὐδὲν ἂν οὔτε καλὸν οὔτε ἀγαθὸν γένοιτο,
ὡς μὲν συνελόντι εἰπεῖν, οὐδαμοῦ, ἐν δὲ δὴ τοῖς πολεμικοῖς παντάπασιν. ἡ μὲν γὰρ εὐταξία σῴζειν δοκεῖ,
39 ἡ δὲ ἀταξία πολλοὺς ἤδη ἀπολώλεκεν. ἐπειδὰν δὲ κατα-
στήσησθε τοὺς ἄρχοντας ὅσους δεῖ, ἢν καὶ τοὺς ἄλλους
στρατιώτας συλλέγητε καὶ παραθαρρύνητε, οἶμαι ἂν
40 ὑμᾶς πάνυ ἐν καιρῷ ποιῆσαι. νῦν γὰρ ἴσως καὶ ὑμεῖς
αἰσθάνεσθε ὡς ἀθύμως μὲν ἦλθον ἐπὶ τὰ ὅπλα, ἀθύμως
δὲ πρὸς τὰς φυλακάς· ὥστε οὕτω γ' ἐχόντων οὐκ οἶδα
ὅ τι ἄν τις χρήσαιτο αὐτοῖς, εἴτε νυκτὸς δέοι εἴτε καὶ
41 ἡμέρας. ἢν δέ τις αὐτῶν τρέψῃ τὰς γνώμας, ὡς μὴ
τοῦτο μόνον ἐννοῶνται τί πείσονται ἀλλὰ καὶ τί ποιή-
42 σουσι, πολὺ εὐθυμότεροι ἔσονται. ἐπίστασθε γὰρ δὴ ὅτι
οὔτε πλῆθός ἐστιν οὔτε ἰσχὺς ἡ ἐν τῷ πολέμῳ τὰς νίκας
ποιοῦσα, ἀλλ' ὁπότεροι ἂν σὺν τοῖς θεοῖς ταῖς ψυχαῖς

ἐρρωμενέστεροι ἴωσιν ἐπὶ τοὺς πολεμίους, τούτους ὡς
ἐπὶ τὸ πολὺ οἱ ἀντίοι οὐ δέχονται. ἐντεθύμημαι δ' 43
ἔγωγε, ὦ ἄνδρες, καὶ τοῦτο, ὅτι ὁπόσοι μὲν μαστεύουσι
ζῆν ἐκ παντὸς τρόπου ἐν τοῖς πολεμικοῖς, οὗτοι μὲν
κακῶς τε καὶ αἰσχρῶς ὡς ἐπὶ τὸ πολὺ ἀποθνήσκουσιν,
ὁπόσοι δὲ τὸν μὲν θάνατον ἐγνώκασι πᾶσι κοινὸν εἶναι
καὶ ἀναγκαῖον ἀνθρώποις, περὶ δὲ τοῦ καλῶς ἀποθνήσκειν ἀγωνίζονται, τούτους δ' ὁρῶ μᾶλλόν πως
εἰς τὸ γῆρας ἀφικνουμένους καί, ἕως ἂν ζῶσιν, εὐδαι-
μονέστερον διάγοντας. ἃ καὶ ἡμᾶς δεῖ νῦν καταμαθόν- 44
τας (ἐν τοιούτῳ γὰρ καιρῷ ἐσμεν) αὐτούς τε ἄνδρας
ἀγαθοὺς εἶναι καὶ τοὺς ἄλλους παρακαλεῖν."

Speech of Cheirisophus.   New generals are chosen.

ὁ μὲν ταῦτα εἰπὼν ἐπαύσατο. μετὰ δὲ τοῦτον εἶπε 45
Χειρίσοφος· "ἀλλὰ πρόσθεν μέν, ὦ Ξενοφῶν, τοσοῦτον
μόνον σε ἐγίγνωσκον ὅσον ἤκουον Ἀθηναῖον εἶναι, νῦν
δὲ καὶ ἐπαινῶ σε ἐφ' οἷς λέγεις τε καὶ πράττεις, καὶ
βουλοίμην ἂν ὅτι πλείστους εἶναι τοιούτους· κοινὸν γὰρ
ἂν εἴη τὸ ἀγαθόν. καὶ νῦν, ἔφη, μὴ μέλλωμεν, ὦ ἄνδρες, 46
ἀλλ' ἀπελθόντες ἤδη αἱρεῖσθε οἱ δεόμενοι ἄρχοντας, καὶ
ἑλόμενοι ἥκετε εἰς τὸ μέσον τοῦ στρατοπέδου καὶ τοὺς
αἱρεθέντας ἄγετε· ἔπειτ' ἐκεῖ συγκαλοῦμεν τοὺς ἄλλους
στρατιώτας. παρέστω δ' ἡμῖν," ἔφη, "καὶ Τολμίδης ὁ
κῆρυξ." καὶ ἅμα ταῦτ' εἰπὼν ἀνέστη, ὡς μὴ μέλλοιτο 47
ἀλλὰ περαίνοιτο τὰ δέοντα. ἐκ τούτου ἡρέθησαν ἄρ-
χοντες ἀντὶ μὲν Κλεάρχου Τιμασίων Δαρδανεύς, ἀντὶ
δὲ Σωκράτους Ξανθικλῆς Ἀχαιός, ἀντὶ δὲ Ἁγίου Κλεάνωρ Ἀρκάς, ἀντὶ δὲ Μένωνος Φιλήσιος Ἀχαιός, ἀντὶ
δὲ Προξένου Ξενοφῶν Ἀθηναῖος.

II.

The soldiers are summoned to meet in general assembly.
Speech of Cheirisophus.

1 Ἐπεὶ δὲ ᾕρηντο, ἡμέρα τε σχεδὸν ὑπέφαινε καὶ
εἰς τὸ μέσον ἧκον οἱ ἄρχοντες· καὶ ἔδοξεν αὐτοῖς προ-
φυλακὰς καταστήσαντας συγκαλεῖν τοὺς στρατιώτας.
ἐπεὶ δὲ καὶ οἱ ἄλλοι στρατιῶται συνῆλθον, ἀνέστη
πρῶτος μὲν Χειρίσοφος ὁ Λακεδαιμόνιος καὶ ἔλεξεν ὧδε·
2 " ἄνδρες στρατιῶται, χαλεπὰ μὲν τὰ παρόντα, ὁπότε
ἀνδρῶν στρατηγῶν τοιούτων στερόμεθα καὶ λοχαγῶν
καὶ στρατιωτῶν, πρὸς δ᾽ ἔτι καὶ οἱ ἀμφὶ Ἀριαῖον οἱ
3 πρόσθεν σύμμαχοι ὄντες προδεδώκασιν ἡμᾶς· ὅμως δὲ
δεῖ ἐκ τῶν παρόντων ἄνδρας ἀγαθοὺς τελέθειν καὶ μὴ
ὑφίεσθαι, ἀλλὰ πειρᾶσθαι ὅπως, ἢν μὲν δυνώμεθα,
καλῶς νικῶντες σῳζώμεθα· εἰ δὲ μή, ἀλλὰ καλῶς γε
ἀποθνήσκωμεν, ὑποχείριοι δὲ μηδέποτε γενώμεθα ζῶν-
τες τοῖς πολεμίοις. οἶμαι γὰρ ἂν ἡμᾶς τοιαῦτα παθεῖν,
οἷα τοὺς ἐχθροὺς οἱ θεοὶ ποιήσειαν."

Speech of Cleanor.

4 ἐπὶ τούτῳ Κλεάνωρ ὁ Ὀρχομένιος ἀνέστη καὶ ἔλεξεν
ὧδε· " ἀλλ᾽ ὁρᾶτε μέν, ὦ ἄνδρες, τὴν βασιλέως ἐπιορκίαν
καὶ ἀσέβειαν, ὁρᾶτε δὲ τὴν Τισσαφέρνους ἀπιστίαν,
ὅστις λέγων ὡς γείτων τε εἴη τῆς Ἑλλάδος καὶ περὶ
πλείστου ἂν ποιήσαιτο σῶσαι ἡμᾶς, καὶ ἐπὶ τούτοις
αὐτὸς ὀμόσας ἡμῖν, αὐτὸς δεξιὰς δούς, αὐτὸς ἐξαπατήσας
συνέλαβε τοὺς στρατηγούς, καὶ οὐδὲ Δία ξένιον ᾐδέσθη,
ἀλλὰ Κλεάρχῳ καὶ ὁμοτράπεζος γενόμενος αὐτοῖς τούτοις
5 ἐξαπατήσας τοὺς ἄνδρας ἀπολώλεκεν. Ἀριαῖος δέ, ὃν

ἡμεῖς ἠθέλομεν βασιλέα καθιστάναι, καὶ ἐδώκαμεν καὶ
ἐλάβομεν πιστὰ μὴ προδώσειν ἀλλήλους, καὶ οὗτος
οὔτε τοὺς θεοὺς δείσας οὔτε Κῦρον τεθνηκότα αἰδεσθείς,
τιμώμενος μάλιστα ὑπὸ Κύρου ζῶντος, νῦν πρὸς τοὺς
ἐκείνου ἐχθίστους ἀποστὰς ἡμᾶς τοὺς Κύρου φίλους
κακῶς ποιεῖν πειρᾶται. ἀλλὰ τούτους μὲν οἱ θεοὶ 6
ἀποτίσαιντο· ἡμᾶς δὲ δεῖ ταῦτα ὁρῶντας μήποτε
ἐξαπατηθῆναι ἔτι ὑπὸ τούτων, ἀλλὰ μαχομένους ὡς
ἂν δυνώμεθα κράτιστα τοῦτο ὅ τι ἂν δοκῇ τοῖς θεοῖς
πάσχειν."

*Xenophon begins to address the soldiers.   He turns
a favourable omen to good account.*

ἐκ τούτου Ξενοφῶν ἀνίσταται ἐσταλμένος ἐπὶ 7
πόλεμον ὡς ἐδύνατο κάλλιστα, νομίζων, εἴτε νίκην δι-
δοῖεν οἱ θεοί, τὸν κάλλιστον κόσμον τῷ νικᾶν πρέπειν,
εἴτε τελευτᾶν δέοι, ὀρθῶς ἔχειν τῶν καλλίστων ἑαυτὸν
ἀξιώσαντα ἐν τούτοις τῆς τελευτῆς τυγχάνειν· τοῦ λόγου
δὲ ἤρχετο· ὧδε· "τὴν μὲν τῶν βαρβάρων ἐπιορκίαν τε 8
καὶ ἀπιστίαν λέγει μὲν Κλεάνωρ, ἐπίστασθε δὲ καὶ ὑμεῖς,
οἶμαι. εἰ μὲν οὖν βουλόμεθα πάλιν αὐτοῖς διὰ φιλίας
ἰέναι, ἀνάγκη ἡμᾶς πολλὴν ἀθυμίαν ἔχειν, ὁρῶντας
καὶ τοὺς στρατηγούς, οἳ διὰ πίστεως αὐτοῖς ἑαυτοὺς
ἐνεχείρισαν, οἷα πεπόνθασιν· εἰ μέντοι διανοούμεθα
σὺν τοῖς ὅπλοις ὧν τε πεποιήκασι δίκην ἐπιθεῖναι αὐτοῖς
καὶ τὸ λοιπὸν διὰ παντὸς πολέμου αὐτοῖς ἰέναι, σὺν
τοῖς θεοῖς πολλαὶ ἡμῖν καὶ καλαὶ ἐλπίδες εἰσὶ σωτηρίας."
τοῦτο δὲ λέγοντος αὐτοῦ πτάρνυταί τις· ἀκούσαντες δ᾽ 9
οἱ στρατιῶται πάντες μιᾷ ὁρμῇ προσεκύνησαν τὸν θεόν·
καὶ ὁ Ξενοφῶν εἶπε· "δοκεῖ μοι, ὦ ἄνδρες, ἐπεὶ περὶ
σωτηρίας ἡμῶν λεγόντων οἰωνὸς τοῦ Διὸς τοῦ σωτῆρος

12 ΞΕΝΟΦΩΝΤΟΣ [II.

ἐφάνη, εὔξασθαι τῷ θεῷ τούτῳ θύσειν σωτήρια, ὅπου ἂν
πρῶτον εἰς φιλίαν χώραν ἀφικώμεθα, συνεπεύξασθαι
δὲ καὶ τοῖς ἄλλοις θεοῖς θύσειν κατὰ δύναμιν. καὶ
ὅτῳ δοκεῖ ταῦτ᾽," ἔφη, "ἀνατεινάτω τὴν χεῖρα." καὶ
ἀνέτειναν ἅπαντες. ἐκ τούτου ηὔξαντο καὶ ἐπαιάνισαν.

*Xenophon continues his address. He shews that the
prospects of the Greeks are good.*

ἐπεὶ δὲ τὰ τῶν θεῶν καλῶς εἶχεν, ἤρχετο πάλιν ὧδε·
10 "ἐτύγχανον λέγων ὅτι πολλαὶ καὶ καλαὶ ἐλπίδες ἡμῖν
εἶεν σωτηρίας. πρῶτον μὲν γὰρ ἡμεῖς μὲν ἐμπεδοῦμεν
τοὺς τῶν θεῶν ὅρκους, οἱ δὲ πολέμιοι ἐπιωρκήκασί τε
καὶ τὰς σπονδὰς παρὰ τοὺς ὅρκους λελύκασιν. οὕτω
δ᾽ ἐχόντων εἰκὸς τοῖς μὲν πολεμίοις ἐναντίους εἶναι
τοὺς θεούς, ἡμῖν δὲ συμμάχους, οἵπερ ἱκανοί εἰσι καὶ
τοὺς μεγάλους ταχὺ μικροὺς ποιεῖν καὶ τοὺς μικρούς,
κἂν ἐν δεινοῖς ὦσι, σῴζειν εὐπετῶς, ὅταν βούλωνται.
11 ἔπειτα δέ, ἀναμνήσω γὰρ ὑμᾶς καὶ τοὺς τῶν προγόνων
τῶν ἡμετέρων κινδύνους, ἵνα εἰδῆτε ὡς ἀγαθοῖς τε ὑμῖν
προσήκει εἶναι, σῴζονταί τε σὺν τοῖς θεοῖς καὶ ἐκ πάνυ
δεινῶν οἱ ἀγαθοί. ἐλθόντων μὲν γὰρ Περσῶν καὶ τῶν
σὺν αὐτοῖς παμπληθεῖ στόλῳ ὡς ἀφανιούντων τὰς Ἀθήνας, ὑποστῆναι αὐτοὶ Ἀθηναῖοι τολμήσαντες ἐνίκησαν
12 αὐτούς. καὶ εὐξάμενοι τῇ Ἀρτέμιδι, ὁπόσους ἂν κατακάνοιεν τῶν πολεμίων, τοσαύτας χιμαίρας καταθύσειν
τῇ θεῷ, ἐπεὶ οὐκ εἶχον ἱκανὰς εὑρεῖν, ἔδοξεν αὐτοῖς κατ᾽
ἐνιαυτὸν πεντακοσίας θύειν, καὶ ἔτι νῦν ἀποθύουσιν.
13 ἔπειτα, ὅτε Ξέρξης ὕστερον ἀγείρας τὴν ἀναρίθμητον
στρατιὰν ἦλθεν ἐπὶ τὴν Ἑλλάδα, καὶ τότε ἐνίκων οἱ
ἡμέτεροι πρόγονοι τοὺς τούτων προγόνους καὶ κατὰ

γῆν καὶ κατὰ θάλατταν. ὧν ἔστι μὲν τεκμήρια ὁρᾶν τὰ τρόπαια, μέγιστον δὲ μνημεῖον ἡ ἐλευθερία τῶν πόλεων ἐν αἷς ὑμεῖς ἐγένεσθε καὶ ἐτράφητε· οὐδένα γὰρ ἄνθρωπον δεσπότην ἀλλὰ τοὺς θεοὺς προσκυνεῖτε. τοιούτων μέν ἐστε προγόνων. οὐ μὲν δὴ τοῦτό γε ἐρῶ 14 ὡς ὑμεῖς καταισχύνετε αὐτούς· ἀλλ᾽ οὔπω πολλαὶ ἡμέ-ραι ἀφ᾽ οὗ ἀντιταξάμενοι τούτοις τοῖς ἐκείνων ἐκγό-νοις πολλαπλασίους ὑμῶν ἐνικᾶτε σὺν τοῖς θεοῖς. καὶ 15 τότε μὲν δὴ περὶ τῆς Κύρου βασιλείας ἄνδρες ἦτε ἀγαθοί· νῦν δ᾽ ὁπότε περὶ τῆς ὑμετέρας σωτηρίας ὁ ἀγών ἐστι, πολὺ δήπου ὑμᾶς προσήκει καὶ ἀμείνονας καὶ προθυμοτέρους εἶναι. ἀλλὰ μὴν καὶ θαρραλεωτέ- 16 ρους νῦν πρέπει εἶναι πρὸς τοὺς πολεμίους. τότε μὲν γὰρ ἄπειροι ὄντες αὐτῶν τό τε πλῆθος ἄμετρον ὁρῶν-τες, ὅμως ἐτολμήσατε σὺν τῷ πατρίῳ φρονήματι ἰέναι εἰς αὐτούς· νῦν δὲ ὁπότε καὶ πεῖραν ἤδη ἔχετε αὐτῶν ὅτι οὐ θέλουσι καὶ πολλαπλάσιοι ὄντες δέχεσθαι ὑμᾶς, τί ἔτι ὑμῖν προσήκει τούτους φοβεῖσθαι; μηδὲ 17 μέντοι τοῦτο μεῖον δόξητε ἔχειν, εἰ οἱ πρόσθεν σὺν ἡμῖν ταττόμενοι νῦν ἀφεστήκασιν. ἔτι γὰρ οὗτοι κακίονές εἰσι τῶν ὑφ᾽ ἡμῶν ἡττημένων· ἔφευγον γοῦν πρὸς ἐκείνους καταλιπόντες ἡμᾶς. τοὺς δ᾽ ἐθέλοντας φυγῆς ἄρχειν πολὺ κρεῖττον σὺν τοῖς πολεμίοις ταττο-μένους ἢ ἐν τῇ ἡμετέρᾳ τάξει ὁρᾶν.

He urges that the want of cavalry is no disadvantage to the Greeks.

" εἰ δέ τις ὑμῶν ἀθυμεῖ ὅτι ἡμῖν μὲν οὐκ εἰσὶν ἱππεῖς, 18 τοῖς δὲ πολεμίοις πολλοὶ πάρεισιν, ἐνθυμήθητε ὅτι οἱ μύριοι ἱππεῖς οὐδὲν ἄλλο ἢ μύριοί εἰσιν ἄνθρωποι· ὑπὸ

μὲν γὰρ ἵππου ἐν μάχῃ οὐδεὶς πώποτε οὔτε δηχθεὶς οὔτε
λακτισθεὶς ἀπέθανεν, οἱ δὲ ἄνδρες εἰσὶν οἱ ποιοῦντες ὅ
19 τι ἂν ἐν ταῖς μάχαις γίγνηται. οὐκοῦν τῶν ἱππέων
πολὺ ἡμεῖς ἐπ᾽ ἀσφαλεστέρου ὀχήματός ἐσμεν· οἱ μὲν
γὰρ ἐφ᾽ ἵππων κρέμανται φοβούμενοι οὐχ ἡμᾶς μόνον
ἀλλὰ καὶ τὸ καταπεσεῖν· ἡμεῖς δ᾽ ἐπὶ γῆς βεβηκότες
πολὺ μὲν ἰσχυρότερον παίσομεν, ἤν τις προσίῃ, πολὺ
δὲ μᾶλλον ὅτου ἂν βουλώμεθα τευξόμεθα. ἑνὶ δὲ μόνῳ
προέχουσιν οἱ ἱππεῖς· φεύγειν αὐτοῖς ἀσφαλέστερόν
ἐστιν ἢ ἡμῖν.

*They must not deplore the want of a guide or a market;
nor must they count the rivers a formidable obstacle.*

20   "εἰ δὲ δὴ τὰς μὲν μάχας θαρρεῖτε, ὅτι δὲ οὐκέτι
ἡμῖν Τισσαφέρνης ἡγήσεται οὐδὲ βασιλεὺς ἀγορὰν
παρέξει, τοῦτο ἄχθεσθε, σκέψασθε πότερον κρεῖττον
Τισσαφέρνην ἡγεμόνα ἔχειν, ὃς ἐπιβουλεύων ἡμῖν φανερός ἐστιν, ἢ οὓς ἂν ἡμεῖς ἄνδρας λαβόντες ἡγεῖσθαι
κελεύωμεν, οἳ εἴσονται ὅτι, ἤν τι περὶ ἡμᾶς ἁμαρτάνωσι,
21 περὶ τὰς ἑαυτῶν ψυχὰς καὶ σώματα ἁμαρτήσονται. τὰ
δὲ ἐπιτήδεια πότερον ὠνεῖσθαι κρεῖττον ἐκ τῆς ἀγορᾶς,
ἧς οὗτοι παρεῖχον, μικρὰ μέτρα πολλοῦ ἀργυρίου, μηδὲ
τοῦτο ἔτι ἔχοντας, ἢ αὐτοὺς λαμβάνειν, ἤνπερ κρατῶμεν,
22 μέτρῳ χρωμένους ὁπόσῳ ἂν ἕκαστος βούληται. εἰ δὲ
ταῦτα μὲν γιγνώσκετε ὅτι κρείττονα, τοὺς δὲ ποταμοὺς
ἄπορον νομίζετε εἶναι καὶ μεγάλως ἡγεῖσθε ἐξαπατηθῆναι διαβάντες, σκέψασθε εἰ ἄρα τοῦτο καὶ μωρότατον
πεποιήκασιν οἱ βάρβαροι. πάντες γὰρ ποταμοί, εἰ καὶ
πρόσω τῶν πηγῶν ἄποροι ὦσι, προϊοῦσι πρὸς τὰς πηγὰς
διαβατοὶ γίγνονται οὐδὲ τὸ γόνυ βρέχοντες.

*At the worst they can settle in the country of the Great
King. But Xenophon does not recommend this course.*

"εἰ δὲ μήθ' οἱ ποταμοὶ διήσουσιν ἡγεμών τε μηδεὶς 23
ἡμῖν φανεῖται, οὐδ' ὡς ἡμῖν γε ἀθυμητέον. ἐπιστάμεθα
μὲν γὰρ Μυσούς, οὓς οὐκ ἂν ἡμῶν φαίημεν βελτίους
εἶναι, ὅτι ἐν τῇ βασιλέως χώρᾳ πολλάς τε καὶ εὐδαίμο-
νας καὶ μεγάλας πόλεις οἰκοῦσιν, ἐπιστάμεθα δὲ Πισίδας
ὡσαύτως, Λυκάονας δὲ καὶ αὐτοὶ εἴδομεν ὅτι ἐν τοῖς
πεδίοις τὰ ἐρυμνὰ καταλαβόντες τὴν τούτων χώραν
καρποῦνται· καὶ ἡμᾶς δ' ἂν ἔφην ἔγωγε χρῆναι μήπω 24
φανεροὺς εἶναι οἴκαδε ὡρμημένους, ἀλλὰ κατασκευά-
ζεσθαι ὡς αὐτοῦ που οἰκήσοντας. οἶδα γὰρ ὅτι καὶ
Μυσοῖς βασιλεὺς πολλοὺς μὲν ἡγεμόνας ἂν δοίη,
πολλοὺς δ' ἂν ὁμήρους τοῦ ἀδόλως ἐκπέμψειν, καὶ
ὁδοποιήσειέ γ' ἂν αὐτοῖς, καὶ εἰ σὺν τεθρίπποις βού-
λοιντο ἀπιέναι. καὶ ἡμῖν γ' ἂν οἶδ' ὅτι τρισάσμενος
ταῦτ' ἐποίει, εἰ ἑώρα ἡμᾶς μένειν κατασκευαζομένους.
ἀλλὰ γὰρ δέδοικα μή, ἂν ἅπαξ μάθωμεν ἀργοὶ ζῆν καὶ 25
ἐν ἀφθόνοις βιοτεύειν, καὶ Μήδων δὲ καὶ Περσῶν καλαῖς
καὶ μεγάλαις γυναιξὶ καὶ παρθένοις ὁμιλεῖν, μή, ὥσπερ
οἱ λωτοφάγοι, ἐπιλαθώμεθα τῆς οἴκαδε ὁδοῦ. δοκεῖ οὖν 26
μοι εἰκὸς καὶ δίκαιον εἶναι πρῶτον εἰς τὴν Ἑλλάδα καὶ
πρὸς τοὺς οἰκείους πειρᾶσθαι ἀφικνεῖσθαι καὶ ἐπιδεῖξαι
τοῖς Ἕλλησιν ὅτι ἑκόντες πένονται, ἐξὸν αὐτοῖς τοὺς νῦν
ἀκλήρους ἐκεῖ πολιτεύοντας ἐνθάδε κομισαμένους πλουσίως ὁρᾶν.

Xenophon's proposals.

"ἀλλὰ γάρ, ὦ ἄνδρες, πάντα ταῦτα τἀγαθὰ δῆλον
ὅτι τῶν κρατούντων ἐστί· τοῦτο δὲ δεῖ λέγειν, ὅπως ἂν 27

πορευοίμεθά τε ὡς ἀσφαλέστατα καί, εἰ μάχεσθαι δέοι, ὡς
κράτιστα μαχοίμεθα. πρῶτον μὲν τοίνυν," ἔφη, " δοκεῖ
μοι κατακαῦσαι τὰς ἁμάξας ἃς ἔχομεν, ἵνα μὴ τὰ ζεύγη
ἡμῶν στρατηγῇ, ἀλλὰ πορευώμεθα ὅπῃ ἂν τῇ στρατιᾷ
συμφέρῃ· ἔπειτα καὶ τὰς σκηνὰς συγκατακαῦσαι. αὗται
γὰρ αὖ ὄχλον μὲν παρέχουσιν ἄγειν, συνωφελοῦσι δ'
οὐδὲν οὔτε εἰς τὸ μάχεσθαι οὔτ' εἰς τὸ τὰ ἐπιτήδεια
28 ἔχειν. ἔτι δὲ καὶ τῶν ἄλλων σκευῶν τὰ περιττὰ ἀπαλ-
λάξωμεν, πλὴν ὅσα πολέμου ἕνεκεν ἢ σίτων ἢ ποτῶν
ἔχομεν, ἵνα ὡς πλεῖστοι μὲν ἡμῶν ἐν τοῖς ὅπλοις ὦσιν,
ὡς ἐλάχιστοι δὲ σκευοφορῶσι. κρατουμένων μὲν γὰρ
ἐπίστασθε ὅτι πάντα ἀλλότρια· ἢν δὲ κρατῶμεν, καὶ
τοὺς πολεμίους δεῖ σκευοφόρους ἡμετέρους νομίζειν.
29 λοιπόν μοι εἰπεῖν ὅπερ καὶ μέγιστον νομίζω εἶναι.
ὁρᾶτε γὰρ καὶ τοὺς πολεμίους, ὅτι οὐ πρόσθεν ἐξ-
ενεγκεῖν ἐτόλμησαν πρὸς ἡμᾶς πόλεμον πρὶν τοὺς
στρατηγοὺς ἡμῶν συνέλαβον, νομίζοντες, ὄντων μὲν
τῶν ἀρχόντων καὶ ἡμῶν πειθομένων, ἱκανοὺς εἶναι
ἡμᾶς περιγενέσθαι τῷ πολέμῳ, λαβόντες δὲ τοὺς ἄρχοντας ἀναρχίᾳ ἂν καὶ ἀταξίᾳ ἐνόμιζον ἡμᾶς ἀπολέ-
30 σθαι. δεῖ οὖν πολὺ μὲν τοὺς ἄρχοντας ἐπιμελεστέρους
γενέσθαι τοὺς νῦν τῶν πρόσθεν, πολὺ δὲ τοὺς ἀρ-
χομένους εὐτακτοτέρους καὶ πειθομένους μᾶλλον τοῖς
31 ἄρχουσι νῦν ἢ πρόσθεν· ἢν δέ τις ἀπειθῇ, ψηφίσασθαι τὸν ἀεὶ ὑμῶν ἐντυγχάνοντα σὺν τῷ ἄρχοντι
κολάζειν· οὕτως οἱ πολέμιοι πλεῖστον ἐψευσμένοι ἔσον-
ται· τῇδε γὰρ τῇ ἡμέρᾳ μυρίους ὄψονται ἀνθ' ἑνὸς
32 Κλεάρχους τοὺς οὐδενὶ ἐπιτρέψοντας κακῷ εἶναι. ἀλλὰ
γὰρ καὶ περαίνειν ἤδη ὥρα· ἴσως γὰρ οἱ πολέμιοι
αὐτίκα παρέσονται. ὅτῳ οὖν ταῦτα δοκεῖ καλῶς ἔχειν,
ἐπικυρωσάτω ὡς τάχιστα, ἵνα ἔργῳ περαίνηται. εἰ δέ

τι ἄλλο βέλτιον ἢ ταύτῃ, τολμάτω καὶ ὁ ἰδιώτης δι-
δάσκειν· πάντες γὰρ κοινῆς σωτηρίας δεόμεθα."

These and other proposals of Xenophon are agreed to.

μετὰ ταῦτα Χειρίσοφος εἶπεν· "ἀλλ' εἰ μέν τινος 33
ἄλλου δεῖ πρὸς τούτοις οἷς λέγει Ξενοφῶν, καὶ αὐτίκα
ἐξέσται ποιεῖν· ἃ δὲ νῦν εἴρηκε δοκεῖ μοι ὡς τάχιστα
ψηφίσασθαι ἄριστον εἶναι· καὶ ὅτῳ δοκεῖ ταῦτα, ἀνατεινάτω τὴν χεῖρα." ἀνέτειναν πάντες. ἀναστὰς δὲ 34
πάλιν εἶπε Ξενοφῶν· "ὦ ἄνδρες, ἀκούσατε ὧν προσδοκεῖ μοι. δῆλον ὅτι πορεύεσθαι ἡμᾶς δεῖ ὅπου ἕξο-
μεν τὰ ἐπιτήδεια· ἀκούω δὲ κώμας εἶναι καλὰς οὐ
πλέον εἴκοσι σταδίων ἀπεχούσας· οὐκ ἂν οὖν θαυμά- 35
ζοιμι εἰ οἱ πολέμιοι (ὥσπερ οἱ δειλοὶ κύνες τοὺς μὲν
παριόντας διώκοντες καὶ δάκνουσιν, ἢν δύνωνται,
τοὺς δὲ διώκοντας φεύγουσιν) εἰ καὶ αὐτοὶ ἡμῖν ἀπ-
ιοῦσιν ἐπακολουθοῖεν. ἴσως οὖν ἀσφαλέστερον ἡμῖν 36
πορεύεσθαι πλαίσιον ποιησαμένους τῶν ὅπλων, ἵνα τὰ
σκευοφόρα καὶ ὁ πολὺς ὄχλος ἐν ἀσφαλεστέρῳ εἴη. εἰ
οὖν νῦν ἀποδειχθείη τίνας χρὴ ἡγεῖσθαι τοῦ πλαισίου
καὶ τὰ πρόσθεν κοσμεῖν καὶ τίνας ἐπὶ τῶν πλευρῶν
ἑκατέρων εἶναι, τίνας δ' ὀπισθοφυλακεῖν, οὐκ ἄν, ὁπότε
οἱ πολέμιοι ἔλθοιεν, βουλεύεσθαι ἡμᾶς δέοι, ἀλλὰ χρώ-
μεθα ἂν εὐθὺς τοῖς τεταγμένοις. εἰ μὲν οὖν ἄλλο 37
τις βέλτιον ὁρᾷ, ἄλλως ἐχέτω· εἰ δέ, Χειρίσοφος μὲν
ἡγοῖτο, ἐπειδὴ καὶ Λακεδαιμόνιός ἐστι· τῶν δὲ πλευρῶν ἑκατέρων δύο τὼ πρεσβυτάτω στρατηγὼ ἐπιμελοί-
σθην· ὀπισθοφυλακοῖμεν δ' ἡμεῖς οἱ νεώτατοι ἐγὼ καὶ
Τιμασίων τὸ νῦν εἶναι. τὸ δὲ λοιπὸν πειρώμενοι ταύ- 38
της τῆς τάξεως βουλευσόμεθα ὅ τι ἂν ἀεὶ κράτιστον
δοκῇ εἶναι. εἰ δέ τις ἄλλο ὁρᾷ βέλτιον, λεξάτω." ἐπεὶ

δ' οὐδεὶς ἀντέλεγεν, εἶπεν· "ὅτῳ δοκεῖ ταῦτα, ἀνατει-
39 νάτω τὴν χεῖρα." ἔδοξε ταῦτα. "νῦν τοίνυν," ἔφη,
"ἀπιόντας ποιεῖν δεῖ τὰ δεδογμένα. καὶ ὅστις τε ὑμῶν
τοὺς οἰκείους ἐπιθυμεῖ ἰδεῖν, μεμνήσθω ἀνὴρ ἀγαθὸς
εἶναι· οὐ γὰρ ἔστιν ἄλλως τούτου τυχεῖν· ὅστις τε ζῆν
ἐπιθυμεῖ, πειράσθω νικᾶν· τῶν μὲν γὰρ νικώντων τὸ
κατακαίνειν, τῶν δὲ ἡττωμένων τὸ ἀποθνήσκειν ἐστί·
καὶ εἴ τις δὲ χρημάτων ἐπιθυμεῖ, κρατεῖν πειράσθω·
τῶν γὰρ νικώντων ἐστὶ καὶ τὰ ἑαυτῶν σώζειν καὶ τὰ
τῶν ἡττωμένων λαμβάνειν."

III.

Mithradates appears on the scene.

1   Τούτων λεχθέντων ἀνέστησαν καὶ ἀπελθόντες κατέ-
καιον τὰς ἁμάξας καὶ τὰς σκηνάς, τῶν δὲ περιττῶν
ὅτου μὲν δέοιτό τις μετεδίδοσαν ἀλλήλοις, τὰ δὲ ἄλλα
εἰς τὸ πῦρ ἐρρίπτουν. ταῦτα ποιήσαντες ἠριστοποιοῦντο.
ἀριστοποιουμένων δὲ αὐτῶν ἔρχεται Μιθραδάτης σὺν
ἱππεῦσιν ὡς τριάκοντα, καὶ καλεσάμενος τοὺς στρατη-
2 γοὺς εἰς ἐπήκοον λέγει ὧδε· "ἐγώ, ὦ ἄνδρες Ἕλληνες,
καὶ Κύρῳ πιστὸς ἦν, ὡς ὑμεῖς ἐπίστασθε, καὶ νῦν ὑμῖν
εὔνους· καὶ ἐνθάδε δ' εἰμὶ σὺν πολλῷ φόβῳ διάγων. εἰ
οὖν ὁρῴην ὑμᾶς σωτήριόν τι βουλευομένους, ἔλθοιμι ἂν
πρὸς ὑμᾶς καὶ τοὺς θεράποντας πάντας ἔχων. λέξατε
οὖν πρός με τί ἐν νῷ ἔχετε ὡς φίλον τε καὶ εὔνουν καὶ
3 βουλόμενον κοινῇ σὺν ὑμῖν τὸν στόλον ποιεῖσθαι." βου-
λευομένοις τοῖς στρατηγοῖς ἔδοξεν ἀποκρίνασθαι τάδε·
καὶ ἔλεγε Χειρίσοφος· "ἡμῖν δοκεῖ, εἰ μέν τις ἐᾷ ἡμᾶς

ἀπιέναι οἴκαδε, διαπορεύεσθαι τὴν χώραν ὡς ἂν δυνώμεθα
ἀσινέστατα· ἢν δέ τις ἡμᾶς τῆς ὁδοῦ ἀποκωλύῃ, διαπολεμεῖν τούτῳ ὡς ἂν δυνώμεθα κράτιστα." ἐκ τού- 4
του ἐπειρᾶτο Μιθραδάτης διδάσκειν ὡς ἄπορον εἴη
βασιλέως ἄκοντος σωθῆναι. ἔνθα δὴ ἐγιγνώσκετο ὅτι
ὑπόπεμπτος εἴη· καὶ γὰρ τῶν Τισσαφέρνους τις οἰ-
κείων παρηκολουθήκει πίστεως ἕνεκα. καὶ ἐκ τούτου 5
ἐδόκει τοῖς στρατηγοῖς βέλτιον εἶναι δόγμα ποιήσασθαι
τὸν πόλεμον ἀκήρυκτον εἶναι, ἔστ' ἐν τῇ πολεμίᾳ εἶεν·
διέφθειρον γὰρ προσιόντες τοὺς στρατιώτας, καὶ ἕνα
γε λοχαγὸν διέφθειραν Νίκαρχον Ἀρκάδα, καὶ ᾤχετο
ἀπιὼν νυκτὸς σὺν ἀνθρώποις ὡς εἴκοσι.

The Greeks cross the Great Zab.   Second appearance of
Mithradates.   A skirmish.   Xenophon in pursuit.

μετὰ ταῦτα ἀριστήσαντες καὶ διαβάντες τὸν Ζα- 6
πάταν ποταμὸν ἐπορεύοντο τεταγμένοι, τὰ ὑποζύγια
καὶ τὸν ὄχλον ἐν μέσῳ ἔχοντες. οὐ πολὺ δὲ προελη-
λυθότων αὐτῶν, ἐπιφαίνεται πάλιν ὁ Μιθραδάτης,
ἱππέας ἔχων ὡς διακοσίους καὶ τοξότας καὶ σφενδονήτας εἰς τετρακοσίους μάλα ἐλαφροὺς καὶ εὐζώνους. καὶ 7
προσῄει μέν, ὡς φίλος ὤν, πρὸς τοὺς Ἕλληνας· ἐπεὶ δ'
ἐγγὺς ἐγένοντο, ἐξαπίνης οἱ μὲν αὐτῶν ἐτόξευον καὶ
ἱππεῖς καὶ πεζοί, οἱ δ' ἐσφενδόνων καὶ ἐτίτρωσκον. οἱ
δὲ ὀπισθοφύλακες τῶν Ἑλλήνων ἔπασχον μὲν κακῶς,
ἀντεποίουν δ' οὐδέν· οἵ τε γὰρ Κρῆτες βραχύτερα τῶν
Περσῶν ἐτόξευον, καὶ ἅμα ψιλοὶ ὄντες εἴσω τῶν ὅπλων
κατεκέκλειντο, οἵ τε ἀκοντισταὶ βραχύτερα ἠκόντιζον
ἢ ὡς ἐξικνεῖσθαι τῶν σφενδονητῶν. ἐκ τούτου Ξενο- 8
φῶντι ἐδόκει διωκτέον εἶναι· καὶ ἐδίωκον τῶν ὁπλιτῶν

καὶ τῶν πελταστῶν οἳ ἔτυχον σὺν αὐτῷ ὀπισθοφυλα-
κοῦντες· διώκοντες δὲ οὐδένα κατελάμβανον τῶν πολε-
9 μίων. οὔτε γὰρ ἱππεῖς ἦσαν τοῖς Ἕλλησιν οὔτε οἱ
πεζοὶ τοὺς πεζοὺς ἐκ πολλοῦ φεύγοντας ἐδύναντο
καταλαμβάνειν ἐν ὀλίγῳ χωρίῳ (πολὺ γὰρ οὐχ οἷόν τε
10 ἦν ἀπὸ τοῦ ἄλλου στρατεύματος διώκειν). οἱ δὲ βάρβαροι ἱππεῖς καὶ φεύγοντες ἅμα ἐτίτρωσκον εἰς τοὔπισθεν τοξεύοντες ἀπὸ τῶν ἵππων, ὁπόσον δὲ διώξειαν
οἱ Ἕλληνες, τοσοῦτον πάλιν ἐπαναχωρεῖν μαχομένους
11 ἔδει. ὥστε τῆς ἡμέρας ὅλης διῆλθον οὐ πλέον πέντε
καὶ εἴκοσι σταδίων, ἀλλὰ δείλης ἀφίκοντο εἰς τὰς
κώμας. ἔνθα δὴ πάλιν ἀθυμία ἦν.

*Xenophon is taken to task for pursuing the enemy.
His answer. Precautions for the future.*

καὶ Χειρίσοφος καὶ οἱ πρεσβύτατοι τῶν στρατηγῶν
Ξενοφῶντα ᾐτιῶντο ὅτι ἐδίωκεν ἀπὸ τῆς φάλαγγος καὶ
αὐτός τε ἐκινδύνευε καὶ τοὺς πολεμίους οὐδὲν μᾶλλον
12 ἐδύνατο βλάπτειν. ἀκούσας δὲ Ξενοφῶν ἔλεγεν ὅτι
ὀρθῶς ᾐτιῶντο καὶ αὐτὸ τὸ ἔργον αὐτοῖς μαρτυροίη.
"ἀλλ᾽ ἐγώ," ἔφη, "ἠναγκάσθην διώκειν, ἐπειδὴ ἑώρων
ἡμᾶς ἐν τῷ μένειν κακῶς μὲν πάσχοντας, ἀντιποιεῖν δὲ
οὐδὲν δυναμένους. ἐπειδὴ δὲ ἐδιώκομεν, ἀληθῆ," ἔφη,
13 "ὑμεῖς λέγετε· κακῶς μὲν γὰρ ποιεῖν οὐδὲν μᾶλλον
ἐδυνάμεθα τοὺς πολεμίους, ἀνεχωροῦμεν δὲ πάνυ χαλε-
14 πῶς. τοῖς οὖν θεοῖς χάρις ὅτι οὐ σὺν πολλῇ ῥώμῃ ἀλλὰ
σὺν ὀλίγοις ἦλθον, ὥστε βλάψαι μὲν μὴ μεγάλα, δηλῶ-
15 σαι δὲ ὧν δεόμεθα. νῦν γὰρ οἱ μὲν πολέμιοι τοξεύουσι
καὶ σφενδονῶσιν ὅσον οὔτε οἱ Κρῆτες ἀντιτοξεύειν
δύνανται οὔτε οἱ ἐκ χειρὸς βάλλοντες ἐξικνεῖσθαι· ὅταν

δὲ αὐτοὺς διώκωμεν, πολὺ μὲν οὐχ οἷόν τε χωρίον ἀπὸ
τοῦ στρατεύματος διώκειν, ἐν ὀλίγῳ δὲ οὐδ' εἰ ταχὺς εἴη
πεζὸς πεζὸν ἂν διώκων καταλαμβάνοι ἐκ τόξου ῥύματος.
ἡμεῖς οὖν εἰ μέλλομεν τούτους εἴργειν ὥστε μὴ δύνασθαι 16
βλάπτειν ἡμᾶς πορευομένους, σφενδονητῶν τὴν ταχίστην
δεῖ καὶ ἱππέων. ἀκούω δ' εἶναι ἐν τῷ στρατεύματι ἡμῶν
Ῥοδίους, ὧν τοὺς πολλούς φασιν ἐπίστασθαι σφενδονᾶν,
καὶ τὸ βέλος αὐτῶν καὶ διπλάσιον φέρεσθαι τῶν Περσι-
κῶν σφενδονῶν. ἐκεῖναι γὰρ διὰ τὸ χειροπληθέσι τοῖς 17
λίθοις σφενδονᾶν ἐπὶ βραχὺ ἐξικνοῦνται, οἱ δὲ Ῥόδιοι
καὶ ταῖς μολυβδίσιν ἐπίστανται χρῆσθαι. ἢν οὖν αὐτῶν 18
ἐπισκεψώμεθα τίνες πέπανται σφενδόνας, καὶ τούτων
μὲν δῶμεν ἀργύριον, τῷ δὲ ἄλλας πλέκειν ἐθέλοντι ἄλλο
ἀργύριον τελῶμεν, καὶ τῷ σφενδονᾶν ἐν τῷ τεταγμένῳ
ἐθέλοντι ἄλλην τινὰ ἀτέλειαν εὑρίσκωμεν, ἴσως τινὲς
φανοῦνται ἱκανοὶ ἡμᾶς ὠφελεῖν. ὁρῶ δὲ ἵππους ὄντας 19
ἐν τῷ στρατεύματι, τοὺς μέν τινας παρ' ἐμοί, τοὺς δὲ
τῶν Κλεάρχου καταλελειμμένους, πολλοὺς δὲ καὶ ἄλλους
αἰχμαλώτους σκευοφοροῦντας. ἂν οὖν τούτους πάντας
ἐκλέξαντες σκευοφόρα μὲν ἀντιδῶμεν, τοὺς δὲ ἵππους
εἰς ἱππέας κατασκευάσωμεν, ἴσως καὶ οὗτοί τι τοὺς
φεύγοντας ἀνιάσουσιν." ἔδοξε καὶ ταῦτα· καὶ ταύτης 20
τῆς νυκτὸς σφενδονῆται μὲν εἰς διακοσίους ἐγένοντο·
ἵπποι δὲ καὶ ἱππεῖς ἐδοκιμάσθησαν τῇ ὑστεραίᾳ εἰς
πεντήκοντα, καὶ σπολάδες καὶ θώρακες αὐτοῖς ἐπορί-
σθησαν, καὶ ἵππαρχος ἐπεστάθη Λύκιος ὁ Πολυστρά-
του Ἀθηναῖος.

IV.

Third appearance of Mithradates.   He is defeated.

1   Μείναντες δὲ ταύτην τὴν ἡμέραν τῇ ἄλλῃ ἐπορεύοντο πρωαίτερον ἀναστάντες· χαράδραν γὰρ ἔδει
αὐτοὺς διαβῆναι, ἐφ᾽ ᾗ ἐφοβοῦντο μὴ ἐπιθοῖντο αὐτοῖς
2 διαβαίνουσιν οἱ πολέμιοι.   διαβεβηκόσι δὲ αὐτοῖς πάλιν
φαίνεται ὁ Μιθραδάτης, ἔχων ἱππέας χιλίους, τοξότας
δὲ καὶ σφενδονήτας εἰς τετρακισχιλίους· τοσούτους γὰρ
ἤτησε Τισσαφέρνην, καὶ ἔλαβεν ὑποσχόμενος, ἂν τούτους λάβῃ, παραδώσειν αὐτῷ τοὺς Ἕλληνας, καταφρονήσας, ὅτι ἐν τῇ πρόσθεν προσβολῇ ὀλίγους ἔχων
ἔπαθε μὲν οὐδέν, πολλὰ δὲ κακὰ ἐνόμιζε ποιῆσαι.
3 ἐπεὶ δὲ οἱ Ἕλληνες διαβεβηκότες ἀπεῖχον τῆς χαράδρας
ὅσον ὀκτὼ σταδίους, διέβαινε καὶ ὁ Μιθραδάτης ἔχων
τὴν δύναμιν.   παρήγγελτο δὲ τῶν πελταστῶν οὓς ἔδει
διώκειν καὶ τῶν ὁπλιτῶν, καὶ τοῖς ἱππεῦσιν εἴρητο
θαρροῦσι διώκειν, ὡς ἐφεψομένης ἱκανῆς δυνάμεως.
4 ἐπεὶ δὲ ὁ Μιθραδάτης κατειλήφει, καὶ ἤδη σφενδόναι
καὶ τοξεύματα ἐξικνοῦντο, ἐσήμηνε τοῖς Ἕλλησι τῇ
σάλπιγγι, καὶ εὐθὺς ἔθεον ὁμόσε οἷς εἴρητο καὶ οἱ
ἱππεῖς ἤλαυνον· οἱ δὲ οὐκ ἐδέξαντο, ἀλλ᾽ ἔφευγον ἐπὶ
5 τὴν χαράδραν.   ἐν ταύτῃ τῇ διώξει τοῖς βαρβάροις τῶν
τε πεζῶν ἀπέθανον πολλοὶ καὶ τῶν ἱππέων ἐν τῇ
χαράδρᾳ ζωοὶ ἐλήφθησαν εἰς ὀκτωκαίδεκα.   τοὺς δὲ
ἀποθανόντας αὐτοκέλευστοι οἱ Ἕλληνες ἠκίσαντο, ὡς
ὅτι φοβερώτατον τοῖς πολεμίοις εἴη ὁρᾶν.

The Greeks continue their march and reach Larissa.

καὶ οἱ μὲν πολέμιοι οὕτω πράξαντες ἀπῆλθον, οἱ δὲ 6
Ἕλληνες, ἀσφαλῶς πορευόμενοι τὸ λοιπὸν τῆς ἡμέρας,
ἀφίκοντο ἐπὶ τὸν Τίγρητα ποταμόν. ἐνταῦθα πόλις ἦν 7
ἐρήμη μεγάλη, ὄνομα δ᾽ αὐτῇ ἦν Λάρισσα· ᾤκουν δ᾽
αὐτὴν τὸ παλαιὸν Μῆδοι. τοῦ δὲ τείχους αὐτῆς ἦν τὸ
εὖρος πέντε καὶ εἴκοσι πόδες, ὕψος δ᾽ ἑκατόν· τοῦ δὲ
κύκλου ἡ περίοδος δύο παρασάγγαι· ᾠκοδόμητο δὲ
πλίνθοις κεραμεαῖς· κρηπὶς δ᾽ ὑπῆν λιθίνη τὸ ὕψος
εἴκοσι ποδῶν. ταύτην βασιλεὺς ὁ Περσῶν, ὅτε παρὰ 8
Μήδων τὴν ἀρχὴν ἐλάμβανον Πέρσαι, πολιορκῶν οὐδενὶ
τρόπῳ ἐδύνατο ἑλεῖν· ἥλιον δὲ νεφέλη προκαλύψασα
ἠφάνισε, μέχρι ἐξέλιπον οἱ ἄνθρωποι, καὶ οὕτως ἑάλω.
παρὰ ταύτην τὴν πόλιν ἦν πυραμὶς λιθίνη, τὸ μὲν εὖρος 9
ἑνὸς πλέθρου, τὸ δὲ ὕψος δύο πλέθρων. ἐπὶ ταύτης
πολλοὶ τῶν βαρβάρων ἦσαν ἐκ τῶν πλησίον κωμῶν
πεφευγότες.

They reach Mespila.

ἐντεῦθεν δ᾽ ἐπορεύθησαν σταθμὸν ἕνα παρασάγγας 10
ἓξ πρὸς τεῖχος ἔρημον μέγα κείμενον· ὄνομα δὲ ἦν τῇ
πόλει Μέσπιλα· Μῆδοι δ᾽ αὐτήν ποτε ᾤκουν. ἦν δὲ ἡ
μὲν κρηπὶς λίθου ξεστοῦ κογχυλιάτου, τὸ εὖρος πεντήκοντα ποδῶν καὶ τὸ ὕψος πεντήκοντα. ἐπὶ δὲ ταύτῃ 11
ἐπῳκοδόμητο πλίνθινον τεῖχος, τὸ μὲν εὖρος πεντήκοντα
ποδῶν, τὸ δὲ ὕψος ἑκατόν· τοῦ δὲ τείχους ἡ περίοδος ἓξ
παρασάγγαι. ἐνταῦθα λέγεται Μήδεια γυνὴ βασιλέως
καταφυγεῖν, ὅτε ἀπώλλυσαν τὴν ἀρχὴν ὑπὸ Περσῶν
Μῆδοι. ταύτην δὲ τὴν πόλιν πολιορκῶν ὁ Περσῶν 12
βασιλεὺς οὐκ ἐδύνατο οὔτε χρόνῳ ἑλεῖν οὔτε βίᾳ· Ζεὺς
δὲ βροντῇ κατέπληξε τοὺς ἐνοικοῦντας, καὶ οὕτως ἑάλω.

The Greeks are harassed by the cavalry of Tissaphernes.

13 ἐντεῦθεν δ' ἐπορεύθησαν σταθμὸν ἕνα παρασάγγας
τέτταρας. εἰς τοῦτον δὲ τὸν σταθμὸν Τισσαφέρνης
ἐπεφάνη, ἄγων οὕς τε αὐτὸς ἱππέας ἦλθεν ἔχων καὶ τὴν
Ὀρόντα δύναμιν τοῦ τὴν βασιλέως θυγατέρα ἔχοντος
καὶ οὓς Κῦρος ἔχων ἀνέβη βαρβάρους καὶ οὓς ὁ
βασιλέως ἀδελφὸς ἔχων βασιλεῖ ἐβοήθει, καὶ πρὸς
τούτοις ὅσους βασιλεὺς ἔδωκεν αὐτῷ· ὥστε τὸ στρά-
14 τευμα πάμπολυ ἐφάνη. ἐπεὶ δ' ἐγγὺς ἐγένετο, τὰς μὲν
τῶν τάξεων ὄπισθεν καταστήσας, τὰς δὲ εἰς τὰ πλάγια
παραγαγών, ἐμβαλεῖν μὲν οὐκ ἐτόλμησεν οὐδ' ἐβούλετο
διακινδυνεύειν, σφενδονᾶν δὲ παρήγγειλε καὶ τοξεύειν.
15 ἐπεὶ δὲ διαταχθέντες οἱ Ῥόδιοι ἐσφενδόνησαν καὶ οἱ
Σκύθαι τοξόται ἐτόξευσαν καὶ οὐδεὶς ἡμάρτανεν
ἀνδρὸς (οὐδὲ γάρ, εἰ πάνυ προυθυμεῖτο, ῥᾴδιον ἦν)
καὶ ὁ Τισσαφέρνης μάλα ταχέως ἔξω βελῶν ἀπεχώρει
16 καὶ αἱ ἄλλαι τάξεις ἀπεχώρησαν. καὶ τὸ λοιπὸν τῆς
ἡμέρας οἱ μὲν ἐπορεύοντο, οἱ δ' εἵποντο καὶ οὐκέτι
ἐσίνοντο οἱ βάρβαροι τῇ τότε ἀκροβολίσει· μακρότερον
γὰρ οἵ τε Ῥόδιοι τῶν Περσῶν ἐσφενδόνων καὶ τῶν
17 τοξοτῶν οἱ Κρῆτες ἐτόξευον. μεγάλα δὲ καὶ τὰ τόξα
τὰ Περσικά ἐστιν· ὥστε χρήσιμα ἦν ὁπόσα ἁλίσκοιτο
τῶν τοξευμάτων τοῖς Κρησί, καὶ διετέλουν χρώμενοι
τοῖς τῶν πολεμίων τοξεύμασι, καὶ ἐμελέτων τοξεύειν
ἄνω ἱέντες μακράν. εὑρίσκετο δὲ καὶ νεῦρα πολλὰ ἐν
ταῖς κώμαις καὶ μόλυβδος, ὥστε χρῆσθαι εἰς τὰς
18 σφενδόνας. καὶ ταύτῃ μὲν τῇ ἡμέρᾳ, ἐπεὶ κατεστρα-
τοπεδεύοντο οἱ Ἕλληνες κώμαις ἐπιτυχόντες, ἀπῆλθον
οἱ βάρβαροι μεῖον ἔχοντες τῇ ἀκροβολίσει· τὴν δ'
ἐπιοῦσαν ἡμέραν ἔμειναν οἱ Ἕλληνες καὶ ἐπεσιτίσαντο·

ἦν γὰρ πολὺς σῖτος ἐν ταῖς κώμαις.   τῇ δὲ ὑστεραίᾳ
ἐπορεύοντο διὰ τοῦ πεδίου, καὶ Τισσαφέρνης εἵπετο
ἀκροβολιζόμενος.

*They find out that marching in a hollow square
is a mistake.*

ἔνθα δὴ οἱ Ἕλληνες ἔγνωσαν πλαίσιον ἰσόπλευρον, 19
ὅτι πονηρὰ τάξις εἴη πολεμίων ἑπομένων.   ἀνάγκη γάρ
ἐστιν, ἢν μὲν συγκύπτῃ τὰ κέρατα τοῦ πλαισίου ἢ ὁδοῦ
στενοτέρας οὔσης ἢ ὀρέων ἀναγκαζόντων ἢ γεφύρας,
ἐκθλίβεσθαι τοὺς ὁπλίτας καὶ πορεύεσθαι πονηρῶς,
ἅμα μὲν πιεζομένους, ἅμα δὲ καὶ ταραττομένους, ὥστε
δυσχρήστους εἶναι ἀτάκτους ὄντας· ὅταν δ᾽ αὖ διάσχῃ 20
τὰ κέρατα, ἀνάγκη διασπᾶσθαι τοὺς τότε ἐκθλιβομένους
καὶ κενὸν γίγνεσθαι τὸ μέσον τῶν κεράτων, καὶ ἀθυμεῖν
τοὺς ταῦτα πάσχοντας πολεμίων ἑπομένων.   καὶ ὁπότε
δέοι γέφυραν διαβαίνειν ἢ ἄλλην τινὰ διάβασιν, ἔσπευ-
δεν ἕκαστος βουλόμενος φθάσαι πρῶτος· καὶ εὐεπίθετον
ἦν ἐνταῦθα τοῖς πολεμίοις.

Their new order of march.

ἐπεὶ δὲ ταῦτ᾽ ἔγνωσαν οἱ στρατηγοί, ἐποίησαν ἓξ 21
λόχους ἀνὰ ἑκατὸν ἄνδρας, καὶ λοχαγοὺς ἐπέστησαν
καὶ ἄλλους πεντηκοντῆρας καὶ ἄλλους ἐνωμοτάρχους.
οὗτοι δὲ πορευόμενοι, ὁπότε μὲν συγκύπτοι τὰ
κέρατα, ὑπέμενον ὕστεροι, ὥστε μὴ ἐνοχλεῖν τοῖς
κέρασι, τότε δὲ παρῆγον ἔξωθεν τῶν κεράτων.   ὁπότε 22
δὲ διάσχοιεν αἱ πλευραὶ τοῦ πλαισίου, τὸ μέσον ἂν
ἐξεπίμπλασαν, εἰ μὲν στενότερον εἴη τὸ διέχον, κατὰ
λόχους, εἰ δὲ πλατύτερον, κατὰ πεντηκοστῦς, εἰ δὲ
πάνυ πλατύ, κατ᾽ ἐνωμοτίας· ὥστε ἀεὶ ἔκπλεων εἶναι.

23 τὸ μέσον. εἰ δὲ καὶ διαβαίνειν τινὰ δέοι διάβασιν ἢ
γέφυραν, οὐκ ἐταράττοντο, ἀλλ' ἐν τῷ μέρει οἱ λοχαγοὶ
διέβαινον· καὶ εἴ που δέοι τι τῆς φάλαγγος, ἐπιπαρῆσαν
οὗτοι.

The Greeks are again hard-pressed by the enemy.
They encamp for three days.

τούτῳ τῷ τρόπῳ ἐπορεύθησαν σταθμοὺς τέτταρας.
24 ἡνίκα δὲ τὸν πέμπτον ἐπορεύοντο, εἶδον βασίλειόν τι καὶ
περὶ αὐτὸ κώμας πολλάς, τὴν δὲ ὁδὸν πρὸς τὸ χωρίον
τοῦτο διὰ γηλόφων ὑψηλῶν γιγνομένην, οἳ καθῆκον
ἀπὸ τοῦ ὄρους, ὑφ' ᾧ ἦν ἡ κώμη. καὶ εἶδον μὲν τοὺς
λόφους ἄσμενοι οἱ Ἕλληνες, ὡς εἰκὸς τῶν πολεμίων
25 ὄντων ἱππέων· ἐπεὶ δὲ πορευόμενοι ἐκ τοῦ πεδίου
ἀνέβησαν ἐπὶ τὸν πρῶτον γήλοφον καὶ κατέβαινον,
ὡς ἐπὶ τὸν ἕτερον ἀναβαίνειν, ἐνταῦθα ἐπιγίγνονται
οἱ βάρβαροι καὶ ἀπὸ τοῦ ὑψηλοῦ εἰς τὸ πρανὲς ἔβαλλον,
26 ἐσφενδόνων, ἐτόξευον ὑπὸ μαστίγων, καὶ πολλοὺς
ἐτίτρωσκον καὶ ἐκράτησαν τῶν Ἑλλήνων γυμνήτων καὶ
κατέκλεισαν αὐτοὺς εἴσω τῶν ὅπλων· ὥστε παντάπασι
ταύτην τὴν ἡμέραν ἄχρηστοι ἦσαν ἐν τῷ ὄχλῳ ὄντες
27 καὶ οἱ σφενδονῆται καὶ οἱ τοξόται. ἐπεὶ δὲ πιεζόμενοι
οἱ Ἕλληνες ἐπεχείρησαν διώκειν, σχολῇ μὲν ἐπὶ τὸ
ἄκρον ἀφικνοῦνται ὁπλῖται ὄντες, οἱ δὲ πολέμιοι ταχὺ
28 ἀπεπήδων. πάλιν δὲ ὁπότε ἀπίοιεν πρὸς τὸ ἄλλο στράτευμα, ταὐτὰ ἔπασχον, καὶ ἐπὶ τοῦ δευτέρου γηλόφου
ταὐτὰ ἐγίγνετο, ὥστε ἀπὸ τοῦ τρίτου γηλόφου ἔδοξεν
αὐτοῖς μὴ κινεῖν τοὺς στρατιώτας, πρὶν ἀπὸ τῆς δεξιᾶς
πλευρᾶς τοῦ πλαισίου ἀνήγαγον πελταστὰς πρὸς τὸ
29 ὄρος. ἐπεὶ δ' οὗτοι ἐγένοντο ὑπὲρ τῶν ἑπομένων πολεμίων, οὐκέτι ἐπετίθεντο οἱ πολέμιοι τοῖς καταβαίνουσι,

δεδοικότες μὴ ἀποτμηθείησαν καὶ ἀμφοτέρωθεν αὐτῶν
γένοιντο οἱ πολέμιοι. οὕτω τὸ λοιπὸν τῆς ἡμέρας πο- 30
ρευόμενοι, οἱ μὲν τῇ ὁδῷ κατὰ τοὺς γηλόφους, οἱ δὲ
κατὰ τὸ ὄρος ἐπιπαριόντες, ἀφίκοντο εἰς τὰς κώμας·
καὶ ἰατροὺς κατέστησαν ὀκτώ· πολλοὶ γὰρ ἦσαν οἱ
τετρωμένοι. ἐνταῦθα ἔμειναν ἡμέρας τρεῖς καὶ τῶν 31
τετρωμένων ἕνεκα καὶ ἅμα ἐπιτήδεια πολλὰ εἶχον,
ἄλευρα, οἶνον, κριθὰς ἵπποις συμβεβλημένας πολλάς.
ταῦτα δὲ συνενηνεγμένα ἦν τῷ σατραπεύοντι τῆς
χώρας.

*The Greeks descend into the plain, and then halt again
to repel the Persian cavalry. They resume their march.*

τετάρτῃ δ' ἡμέρᾳ καταβαίνουσιν εἰς τὸ πεδίον. ἐπεὶ 32
δὲ κατέλαβεν αὐτοὺς Τισσαφέρνης σὺν τῇ δυνάμει,
ἐδίδαξεν αὐτοὺς ἡ ἀνάγκη κατασκηνῆσαι οὗ πρῶτον
εἶδον κώμην καὶ μὴ πορεύεσθαι ἔτι μαχομένους· πολλοὶ
γὰρ ἦσαν οἱ ἀπόμαχοι, οἵ τε τετρωμένοι καὶ οἱ
ἐκείνους φέροντες καὶ οἱ τῶν φερόντων τὰ ὅπλα δεξά-
μενοι. ἐπεὶ δὲ κατεσκήνησαν καὶ ἐπεχείρησαν αὐτοῖς 33
ἀκροβολίζεσθαι οἱ βάρβαροι πρὸς τὴν κώμην προσιόντες, πολὺ περιῆσαν οἱ Ἕλληνες· πολὺ γὰρ διέφερεν
ἐκ χώρας ὁρμῶντας ἀλέξασθαι ἢ πορευομένους ἐπιοῦσι
τοῖς πολεμίοις μάχεσθαι. ἡνίκα δ' ἦν ἤδη δείλη, ὥρα 34
ἦν ἀπιέναι τοῖς πολεμίοις· οὔποτε γὰρ μεῖον ἀπεστρα-
τοπεδεύοντο οἱ βάρβαροι τοῦ Ἑλληνικοῦ ἑξήκοντα
σταδίων, φοβούμενοι μὴ τῆς νυκτὸς οἱ Ἕλληνες ἐπιθῶνται αὐτοῖς. πονηρὸν γὰρ νυκτός ἐστι στράτευμα 35
Περσικόν. οἵ τε γὰρ ἵπποι αὐτοῖς δέδενται καὶ ὡς ἐπὶ
τὸ πολὺ πεποδισμένοι εἰσί, τοῦ μὴ φεύγειν ἕνεκα εἰ
λυθείησαν· ἐάν τέ τις θόρυβος γίγνηται, δεῖ ἐπισάξαι

τὸν ἵππον Πέρσῃ ἀνδρὶ καὶ χαλινῶσαι, δεῖ καὶ θωρακισθέντα ἀναβῆναι ἐπὶ τὸν ἵππον. ταῦτα δὲ πάντα
χαλεπὰ νύκτωρ καὶ θορύβου ὄντος. τούτου ἕνεκα πόρρω
36 ἀπεσκήνουν τῶν Ἑλλήνων. ἐπεὶ δὲ ἐγίγνωσκον αὐτοὺς
οἱ Ἕλληνες βουλομένους ἀπιέναι καὶ διαγγελλομένους,
ἐκήρυξε τοῖς Ἕλλησι συσκευάζεσθαι ἀκουόντων τῶν
πολεμίων. καὶ χρόνον μέν τινα ἐπέσχον τῆς πορείας
οἱ βάρβαροι, ἐπειδὴ δὲ ὀψὲ ἐγίγνετο, ἀπῇσαν· οὐ γὰρ
ἐδόκει λύειν αὐτοὺς νυκτὸς πορεύεσθαι καὶ κατάγεσθαι
ἐπὶ τὸ στρατόπεδον.

*The Persians occupy a strong position. Xenophon makes
a flank attack upon them.*

37 ἐπειδὴ δὲ σαφῶς ἀπιόντας ἤδη ἑώρων οἱ Ἕλληνες,
ἐπορεύοντο καὶ αὐτοὶ ἀναζεύξαντες καὶ διῆλθον ὅσον
ἑξήκοντα σταδίους. καὶ γίγνεται τοσοῦτον μεταξὺ τῶν
στρατευμάτων, ὥστε τῇ ὑστεραίᾳ οὐκ ἐφάνησαν οἱ πολέμιοι οὐδὲ τῇ τρίτῃ, τῇ δὲ τετάρτῃ νυκτὸς προελθόντες
καταλαμβάνουσι χωρίον ὑπερδέξιον οἱ βάρβαροι, ᾗ
ἔμελλον οἱ Ἕλληνες παριέναι, ἀκρωνυχίαν ὄρους, ὑφ'
38 ἦν ἡ κατάβασις ἦν εἰς τὸ πεδίον. ἐπειδὴ δὲ ἑώρα
Χειρίσοφος προκατειλημμένην τὴν ἀκρωνυχίαν, καλεῖ
Ξενοφῶντα ἀπὸ τῆς οὐρᾶς καὶ κελεύει λαβόντα τοὺς
πελταστὰς παραγενέσθαι εἰς τὸ πρόσθεν. ὁ δὲ Ξενοφῶν
39 τοὺς μὲν πελταστὰς οὐκ ἦγεν· ἐπιφαινόμενον γὰρ
ἑώρα Τισσαφέρνην καὶ τὸ στράτευμα πᾶν· αὐτὸς δὲ
προσελάσας ἠρώτα· "τί καλεῖς;" ὁ δὲ λέγει αὐτῷ·
"ἔξεστιν ὁρᾶν· προκατείληπται γὰρ ἡμῖν ὁ ὑπὲρ τῆς
καταβάσεως λόφος, καὶ οὐκ ἔστι παρελθεῖν, εἰ μὴ
40 τούτους ἀποκόψομεν. ἀλλὰ τί οὐκ ἦγες τοὺς πελταστάς;" ὁ δὲ λέγει ὅτι οὐκ ἐδόκει αὐτῷ ἔρημα

καταλιπεῖν τὰ ὄπισθεν πολεμίων ἐπιφαινομένων. "ἀλλὰ
μὴν ὥρα γ'," ἔφη, " βουλεύεσθαι πῶς τις τοὺς ἄνδρας
ἀπελᾷ ἀπὸ τοῦ λόφου." ἐνταῦθα Ξενοφῶν ὁρᾷ τοῦ 41
ὄρους τὴν κορυφὴν ὑπὲρ αὐτοῦ τοῦ ἑαυτῶν στρατεύματος οὖσαν, καὶ ἀπὸ ταύτης ἔφοδον ἐπὶ τὸν λόφον
ἔνθα ἦσαν οἱ πολέμιοι, καὶ λέγει· " κράτιστον, ὦ
Χειρίσοφε, ἡμῖν ἵεσθαι ὡς τάχιστα ἐπὶ τὸ ἄκρον· ἢν
γὰρ τοῦτο λάβωμεν, οὐ δυνήσονται μένειν οἱ ὑπὲρ τῆς
ὁδοῦ. ἀλλά, εἰ βούλει, μένε ἐπὶ τῷ στρατεύματι, ἐγὼ
δ' ἐθέλω πορεύεσθαι· εἰ δὲ χρῄζεις, πορεύου ἐπὶ τὸ
ὄρος, ἐγὼ δὲ μενῶ αὐτοῦ." " ἀλλὰ δίδωμί σοι," ἔφη ὁ 42
Χειρίσοφος, " ὁπότερον βούλει ἑλέσθαι." εἰπὼν ὁ Ξενοφῶν ὅτι νεώτερός ἐστιν αἱρεῖται πορεύεσθαι, κελεύει
δέ οἱ συμπέμψαι ἀπὸ τοῦ στόματος ἄνδρας· μακρὸν
γὰρ ἦν ἀπὸ τῆς οὐρᾶς λαβεῖν. καὶ ὁ Χειρίσοφος 43
συμπέμπει τοὺς ἀπὸ τοῦ στόματος πελταστάς, ἔλαβε δὲ
τοὺς κατὰ μέσον τοῦ πλαισίου. συνέπεσθαι δ' ἐκέλευσεν αὐτῷ καὶ τοὺς τριακοσίους οὓς αὐτὸς εἶχε τῶν
ἐπιλέκτων ἐπὶ τῷ στόματι τοῦ πλαισίου. ἐντεῦθεν 44
ἐπορεύοντο ὡς ἐδύναντο τάχιστα. οἱ δ' ἐπὶ τοῦ λόφου
πολέμιοι ὡς ἐνόησαν αὐτῶν τὴν πορείαν ἐπὶ τὸ ἄκρον,
εὐθὺς καὶ αὐτοὶ ὥρμησαν ἁμιλλᾶσθαι ἐπὶ τὸ ἄκρον.
καὶ ἐνταῦθα πολλὴ μὲν κραυγὴ ἦν τοῦ Ἑλληνικοῦ 45
στρατεύματος διακελευομένων τοῖς ἑαυτῶν, πολλὴ δὲ
κραυγὴ τῶν ἀμφὶ Τισσαφέρνην τοῖς ἑαυτῶν διακελευομένων.

Prowess of Xenophon. Victory of the Greeks.

Ξενοφῶν δὲ παρελαύνων ἐπὶ τοῦ ἵππου παρεκε- 46
λεύετο· " ἄνδρες, νῦν ἐπὶ τὴν Ἑλλάδα νομίζετε ἁμιλλᾶσθαι, νῦν πρὸς τοὺς παῖδας καὶ τὰς γυναῖκας, νῦν

ὀλίγον πονήσαντες ἀμαχεὶ τὴν λοιπὴν πορευσόμεθα."

47 Σωτηρίδας δὲ ὁ Σικυώνιος εἶπεν· "οὐκ ἐξ ἴσου, ὦ
Ξενοφῶν, ἐσμέν· σὺ μὲν γὰρ ἐφ' ἵππου ὀχεῖ, ἐγὼ δὲ
48 χαλεπῶς κάμνω τὴν ἀσπίδα φέρων." καὶ ὃς ἀκούσας
ταῦτα καταπηδήσας ἀπὸ τοῦ ἵππου ὠθεῖται αὐτὸν ἐκ
τῆς τάξεως καὶ τὴν ἀσπίδα ἀφελόμενος, ὡς ἐδύνατο
τάχιστα, ἔχων ἐπορεύετο· ἐτύγχανε δὲ καὶ θώρακα ἔχων
τὸν ἱππικόν· ὥστ' ἐπιέζετο. καὶ τοῖς μὲν ἔμπροσθεν
ὑπάγειν παρεκελεύετο, τοῖς δὲ ὄπισθεν παριέναι μόλις
49 ἑπόμενος. οἱ δ' ἄλλοι στρατιῶται παίουσι καὶ βάλ-
λουσι καὶ λοιδοροῦσι τὸν Σωτηρίδαν, ἔστε ἠνάγκασαν
λαβόντα τὴν ἀσπίδα πορεύεσθαι. ὁ δὲ ἀναβάς, ἕως
μὲν βάσιμα ἦν, ἐπὶ τοῦ ἵππου ἦγεν, ἐπεὶ δὲ ἄβατα ἦν,
καταλιπὼν τὸν ἵππον ἔσπευδε πεζῇ. καὶ φθάνουσιν ἐπὶ
τῷ ἄκρῳ γενόμενοι τοὺς πολεμίους.

V.

After the battle.

1 Ἔνθα δὴ οἱ μὲν βάρβαροι στραφέντες ἔφευγον ᾗ
ἕκαστος ἐδύνατο, οἱ δὲ Ἕλληνες εἶχον τὸ ἄκρον. οἱ δὲ
ἀμφὶ Τισσαφέρνην καὶ Ἀριαῖον ἀποτραπόμενοι ἄλλην
ὁδὸν ᾤχοντο. οἱ δὲ ἀμφὶ Χειρίσοφον καταβάντες
ἐστρατοπεδεύοντο ἐν κώμῃ μεστῇ πολλῶν ἀγαθῶν.
ἦσαν δὲ καὶ ἄλλαι κῶμαι πολλαὶ πλήρεις πολλῶν
ἀγαθῶν ἐν τούτῳ τῷ πεδίῳ παρὰ τὸν Τίγρητα ποταμόν.
2 ἡνίκα δ' ἦν δείλη ἐξαπίνης οἱ πολέμιοι ἐπιφαίνονται ἐν
τῷ πεδίῳ, καὶ τῶν Ἑλλήνων κατέκοψάν τινας τῶν
ἐσκεδασμένων ἐν τῷ πεδίῳ καθ' ἁρπαγήν· καὶ γὰρ

νομαὶ πολλαὶ βοσκημάτων διαβιβαζόμεναι εἰς τὸ πέραν
τοῦ ποταμοῦ κατελήφθησαν. ἐνταῦθα Τισσαφέρνης 3
καὶ οἱ σὺν αὐτῷ καίειν ἐπεχείρησαν τὰς κώμας. καὶ
τῶν Ἑλλήνων μάλα ἠθύμησάν τινες, ἐννοούμενοι μὴ τὰ
ἐπιτήδεια, εἰ καίοιεν, οὐκ ἔχοιεν ὁπόθεν λαμβάνοιεν.
καὶ οἱ μὲν ἀμφὶ Χειρίσοφον ἀπῆσαν ἐκ τῆς βοηθείας· ὁ 4
δὲ Ξενοφῶν ἐπεὶ κατέβη, παρελαύνων τὰς τάξεις, ἡνίκα
ἀπὸ τῆς βοηθείας ἀπήντησαν οἱ Ἕλληνες, ἔλεγεν·
"ὁρᾶτε, ὦ ἄνδρες, ὑφιέντας τὴν χώραν ἤδη ἡμετέραν 5
εἶναι; ἃ γάρ, ὅτε ἐσπένδοντο, διεπράττοντο, μὴ καίειν τὴν
βασιλέως χώραν, νῦν αὐτοὶ καίουσιν ὡς ἀλλοτρίαν. ἀλλ'
ἐάν που καταλίπωσί γε αὐτοῖς τὰ ἐπιτήδεια, ὄψονται
καὶ ἡμᾶς ἐνταῦθα πορευομένους. ἀλλ', ὦ Χειρίσοφε," 6
ἔφη, "δοκεῖ μοι βοηθεῖν ἐπὶ τοὺς καίοντας, ὡς ὑπὲρ τῆς
ἡμετέρας." ὁ δὲ Χειρίσοφος εἶπεν· "οὔκουν ἔμοιγε
δοκεῖ· ἀλλὰ καὶ ἡμεῖς," ἔφη, "καίωμεν, καὶ οὕτω θᾶττον
παύσονται."

*Difficulties of the Greeks as to their route. Ingenious
proposal of a Rhodian soldier.*

ἐπεὶ δὲ ἐπὶ τὰς σκηνὰς ἦλθον, οἱ μὲν ἄλλοι 7
περὶ τὰ ἐπιτήδεια ἦσαν, στρατηγοὶ δὲ καὶ λοχαγοὶ
συνῆσαν. καὶ ἐνταῦθα πολλὴ ἀπορία ἦν. ἔνθεν μὲν
γὰρ ὄρη ἦν ὑπερύψηλα, ἔνθεν δὲ ὁ ποταμὸς τοσοῦτος
τὸ βάθος ὡς μηδὲ τὰ δόρατα ὑπερέχειν πειρωμένοις
τοῦ βάθους. ἀπορουμένοις δ' αὐτοῖς προσελθών τις 8
ἀνὴρ Ῥόδιος εἶπεν· "ἐγὼ θέλω, ὦ ἄνδρες, διαβιβάσαι
ὑμᾶς κατὰ τετρακισχιλίους ὁπλίτας, ἂν ἐμοὶ ὧν δέομαι
ὑπηρετήσητε καὶ τάλαντον μισθὸν πορίσητε." ἐρωτώ- 9
μενος δὲ ὅτου δέοιτο, "ἀσκῶν," ἔφη, "δισχιλίων δεήσο-
μαι· πολλὰ δ' ὁρῶ ταῦτα πρόβατα καὶ αἶγας καὶ βοῦς καὶ

ὄνους, ἃ ἀποδαρέντα καὶ φυσηθέντα ῥᾳδίως ἂν παρέχοι
10 τὴν διάβασιν. δεήσομαι δὲ καὶ τῶν δεσμῶν οἷς χρῆσθε
περὶ τὰ ὑποζύγια· τούτοις ζεύξας τοὺς ἀσκοὺς πρὸς
ἀλλήλους, ὁρμίσας ἕκαστον ἀσκὸν λίθους ἀρτήσας καὶ
ἀφεὶς ὥσπερ ἀγκύρας εἰς τὸ ὕδωρ, διαγαγὼν καὶ
ἀμφοτέρωθεν δήσας, ἐπιβαλῶ ὕλην καὶ γῆν ἐπιφορήσω·
11 ὅτι μὲν οὖν οὐ καταδύσεσθε αὐτίκα μάλα εἴσεσθε·
πᾶς γὰρ ἀσκὸς δύο ἄνδρας ἕξει τοῦ μὴ καταδῦναι.
12 ὥστε δὲ μὴ ὀλισθάνειν ἡ ὕλη καὶ ἡ γῆ σχήσει." ἀκού-
σασι ταῦτα τοῖς στρατηγοῖς τὸ μὲν ἐνθύμημα χαρίεν
ἐδόκει εἶναι, τὸ δ' ἔργον ἀδύνατον· ἦσαν γὰρ οἱ κω-
λύσοντες πέραν πολλοὶ ἱππεῖς, οἳ εὐθὺς τοῖς πρώτοις
οὐδὲν ἂν ἐπέτρεπον τούτων ποιεῖν.

The generals decide to make for the Carduchian territory.

13 ἐνταῦθα τὴν μὲν ὑστεραίαν ὑπανεχώρουν εἰς τοὔμπαλιν ἢ πρὸς Βαβυλῶνα, εἰς τὰς ἀκαύστους κώμας,
κατακαύσαντες ἔνθεν ἐξῆσαν· ὥστε οἱ πολέμιοι οὐ
προσήλαυνον, ἀλλὰ ἐθεῶντο καὶ ὅμοιοι ἦσαν θαυμάζειν
ὅποι ποτὲ τρέψονται οἱ Ἕλληνες καὶ τί ἐν νῷ ἔχοιεν.
14 ἐνταῦθα οἱ μὲν ἄλλοι στρατιῶται ἐπὶ τὰ ἐπιτήδεια
ἦσαν· οἱ δὲ στρατηγοὶ πάλιν συνῆλθον, καὶ συναγα-
γόντες τοὺς ἑαλωκότας ἤλεγχον τὴν κύκλῳ πᾶσαν
15 χώραν, τίς ἑκάστη εἴη. οἱ δὲ ἔλεγον ὅτι τὰ μὲν πρὸς
μεσημβρίαν τῆς ἐπὶ Βαβυλῶνα εἴη καὶ Μηδίαν, δι'
ἧσπερ ἥκοιεν, ἡ δὲ πρὸς ἕω ἐπὶ Σοῦσά τε καὶ
Ἐκβάτανα φέροι, ἔνθα θερίζειν καὶ ἐαρίζειν λέγεται
βασιλεύς, ἡ δὲ διαβάντι τὸν ποταμὸν πρὸς ἑσπέραν
ἐπὶ Λυδίαν καὶ Ἰωνίαν φέροι, ἡ δὲ διὰ τῶν ὀρέων
καὶ πρὸς ἄρκτον τετραμμένη ὅτι εἰς Καρδούχους
16 ἄγοι. τούτους δὲ ἔφασαν οἰκεῖν ἀνὰ τὰ ὄρη καὶ

πολεμικοὺς εἶναι, καὶ βασιλέως οὐκ ἀκούειν, ἀλλὰ καὶ
ἐμβαλεῖν ποτε εἰς αὐτοὺς βασιλικὴν στρατιὰν δώδεκα
μυριάδας· τούτων δ᾽ οὐδένα ἀπονοστῆσαι διὰ τὴν
δυσχωρίαν. ὁπότε μέντοι πρὸς τὸν σατράπην τὸν ἐν
τῷ πεδίῳ σπείσαιντο, καὶ ἐπιμιγνύναι σφῶν τε πρὸς
ἐκείνους καὶ ἐκείνων πρὸς ἑαυτούς. ἀκούσαντες ταῦτα 17
οἱ στρατηγοὶ ἐκάθισαν χωρὶς τοὺς ἑκασταχόσε φάσκον-
τας εἰδέναι, οὐδὲν δῆλον ποιήσαντες ὅποι πορεύεσθαι
ἔμελλον. ἐδόκει δὲ τοῖς στρατηγοῖς ἀναγκαῖον εἶναι
διὰ τῶν ὀρέων εἰς Καρδούχους ἐμβάλλειν· τούτους
γὰρ διελθόντας ἔφασαν εἰς Ἀρμενίαν ἥξειν, ἧς Ὀρόντας ἦρχε πολλῆς καὶ εὐδαίμονος. ἐντεῦθεν δ᾽ εὔπορον
ἔφασαν εἶναι ὅποι τις ἐθέλοι πορεύεσθαι. ἐπὶ τούτοις 18
ἐθύσαντο, ὅπως ἡνίκα καὶ δοκοίη τῆς ὥρας τὴν πορείαν
ποιοῖντο· τὴν γὰρ ὑπερβολὴν τῶν ὀρέων ἐδεδοίκεσαν,
μὴ προκαταληφθείη· καὶ παρήγγειλαν, ἐπειδὴ δειπνήσειαν, συσκευασαμένους πάντας ἀναπαύεσθαι, καὶ ἕπεσθαι ἡνίκ᾽ ἄν τις παραγγέλλῃ.

NOTES.

I.

1. ἀναβάσει, the march *up country* from Sardis to Babylonia; cf. § 8 τὴν ἄνω ὁδόν.

τῆς μάχης, the battle of Cunaxa, in which Cyrus was killed, described at the end of Book 1; see Introduction, p. xiv.

ἀπιόντων—σπονδαῖς, 'while the Greeks were retreating in company with Tissaphernes as long as the truce lasted.' The truce was broken by the treacherous seizure of the Greek generals by Tissaphernes.

2. οἱ στρατηγοί, five in number, Clearchus the Spartan, Proxenus the Boeotian, Menon the Thessalian, Agias the Arcadian, and Socrates the Achaean.

συνειλημμένοι. The generals were seized when on a visit to the tent of Tissaphernes, and after an interval put to death. Their companions, i.e. 20 captains and 200 soldiers, were almost all massacred on the spot.

λοχαγῶν—στρατιωτῶν, partitive genitives, 'those of the captains and soldiers who accompanied them.' Cf. § 35, iii. 8.

ἐννοούμενοι μέν, as if ἐννοούμενοι δὲ ὅτι κύκλῳ were to follow.

ἐπὶ ταῖς βασιλέως θύραις, an oriental hyperbole, as they were now a long way from Babylon.

βασιλέως, without the article, as usual when it denotes the 'Great King'; cf. Ἰσθμός 'the well known Isthmus,' i.e. of Corinth.

πολλὰ—πολέμιαι. In sense these words go both with ἔθνη and πόλεις. In syntax each of the two epithets is attracted to the substantive nearest to it. Translate:—'and that all around them there were many hostile tribes and cities.' Cf. § 42.

ἦσαν. Instead of this and the imperfects following the student might expect either the present indicative or the present optative. But the rules of *oratio obliqua* are much more elastic in Greek than in Latin. Cf. §§ 6, 9, iii. 12.

ἀγοράν—ἡγεμὼν δ' οὐδείς. The two great difficulties of the Greeks are here put side by side,—(1) want of supplies, (2) ignorance of the route from Babylonia to the Euxine.

τῆς Ἑλλάδος, i.e. Ionia, part of the Hellenic world.

μύρια στάδια, a rough estimate of the distance. The distance from Sardis to Cunaxa is said to be 1464 miles.

ποταμοὶ—ὁδοῦ, 'and that impassable rivers barred their progress, intervening between (them and) their homeward route.'

ἐν μέσῳ, sometimes, as here, in the sense of 'standing in the way of'; cf. Demosth. p. 682 οὐδὲν ἦν ἐν μέσῳ πολεμεῖν ἡμᾶς 'nothing stood in the way of our going to war.'

οἱ σὺν Κύρῳ—βάρβαροι, the 100,000 Asiatic troops, who accompanied Cyrus from Sardis under the command of his friend Ariaeus the Persian.

οὐδὲ ἱππέα—λειφθείη, 'with not one single horseman on their side, so that it was quite clear that, if they won a victory, they could kill none of the enemy, while, if they were defeated, not a man of them would be left (alive).' This is very exaggerated language. It is of course quite true that cavalry are generally necessary for the completion of a victory by a pursuit. Note also that the Persians were strong in cavalry, as we shall see later on.

νικῶντες—ἡττηθέντων. These participles denote a condition. The tense of νικῶντες is to be accounted for by the fact that νικᾶν is often used idiomatically for 'to be a conqueror'; cf. ἀδικεῖν 'to be a wrong-doer.'

3. ταῦτ' ἐννοούμενοι. ταῦτ' sums up the melancholy reflections of the last ten lines.

ὀλίγοι μὲν—ὀλίγοι δέ. Xenophon is very fond of this little trick of style; cf. § 13 πάντα μὲν—πάντα δέ and § 40.

εἰς τὴν ἑσπέραν, 'for that evening'; cf. I. vii. 1 εἰς τὴν ἐπιοῦσαν ἕω.

τὰ ὅπλα, properly the place in front of the camp, where the arms were piled; here 'their quarters' generally, as is clear from the next words. The Greek camp was now near the Great Zab river not far from its confluence with the Tigris; see Map of Route.

ἀνεπαύοντο—ἕκαστος, 'but they lay down to rest just where each chanced to be.'

ἐτύγχανεν. For the omission of the participle ὤν cf. Soph. *Ajax* 9
ἔνδον γὰρ ἀνὴρ τυγχάνει.

πατρίδων—παίδων, objective genitives after πόθου, 'yearning for
fatherlands, etc.' Cf. §§ 10, 18, 21.   Notice the *asyndeton,* which is far
less common in Greek than in Latin.

πατρίδων, plural because the Ten Thousand came from many
different Greek communities.

4. ἦν δέ τις—Ξενοφῶν. Thus Xenophon with characteristic
modesty introduces himself to the reader, now that he is about to be
the leading figure among the Ten Thousand.

οὔτε στρατηγὸς—στρατιώτης.   On Xenophon's position in the
expedition see Introduction, p. x.

ὑπισχνεῖτο—πατρίδος, 'And he promised Xenophon that, if he
came, he would make him a friend of Cyrus, whom he said he himself
counted as a better (friend) to himself than his own country.'   On the
decay of Greek patriotism during this epoch see Introduction,
p. ix.

5. ὑποπτεύσας—συμπολεμῆσαι, 'having misgivings that becoming
a friend of Cyrus might in some degree be a ground of accusation on the
part of the city, because Cyrus was thought to have vigorously aided the
Lacedaemonians in the war against Athens.'   He feared that Xenophon's
conduct would be considered unpatriotic.

ὑποπτεύσας μή, on the analogy of μή after verbs of fearing. Cf. v. 3.

τι, adverbial, 'in some degree'; cf. § 37 and Herod. I. 32 οὐ γάρ τι
ὁ μέγα πλούσιος ὀλβιώτερός ἐστι 'the very rich man is not in any way
more happy.'

πρὸς τῆς πόλεως, 'from the side of the city'; cf. Hom. *Il.* VI. 525
αἴσχε' ἀκούω πρὸς Τρώων 'I hear taunts from the Trojans.'

συμπολεμῆσαι.   During the last years of the Peloponnesian war
Cyrus had helped the Spartans with large sums of money, which he
sent through Lysander.

6. τίνι—σωθείη, literally 'to which of the gods sacrificing and
praying he would go...and...be saved,' i.e. 'to which of the gods he was
to sacrifice and pray in order to make the journey he had in view most
honourable and successful, and to secure a prosperous return.'   Note
that the stress of the sentence is on the participles θύων and εὐχόμενος.
This is often the case in Greek. Cf. ii. 25.

τίνι ἄν.   This ἄν does not go with the participles, but merely
anticipates the ἄν later on in the sentence which goes with ἔλθοι.   The
Greeks are fond of thus giving an early intimation of the conditional

character of a sentence; cf. Eurip. *Alcestis* 72 πόλλ' ἃν σὺ λέξας οὐδὲν
ἃν πλέον λάβοις.

τὴν ὁδόν, cognate accusative with ἔλθοι, 'go his way'; cf. § 8
ὁρμᾶν ὁδόν.

ἐπινοεῖ. The Greeks like the vivid effect produced in Greek *oratio
obliqua* by the retention of the tense of the *recta*. Cf. § 9.

σωθείη. σῴζειν often means 'bring safely'; cf. ii. 4 and II. iv. 19
ὅποι φυγόντες σωθῶμεν.

ἀνεῖλεν—θύειν, 'Apollo named in his reply the gods to whom he
ought to sacrifice.'

θεοῖς, an instance of *inverse attraction,* the antecedent being attracted
into the case of the relative. The gods in question are Zeus, Hermes,
and Heracles, the special protectors of travellers.

7. ἀλλ' αὐτὸς—πορευθείη, 'instead he had decided for himself
that he ought to go and then asked this question, how he should go best.'

8. θυσάμενος—θεός, 'having got sacrifices offered to the deities
mentioned in Apollo's response.' This *causal* force of the middle
voice is rare, except in the case of θύομαι which is so used often in
Xenophon. Cf. ii. 25. The often-quoted διδάσκομαι τὸν υἱόν 'I get
my son taught' is a mere figment of grammarians, based on a misconception of the meaning of a passage in Plato *Meno* p. 93 D, where
διδάσκομαι simply means 'I teach for myself.'

τὴν—ὁδόν, cognate accusative; cf. § 6, and *Cyropaedeia* VIII. vi. 20
ὁρμᾶν τὴν στρατείαν.

ἄνω, 'up country' from the sea; cf. I. ii. 1 πορεύεσθαι ἄνω. See
note on § 1.

συνεστάθη, 'was introduced'; cf. Plato *Laches* 200 D ἄλλους μοι
συνίστησιν.

9. προθυμουμένου—αὐτόν, 'When Proxenus was anxious that
Xenophon should remain, Cyrus also joined in urging that he should
do so.'

λήξῃ—ἀποπέμψει. The moods of the *oratio recta* are here retained,
as the tense is in § 6 ἐπινοεῖ. Cf. iv. 1.

Πισίδας. Cf. Introduction, p. xii, and see Map of Route.

10. μὲν δή, often used in closing a narrative or discussion.
Translate:—'*So then* Xenophon took part in the expedition deceived in
this way,—(but) not by Proxenus; for Proxenus knew nothing of the
(intended) attack upon the Great King.' For μὲν δή cf. §§ 3, 13 and
Aesch. *P. V.* 500 τοιαῦτα μὲν δὴ ταῦτα 'so much then for this.'

οὐδὲ ἄλλος οὐδείς, 'nor did any other.' Note that as a rule in

Greek accumulated negatives do not destroy, but strengthen the nega-
tion; cf. § 38 and Eurip. *Cyclops* 120 ἀκούει δ' οὐδὲν οὐδεὶς οὐδενός
'no one listens to anyone in anything.'

Κλέαρχον, commander-in-chief of the Greek force, and the con-
fidential friend of Cyrus.

εἰς Κιλικίαν ἦλθον. See Introduction, pp. xii, xiii.

ἄκοντες ὅμως οἱ πολλοί, 'though unwilling most of them.' ὅμως
'nevertheless' in sense goes with the principal verb; but in position it is
often attracted to a concessive participle, as here; cf. Eurip. *Medea* 280
ἐρήσομαι δὲ καὶ κακῶς πάσχουσ' ὅμως 'I will ask, ill-treated though I am.'

οἱ πολλοί, not subject of the sentence, but in apposition to the
subject 'they'; cf. Hom. *Il.* XVIII. 496 αἱ δὲ γυναῖκες θαύμαζον ἑκάστη
'the women marvelled, each one of them.'

ἀλλήλων καὶ Κύρου, objective genitives; cf. § 3 πόθον πατρίδων.
Translate :—' owing to mere shame of one another and of Cyrus,' i.e.
they had too much self-respect to appear cowards in the eyes of their
comrades or to desert Cyrus their benefactor.

11. The main narrative is now resumed after the digression in
§§ 4—10.

μικρόν, 'for a little while,' accusative of duration of time.

ὕπνου, partitive genitive, as often after λαγχάνω, 'having obtained
some sleep'; cf. *Cyropaedeia* I. iv. 16 οὔτε σίτου οὔθ' ὕπνου δύνανται
λαγχάνειν.

ἔδοξεν, used *personally* in the first part of the sentence, 'a thunderbolt seemed to fall'; then *impersonally*, 'it seemed that the house was
all in a blaze.'

12. ἔκρινεν, aorist (not imperfect, since ἔδοξε follows) expressing a
final decision. Contrast with this the imperfects in the next sentence,
ἐφοβεῖτο and ἐδόκει.

τῇ δὲ καὶ—ἀποριῶν, 'But partly also he was fearing—(1) because the
dream seemed to him to come from Zeus *as King*, and (2) because *all
around him* the fire seemed to blaze—that he might be unable to escape
from the country of the Great King, but be hemmed in by some
perplexities on all sides.' Note (*a*) that Zeus is the patron of kings in
general and of the Kings of Persia in particular (Ζεὺς Πατρῷος, *Cyropaedeia* I. vi. 1); (*b*) that κύκλῳ is emphatic by position and explains
εἴργοιτο πάντοθεν.

μὴ οὐ δύναιτο. The μή depends on ἐφοβεῖτο 'was fearing lest...';
the οὐ negatives δύναιτο.

13. ὁποῖόν τι—τὸ ὄναρ, 'what kind of thing then it is (i.e. what it amounts to) to see such a dream as this may be judged from what happened after it.'

μὲν δή. See above, § 10.

εἰ δὲ—ἐπὶ βασιλεῖ, 'but if we mean to come into the King's power.' *εἰ γενησόμεθα* is sometimes said to be equivalent to *ἐὰν γενώμεθα* 'if we become.' Rather it signifies 'if we *will* become,' 'if we are determined to become.' Cf. Aristoph. *Birds* 759 αἶρε πλῆκτρον εἰ μαχεῖ (addressed to a cock) 'Up with your spur *if you mean to fight,*' a signification which would not be given by *ἐὰν μάχῃ*.

ἐπὶ βασιλεῖ, literally 'dependent on the King'; cf. v. viii. 17 εἰ ἐπὶ τοῖς πολεμίοις ἐγένοντο, τί ἂν ἔπαθον ;

τί ἐμποδὼν—ἀποθανεῖν, 'what is to prevent us being tortured to death after having lived through all the most cruel sights and having endured the most terrible sufferings.'

μὴ οὐχὶ—ἀποθανεῖν. After expressions implying *hindering, desisting,* etc., when negatived, or *virtually negatived* as here, an infinitive has the double redundant negative μὴ οὐ instead of μή. Cf. Soph. *Electra* 107 οὐ λήξω μὴ οὐ πᾶσι προφωνεῖν 'I will not cease from publishing to all.' Cf. v. 11.

ἐπιδόντας, properly 'having lived to see,' the ordinary sense of the word ; e.g. Demosth. p. 296 τὴν πατρίδα ἐπιδεῖν δουλεύουσαν 'to live to see one's country in slavery.'

ὑβριζομένους, to be taken closely with ἀποθανεῖν. It expresses the *mode* of death.

14. ὅπως δ' ἀμυνούμεθα—παρασκευάζεται, 'None of us are taking measures *to* (lit. *how we are to*) defend ourselves.' For the construction cf. ὅπως ἀγωνιούμεθα, § 16 and ὅπως μὴ γενησόμεθα, § 18.

ὥσπερ ἐξὸν—ἄγειν, 'as if it were possible for us to rest' (ἐξὸν accusative absolute) ; cf. ii. 25.

ἐγὼ οὖν—πράξειν, 'For myself then (ἐγώ emphatic), what state's general (lit. *the general coming from what state*) do I expect to undertake this?' Two interrogations are here compressed into one; cf. Hom. *Od.* I. 170 τίς πόθεν εἶς ἀνδρῶν; 'who art thou and whence dost thou come?'

στρατηγόν. Xenophon is evidently thinking of Cheirisophus, who had been commissioned to take part in the expedition by Sparta, the leading state of Greece. It was natural that he should succeed to the command of an army mainly Peloponnesian. Probably, however, Cheirisophus, like most of his countrymen, was lacking in initiative and not qualified to cope with the present crisis.

προσδοκῶ, indicative; or, less probably, deliberative subjunctive, 'am I to expect?'

ἡλικίαν, here 'maturity.' Xenophon was, almost certainly, about 35 at this time; see Introduction, p. i, and § 25 of this chapter, where ἡλικία has a different sense.

15. Προξένου. Xenophon had joined the expedition as the friend of Proxenus, and would on that account be well acquainted with the captains of his division.

ὥσπερ οἶμαι οὐδ' ὑμεῖς, 'as, I suppose, you cannot *either.*' οὐδέ not unfrequently has the sense of 'not—either.'

16. τὸν πόλεμον ἐξέφηναν, 'unmasked their hostility,' treacherously veiled during the truce, which was finally broken by the seizure of the Greek generals.

17. εἰ ὑφησόμεθα, 'if we mean to give in'; cf. εἰ γενησόμεθα, § 13.

ὅς, 'seeing that he,'—a meaning generally given by ὅστις. Cf. ii. 4. ἀδελφοῦ, i.e. Cyrus.

καὶ τεθνηκότος ἤδη, 'aye even after he was dead.' The mutilation of the dead was most revolting to the Greek mind.

ἡμᾶς δέ—παθεῖν, 'while as for us, who have no one to care for us and who marched against him intending to make him a slave instead of a king and to kill him if we could, what treatment do we think we should receive?'

ἡμᾶς, if it is subject of παθεῖν, should strictly be ἡμεῖς according to the rule exemplified in Thuc. IV. 28 οὐκ ἔφη αὐτὸς ἀλλ' ἐκεῖνον στρατηγεῖν. It is better to take it as the loose 'anticipatory accusative,' which comes at the beginning of a sentence, unconnected with its construction.

κηδεμὼν οὐδείς, as Parysatis, the queen mother, cared for Cyrus her favourite son; see Introduction, p. ix.

ἐστρατεύσαμεν δέ, subject οἵ to be understood from οἷς which precedes. For the construction cf. ii. 5 below. So in Cicero, *mancipium quo et omnes utimur et* (*quod* understood) *non praebetur a publico.*

ἄν, to be taken with παθεῖν. The magnetic power of interrogatives over ἄν often attracts it out of its natural syntactical position. Negatives have a similar power; e.g. in the next sentence, οὐκ ἂν ἐπὶ πᾶν ἔλθοι.

18. τὰ ἔσχατα, cognate accusative with αἰκισάμενος, 'having inflicted the most exquisite tortures upon us.'

πᾶσιν—αὐτόν, 'inspire all men with fear of ever marching against him.' τοῦ στρατεῦσαι is objective genitive after φόβον, cf. § 3.

19. διαθεώμενος—ἐπιτήδεια, 'observing with regard to them what a large and rich country they had and what bountiful supplies.'

αὐτῶν. For this genitive of *connexion* after verbs of *perceiving*, etc. cf. *Cyropaedeia* v. ii. 18 ἐπενόησε δ' αὐτῶν ὡς ἐπηρώτων 'he noticed with regard to them how they asked.' Thuc. IV. 6 ἐπύθοντο τῆς Πύλου κατειλημμένης 'they learnt about the capture of Pylos.'

20. ἐνθυμοίμην, optative of frequency, 'whenever I thought of the plight of the (Greek) soldiers'; cf. § 32.

οὐδενός, partitive genitive after μετείη, 'that we had a share in none of these blessings'; cf. § 31 τῆς Βοιωτίας προσήκει.

ὅτου—ἡμᾶς, 'And I knew that few of us any longer had the wherewithal to buy them, and that oaths now restrained us from furnishing ourselves with supplies by any other means than purchase.'

ὅτου, genitive of price; cf. iii. 18 and Plato *Phaedo* 98 B οὐκ ἂν ἀπεδόμην πολλοῦ τὰς ἐλπίδας 'I would not have sold my hopes *for much.*'

ὅρκους, the oaths taken when the truce was ratified; see II. iii. 27.

ἤδη, i.e. after the truce.

21. λελύσθαι, 'to have been ended' *there and then.* Such is the force of the perfect.

ἐν μέσῳ—ὦσιν, 'For now these good things have been set as prizes in the midst (of the arena) for whichever side of us (combatants) prove better men.' Cf. Demosth. p. 41 ταῦτα μέν ἐστιν ἅπαντα τὰ χωρία ἆθλα τοῦ πολέμου κείμενα ἐν μέσῳ. In our passage the metaphor is continued in ἀγωνοθέται 'umpires.'

κεῖται, not 'lie,' but 'have been placed,' κεῖμαι being quite regularly used as perfect passive of τίθημι.

ὁπότεροι. An antecedent, ἐκείνοις, must be understood.

22. ὁρῶντες. The participle is concessive, 'though we saw.' Cf. § 10 and ii. 5.

τοὺς τῶν θεῶν ὅρκους, 'oaths to the gods,' objective genitive; cf. § 3.

πολύ, to be taken with μείζονι, 'much greater spirit.'

τούτοις, dative because it depends on ἐξεῖναι understood, 'than is possible for them.'

23. οἱ ἄνδρες, the Persians.

θνητοί, 'liable to death,' as being weak effeminate Asiatics opposed to hardy vigorous Greeks.

24. καὶ ἄλλοι, 'others also' in other divisions of the army, in which case we shall lose the credit of beginning.

πρὸς τῶν θεῶν—ἀρετήν, 'In Heaven's name, let us not wait for others to come to us to summon us to the noblest deeds, but let *us* begin the work of stirring up our comrades too to valour.'

παρακαλοῦντας, future, *not* present, participle (cf. § 46), denoting purpose; cf. ὡς ποιήσοντες, § 17.

25. ἐξορμᾶν, either (1) *neuter*, 'to make a move'; or (2), less probably, *active*, 'to stir up (others),' as in the last section.

οὐδὲν—ἡλικίαν, 'In no wise do I plead my youth as an excuse.' Xenophon was now apparently about 35. But four of the late generals were younger. Proxenus was only 30 (II. vi. 20); Agias and Socrates both about 35 (II. vi. 30); Menon also was quite young (II. vi. 28).

ἀκμάζειν—ἐρύκειν, 'I consider that I am of full age so as to avert....' The contrast between ἀκμάζειν and ἡλικία in this passage is a decisive argument against the ordinary view that Xenophon was about 45 at this time.

26. πλὴν Ἀπολλωνίδης—τὰς ἀπορίας, 'except that there was one Apollonides speaking the Boeotian dialect; and he maintained that anyone was playing the fool who said that he would attain safety by any other means than by conciliating the Great King if he possibly could; and at the same time he began to enlarge on the difficulties (of the Greeks).'

βοιωτιάζων. Apparently he was a Lydian slave of the Boeotian Proxenus, who had liberated him and made him one of his captains; cf. § 31.

πείσας, nominative according to rule, because it refers to the subject of λέγοι. Cf. § 17.

27. μεταξὺ ὑπολαβών, 'interrupting him in the middle of his remarks.'

οὐδὲ—οὐδέ. The first οὐδέ means 'not even,' the second 'nor... either.' οὐδὲ—οὐδέ never mean 'neither—nor' like οὔτε—οὔτε.

ἐν ταὐτῷ—ὅπλα, 'However you were at any rate in company with these officers when the King, after the death of Cyrus, despising us on this account, was sending and bidding us surrender our arms.'

ἐν ταὐτῷ—τούτοις, 'in the same place with these'; cf. § 30 εἰς ταὐτὸν ἡμῖν αὐτοῖς, and II. vi. 22 τὸ ἀληθὲς ἐνόμιζε τὸ αὐτὸ τῷ ἠλιθίῳ εἶναι 'thought that truth was the same as silliness.' The dative is similar to that after ὁμοῖος and other words expressing similarity.

29. ὥσπερ δή, 'as forsooth'; cf. Aesch. *Agam.* 1616 ὡς δὴ σύ μοι τύραννος Ἀργείων ἔσει 'as if forsooth I shall ever see *you* king of Argos.'

εἰς λόγους αὐτοῖς ἦλθον. The dative is probably one of accompaniment, 'with them'; or it may be dative of interest, 'for them,' 'to oblige them.'

οὐ νῦν—τούτου, 'is it not the case that now they, poor fellows,...are not allowed even the privilege of death, though, I imagine, they are earnestly desiring it?'

πείθειν, 'attempt to persuade'; contrast the tense of πείσας, § 26.

πάλιν, to be taken with πείθειν ἰόντας, not with κελεύεις.

30. ἐμοὶ—χρῆσθαι, 'I think we should not admit this fellow to our company, but, having deprived him of his captaincy, pack baggage upon him and employ him in this capacity' (i.e. ὡς σκευοφόρῳ). There is a good parallel to this passage in *Cyropaedeia* IV. ii. 25 ὁ τοῦτο ποιῶν οὐκέτ' ἀνήρ ἐστιν ἀλλὰ σκευοφόρος, καὶ ἔξεστι τῷ βουλομένῳ χρῆσθαι δὴ τούτῳ ὡς ἀνδραπόδῳ 'he who acts thus is no longer a man, but a porter; and anyone who likes may employ him as a slave.'

Ἑλλάδα—Ἕλλην. Throughout all their troubles the Ten Thousand never lose the proud consciousness that they are Greeks. So the Scottish soldiers of fortune, of whom we read in *Quentin Durward* as serving under Louis XI. of France, continue Scotchmen to the backbone with a haughty contempt for the French.

31. ἀλλὰ—παντάπασιν 'Yes, but this fellow has nothing to do with Boeotia or with Greece, nothing whatever.' For the partitive genitives after προσήκει cf. § 20 οὐδενὸς ἡμῖν μετείη.

Λυδόν. This probably means that Apollonides was a Lydian by birth; but it is thought by some that Λυδός may be a generic term for an Asiatic slave like *Syrus* in the Latin comic poets.

ἀμφότερα τὰ ὦτα τετρυπημένον. For the accusative after a passive verb cf. II. vi. 1 ἀποτμηθέντας τὰς κεφαλάς 'having had their heads cut off.' The Greeks looked upon the wearing of ear-rings as effeminate. So his pierced ears are a proof that Apollonides is a barbarian.

32. παρὰ τὰς τάξεις. παρά with accusative is sometimes used to denote *motion along* as well as *to along side of.*

εἴη—οἴχοιτο— εἴη, optatives of frequency ; cf. i. 20, 32.

ὁπόθεν—λοχαγόν, 'from whatever division the general was missing (they summoned) the lieutenant-general, and where a captain alone was left alive (they summoned) the captain.'

οἴχοιτο, 'was gone,' a euphemism characteristic of the Greek language. So Socrates says (in Plato *Phaedo* 115 D) οἰχήσομαι ἀπιὼν εἰς μακάρων τινὰς εὐδαιμονίας.

33. εἰς τὸ πρόσθεν—ἐκαθέζοντο, 'they went and sat down in the front of the camp.' For this so-called 'pregnant construction' cf. iv. 13 and I. ii. 2 παρῆσαν εἰς Σάρδεις.

τὸ πρόσθεν τῶν ὅπλων, strictly 'the place in front of where the arms were piled'; cf. § 3. It was a large open space suitable for a meeting.

τοὺς ἑκατόν. The use of the article with numerals, when a round number is given, is idiomatic; it must be neglected in translation. Cf. ii. 18.

μέσαι νύκτες, plural because the night was divided into watches.

34. πρεσβύτατος ὤν. The participle here gives a reason, as often in Greek,—'since he was oldest.' Cf. iii. 7.

ὁρῶσι—παρακαλέσαι, 'in view of the present crisis we determined both to come together ourselves and to summon you.'

ἅπερ καὶ πρὸς ἡμᾶς, 'just what you said to *us*.'

35. ἡμῶν, partitive genitive depending on οὕς, 'those of us whom they could.' Cf. § 2 and iii. 8, 18.

ἐπὶ τοῖς βαρβάροις. Cf. § 13 ἐπὶ βασιλεῖ.

36. εὖ τοίνυν—καιρόν, 'Be well assured then that you, assembled in such numbers before me, have a splendid opportunity.'

ἢν δὲ ὑμεῖς—παρακαλῆτε, 'but if you make it clear to them that you are yourselves preparing to face the enemy and if you cheer on the rest (to do the same).'

37. ἴσως δέ τοι—τούτων, 'And perhaps, *you know* (τοι), it is only right that you should *in a measure* (τι) excel these soldiers.' Notice the delicate and conciliatory tone of this typically Greek sentence. Cf. iii. 19.

καὶ χρήμασι—ἐπλεονεκτεῖτε, 'you had the advantage of them in point of wealth and honour.' τούτων is genitive of comparison, just like διαφέρειν τούτων above, which strictly means 'differ *from these*.'

ἀξιοῦν δεῖ—εἶναι, 'it is but right that we should expect that you should yourselves be braver than the rank and file.'

38. ἄν, to be taken with ὠφελῆσαι. Cf. § 39 οἶμαι ἄν—ποιῆσαι.

οὐδὲν ἄν. Cf. note on § 17.

οὐδὲν—οὔτε—οὔτε—οὐδαμοῦ. For the accumulation of negatives cf. § 10. Translate: 'For without commanders nothing honourable or good would be achieved—to speak comprehensively, *anywhere*; and particularly (δή) in military matters this is absolutely true.'

ὡς συνελόντι εἰπεῖν, literally 'so—for a man having summed up the matter—to speak.' Cf. the simple phrase ὡς εἰπεῖν 'so to speak'; also ὡς εἰκάσαι 'to make a guess,' ὡς συντόμως εἰπεῖν 'to speak briefly.' The infinitive is often thus used to limit an assertion; cf. ii. 37 τὸ νῦν εἶναι. ἤδη, 'ere now'; cf. Soph. *Ajax* 1142 ἤδη ποτ' εἶδον 'I have seen ere now.'

40. ἀθύμως μὲν—ἀθύμως δέ. See § 3 ὀλίγοι μὲν—ὀλίγοι δέ.

ὥστε—ἡμέρας, 'So much so that, while they are in *this* condition, I know not what use any one could make of them, whether by night, if need were, or even by day.'

οὕτω γ' ἐχόντων, genitive absolute with τῶν στρατιωτῶν understood. Strict syntax would require ἔχουσιν in agreement with αὐτοῖς. But the present form of sentence is admissible and indeed quite natural in a language which dislikes rigid uniformity of structure; cf. an exact parallel in I. ii. 17 θᾶττον προϊόντων—δρόμος ἐγένετο τοῖς στρατιώταις.

ὅ τι, cognate accusative with χρήσαιτο. Cf. II. i. 14 ἄλλο τι χρῆσθαι 'to make any other use of.'

42. οὔτε πλῆθος—ποιοῦσα, 'it is neither numbers nor strength which brings about victories.' ἡ—ποιοῦσα agrees with the substantive nearest to it; cf. § 2 πολλὰ καὶ ἔθνη καὶ πόλεις πολέμιαι.

43. ζῆν ἐκ παντὸς τρόπου, 'to keep alive at all hazards.'

ἐγνώκασι, 'have made up their minds,' 'have decided.' When γιγνώσκω has this particular meaning, it takes the infinitive, as here, and not the participial construction which is the rule after verbs of *knowing.* Cf. Thuc. I. 43 γνόντες τοῦτον ἐκεῖνον εἶναι τὸν καιρόν 'having determined that this was that crisis.'

τούτους δ' ὁρῶ. δέ here simply marks the apodosis, as often; and must be neglected in translation. So also μέν marks an apodosis in οὗτοι μὲν κακῶς above. But μέν *in apodosi* is comparatively rare. Both uses are combined, as here, in Herod. II. 42 ὅσοι μὲν νομοῦ τοῦ Θηβαίου εἰσί, οὗτοι μὲν αἶγας θύουσι· ὅσοι δὲ νομοῦ τοῦ Μενδησίου εἰσί, οὗτοι δὲ ὄϊς θύουσι.

44. αὐτούς, 'ourselves'; cf. § 37.

45. τοσοῦτον—Ἀθηναῖον εἶναι, literally 'I only knew so much of you as that I heard you were an Athenian.'

βουλοίμην ἄν—τοιούτους, 'I could wish that as many as possible were such as you are.'

46. οἱ δεόμενοι, 'you who need them.'

συγκαλοῦμεν, Attic future; cf. § 24.

47. ὡς μὴ μέλλοιτο—τὰ δέοντα, 'so that what was wanted might not be delayed, but be accomplished.' The passive μέλλομαι is very rare; cf. Demosth. p. 50 ταῦτα μέλλεται 'these delays are going on.'

Τιμασίων Δαρδανεύς, belonging to Dardanus in the Troad, and on that account selected to succeed Clearchus, whose troops came from the north-west of Asia Minor. Similarly the Arcadian Cleanor succeeds the Arcadian Agias, and the Achaean Xanthicles is chosen by his fellow-countrymen to take the place of Socrates. Menon, however, a Thessalian is succeeded by the Achaean Philesius, and Proxenus the Boeotian by Xenophon the Athenian.

II.

1. **ἡμέρα τε—καί**, 'day was nearly breaking *when....*' For this idiom cf. II. i. 7 'It was already about full-market time—**καί ἔρχονται κήρυκες**, *when* heralds came.'

πρῶτος—Χειρίσοφος, because (1) he had been officially commissioned by Sparta, premier state of Greece, (2) he was probably the senior remaining general—*perhaps the only remaining general*, after the seizure of Clearchus and the four others.

2. **ὁπότε—στερόμεθα**, 'now that we are deprived'; cf. § 15 **νῦν δ' ὁπότε—ὁ ἀγών ἐστι**.

πρὸς δ' ἔτι καί, 'and still further also.' **πρός** is sometimes used adverbially, as here.

οἱ ἀμφὶ 'Αριαῖον, 'Ariaeus and his men.' For this idiom cf. II. iv. 2 **οἱ περὶ 'Αριαῖον**.

3. **ἐκ τῶν παρόντων**, strictly 'starting from the present state,' i.e. 'notwithstanding the present distress.'

εἰ δὲ μή, ἀλλά—γε, 'failing that, yet at least.'

οἶμαι γὰρ—ποιήσειαν, 'For I imagine that (if we were to surrender) we should receive such treatment as I pray the gods may deal out to our foes.'

ποιήσειαν, pure optative denoting a wish; cf. § 6 **ἀποτίσαιντο**. Note the frequent use of **ποιεῖν** and **πάσχειν** as correlatives; cf. i. 41 **πείσονται—ποιήσουσι**.

4. **ὅστις λέγων—ἡδέσθη**, 'in as much as (lit. a man who), while he was saying that he was neighbour of Greece and would count it of the highest importance to preserve us, yes and in confirmation of this (**ἐπὶ τούτοις**) himself swore oaths to us and gave us solemn pledges,—he himself cheated and seized our generals, and paid no respect even to Zeus, Protector of Strangers.'

λέγων. Contrast this imperfect participle with the aorist participles which follow. The reference is to Tissaphernes' remarks in II. iii. 18.

γείτων—τῆς Ἑλλάδος, i.e. as Satrap of Caria.

σῶσαι ἡμᾶς. Tissaphernes had said :—'I counted it a godsend if by any means I could prevail on the King to allow me to send you safe home to Greece.'

αὐτὸς—αὐτὸς—αὐτός. The use of this word at the beginning of three successive clauses gives great solemnity to the passage ; cf. below iv. 46.

Δία ξένιον. The special outrage against the god is explained by the words which follow.

αὐτοῖς τούτοις, instrumental dative, 'by these very means,' i.e. by his solemn assurances.

5. Ἀριαῖος—βασιλέα καθιστάναι. See Introduction, p. xv.

ἐδώκαμεν καὶ ἐλάβομεν πιστά, '(to whom) we gave and (from whom) we received pledges'; cf. note on i. 17.

καὶ οὗτος, 'even he,' an emphatic resumption of the subject Ἀριαῖος.

τιμώμενος, 'though he was being honoured,' imperfect participle, as λέγων above, § 4. For the concessive use of the participle cf. i. 10, 22.

7. εἴτε τελευτᾶν—τυγχάνειν, 'and if he must die, it was right to count himself worthy of the noblest attire and meet his end in it.' He thought to himself:—' If we win, my fine uniform will be quite in place. If I am killed, I shall be killed in it after *doing my duty* in a way worthy of it.' Cf. Nelson's answer to those who urged him to conceal the stars of his four orders which made him such a conspicuous mark for the enemy :—'*In honour I gained them, and in honour I will die with them.*'

8. αὐτοῖς διὰ φιλίας ἰέναι, literally 'to pass through a state of friendship in regard to them.' Cf. below διὰ παντὸς πολέμου αὐτοῖς ἰέναι 'to be at downright war with them,' and Soph. *O. T.* 773 διὰ τύχης τοιᾶσδ' ἰών 'passing through such a fortune as this.' Soph. *Electra* 1509 δι' ἐλευθερίας ἐξῆλθες.

ὁρῶντας τοὺς στρατηγούς—οἷα πεπόνθασιν. For the form of sentence cf. St Luke iv. 34 οἶδά σε τίς εἶ ' I know thee who thou art.'

διὰ πίστεως, certainly not '*because of* confidence,' which meaning would be given by διὰ πίστιν, but '*in a state of* confidence,' like διὰ φιλίας above. Translate :—' who in full confidence put themselves in the power of the Persians.' An exact parallel is furnished by Caesar *Bell. Gall.* I. 46 *per fidem in colloquio circumventos* 'taken prisoners at a conference (to which they went) in confidence.' Cf. also δι' ὀργῆς and *per iram*, both used for 'in anger' and both meaning literally 'passing through a state of anger.'

σὺν τοῖς ὅπλοις, much stronger than μετὰ τῶν ὅπλων. It practically personifies their arms as trusty comrades who have stood them in good stead and will do so again; cf. σὺν τοῖς θεοῖς below. II. i. 12 σὺν τούτοις (these arms) μαχούμεθα. See note on § 15.

ὧν τε—ἐπιθεῖναι αὐτοῖς, 'to inflict punishment upon them for their crimes.'

πτάρνυταί τις. Note that a sneeze was only a good omen in so far as it occurred in connexion with lucky words or circumstances; cf. Catullus xlv. 6 *Amor dextram sternuit approbationem* 'Love sneezed a blessing *on the right*' (the lucky side),—there too after lucky words, as in our passage the sneeze comes immediately after the lucky word σωτηρίας. Sneezing was regarded as an omen even in Homeric times; e.g. *Od.* XVII. 545, where Penelope says 'Seest thou not that my son sneezed a blessing on every word?'

9. σωτηρίας—σωτῆρος—σωτήρια. Cf. *Palatine Anthology* xi. 268 οὐδὲ λέγει Ζεῦ σῶσον, ἐὰν πτάρῃ 'and he won't say *God bless you* if he sneezes.' It was supposed that a sneeze was an omen sent by Zeus the Saviour.

οἰωνός, 'omen,' strictly 'bird'; appearances of birds being the ordinary omens; so Latin *auspex* is contracted for *avispex*. Cf. the noble words of Hector, scorning the omen furnished by an eagle, *Il.* XII. 243 εἷς οἰωνὸς ἄριστος ἀμύνεσθαι περὶ πάτρης 'the one best omen is to fight for fatherland.' Aristophanes makes merry over the use of the word ὄρνις for all kinds of omens, and says (*Birds* 720) πταρμόν τ' ὄρνιθα καλεῖτε 'and you call a sneeze a bird,'—a good illustration of our passage.

εὔξασθαι—κατὰ δύναμιν, 'that we vow to sacrifice to this god thank-offerings for our preservation wherever we first reach friendly territory, and that at the same time we make another vow (συν-επ-εύξασθαι) to sacrifice also to the rest of the gods to the best of our ability.' The vow was paid when they reached Trapezus on the Euxine; see IV. viii. 25.

ἀνατεινάτω τὴν χεῖρα. The forms of the Greek citizen-assemblies are preserved in the meetings of the Ten Thousand, who are a wandering political community. The following passage from Dr Holm's recently published History of Greece is a good commentary on the present chapter :—'It is worthy of note that an Athenian kept them together; and he did it *in genuine Greek fashion by the example of his own*

personal bravery and by a proper use of the art of speech.... These
mercenaries were by no means the moral flower of the nation ; and if a
chance collection of men like this behaved in such an exemplary
manner, what might not be expected from the Greeks as a whole, if
they were well led ? The Retreat is also a proof that democracy was
after all the best constitution for the Greeks ; *for freely-rendered
obedience, secured by the oratorical power of an energetic man, was the
salvation of the Ten Thousand.'*

10. ἐτύγχανον λέγων, 'I happened to be saying,' 'I was just
saying,' when I was interrupted by the sneeze.

οὔτω δ' ἐχόντων. The same difficulty arises here as in i. 40.

11. ἔπειτα δέ, answering to πρῶτον μέν above. The parenthesis
which follows interrupts the construction, and causes an *anacoluthon.*

ἀναμνήσω—ὑμᾶς—κινδύνους, double accusative ; cf. iv. 2.

ἐλθόντων Περσῶν, the first Persian expedition against Greece under
Datis and Artaphernes, defeated at Marathon 490 B.C.

παμπληθεῖ στόλῳ, 'with a very large force.' For this dative of
accompaniment cf. II. ii. 12 ὀλίγῳ στρατεύματι ἐφέπεσθαι 'to pursue
with a small force.'

ὡς ἀφανιούντων, 'intending to make Athens disappear,' to blot it
out of the map of Greece.

αὐτοὶ 'Αθηναῖοι, 'Athenians alone.' Notice that there is no article
with 'Αθηναῖοι. For the idiomatic use of αὐτός cf. Aristophanes *Ach.*
504 αὐτοὶ γὰρ ἐσμεν 'for we are by ourselves.'

ἐνίκησαν, though they had only 10,000 men against an army of
over 100,000.

12. εὐξάμενοι—ἔδοξεν αὐτοῖς, an *anacoluthon* ; the participle being
constructed as if a personal verb 'they determined' was going to follow,
instead of ἔδοξεν αὐτοῖς.

ὁπόσους ἂν κατακάνοιεν. According to the ordinary syntax, ὁπόσους
ἂν κατακάνωμεν ('as many as we kill') in *oratio recta* would become
ὁπόσους κατακάνοιεν when turned into the *obliqua.* But sometimes, as
here, though the mood is changed, the ἄν remains. Cf. I. iv. 9 νομίζων,
ὅσῳ μὲν ἂν θᾶττον ἔλθοι....

χιμαίρας. It is said that Callimachus, the Athenian Polemarch,
vowed before the battle of Marathon that he would sacrifice to the
goddess Artemis heifers as many in number as the Persians who should
be slain. Since more than 6000 were killed, he could not obtain
sufficient heifers ; so he sacrificed goats instead. And from our
passage it appears that even of these enough were not forthcoming ;

unless this was a pious fiction for the establishment of an annual sacrifice to satisfy the national vanity.

ἔτι νῦν, after the lapse of 90 years.

13. τὴν ἀναρίθμητον στρατιάν, more than two and a half million soldiers, according to the estimate of Herodotus, excluding camp followers. The inscription commemorating those who fell at Thermopylae gave the number as three millions.

ἐνίκων, idiomatic, 'they were conquerors over'; see note on i. 2 and cf. § 14 ἐνικᾶτε.

κατὰ γῆν, PLATAEA, 479 B.C.

κατὰ θάλατταν, ARTEMISIUM, 480 B.C.; SALAMIS, 480 B.C.; MYCALÉ, 479 B.C.

ὧν ἔστι—τρόπαια, 'And of these things it is possible to see proofs, viz. the trophies.' This use of ἔστι is common in Xenophon, e.g. § 39.

τοιούτων—προγόνων, 'such are the ancestors from whom you come,' —genitive of origin.

14. οὐ μὲν δὴ—ἀφ' οὗ, 'I am not of course going to say that you are disgracing them. On the contrary, it is not many days since....' The reference is to the battle of Cunaxa.

πολλαπλασίους ὑμῶν, 'many times more numerous than you.' The genitive is similar to that after comparatives and other words denoting *difference*; i. 37, iii. 16.

15. νῦν δ' ὁπότε—ἐστι. Cf. § 2 and νῦν δὲ ὁπότε—ἔχετε (next section).

πολύ, to be taken with καὶ ἀμείνονας καὶ προθυμοτέρους, from which it is separated in order to give greater emphasis; cf. i. 22.

16. ἄμετρον, a predicate, 'seeing that their number is measureless.'

σὺν τῷ πατρίῳ φρονήματι, an unusual use of σύν. This expression (far more forcible than the commonplace μετὰ τοῦ πατρίου φρονήματος) denotes that *their spirit is an ally in battle*, more than a match for the hosts of the enemy. Cf. II. vi. 18 οὐδὲν μετὰ ἀδικίας, ἀλλὰ σὺν τῷ δικαίῳ καὶ καλῷ, where the contrast between the two constructions is well exemplified. See also note on § 8.

17. μηδὲ μέντοι—ἀφεστήκασιν, 'Nor yet consider that you have this as a disadvantage, viz. that those who were formerly arrayed on your side have now deserted you.'

τοῦτο μεῖον ἔχειν εἰ. The εἰ is idiomatic; cf. θαυμάζω εἰ...'I wonder that,' ἀγανακτῶ εἰ...'I am indignant that.'

οἱ πρόσθεν—ταττόμενοι, especially Ariaeus and his Asiatic troops.

ἔφευγον. Mark the force of the imperfect, 'they were for running away,' 'they were disposed to run away,' i.e. they were, in the words of the next sentence, men ready to set an example of flight. There is no need to read ἔφυγον, as some do.

γοῦν, 'at any rate,' often introduces a special illustration of a general statement. Cf. Thuc. I. 2, where, after laying down some general principles about changes of population, the historian says :—τὴν γοῦν Ἀττικὴν ᾤκουν οἱ αὐτοὶ ἀεί 'Attica at all events was always inhabited by the same race.'

18. οἱ μύριοι ἱππεῖς. The use of the article here is idiomatic; cf. i. 33. The statement is a general one, and does not refer to the number of the Persian cavalry. Translate, ' *a* (not *the*) body of 10,000 cavalry.'

γίγνηται, 'is done.' γίγνομαι is often used as the passive of ποιέω.

19. πολὺ—ἀσφαλεστέρου, cf. § 15.

ἐπὶ γῆς βεβηκότες, 'with feet firmly planted on the ground.' The perfect here denotes a lasting condition or attitude, as opposed to βαίνοντες 'walking.' Cf. εὖ βεβηκώς, metaphorically, 'on a good footing.' In Homer especially many perfects denote a state, e.g. κέκμηκα 'I am weary,' τέτηκα 'I am wasting,' ἔολπα 'I hope.'

20. τὰς μὲν μάχας θαρρεῖτε, 'you are confident about fighting,' accusative of reference; cf. Homer *Od.* VIII. 197 σὺ δὲ θάρσει τόνδε γ' ἄεθλον ' be of good heart about this contest.'

τοῦτο ἄχθεσθε, 'you are annoyed at this.' τοῦτο is a cognate accusative used *adverbially*, i.e. to define the action of the verb. So often in Homer, e.g. τόδε χώεο 'be angry at this,' τό γε δείδιθι 'have this fear,' τάδε μαίνεται ' does these mad acts.'

ἢ οὓς ἄν—κελεύωμεν, ' or (to employ as guides) any of the natives we can catch and order them to lead us.'

περὶ ἡμᾶς ἁμαρτάνωσι, 'make a mistake in our case ': cf. I. iv. 8 κακίους εἰσὶ περὶ ἡμᾶς (worse in dealing with us) ἢ ἡμεῖς περὶ ἐκείνους.

21. τὰ δὲ ἐπιτήδεια—βούληται, 'And as to provisions, (consider) whether it is better to purchase them from the market which the Persians used to provide—small measures for much money—, without even this (money) to pay with any longer, or to seize them ourselves, if we gain the upper hand, employing any measure that each man chooses.'

ἧς, attracted into the case of its antecedent ἀγορᾶς. Cf. i. 6, ii. 21.

μικρὰ μέτρα, in apposition to τὰ ἐπιτήδεια.

ἀργυρίου, genitive of price; cf. i. 20.

22. ἄπορον, 'a difficulty '; cf. Virg. *Ecl.* iii. 80 *triste lupus stabulis.*

διαβάντες. He is alluding to (1) the Euphrates which they crossed at Thapsacus, (2) the Tigris which they crossed before reaching Opis. See Map of Route.

σκέψασθε—βάρβαροι, 'Consider whether after all the barbarians have not in this acted really (καὶ) very foolishly.' The English idiom requires the insertion of a negative.

εἰ—ὦσι, the reading of the MSS., a very unusual construction in Attic Greek, instead of the ordinary ἐὰν ὦσι. It is quite common in Homer and, if we are to trust the best MSS., it survived to a small extent in Attic. Sophocles has the construction several times; e.g. *Oed. Col.* 1442 δυστάλαινά τἄρ' ἐγώ, εἰ σοῦ στερηθῶ 'if I am deprived of you.' In Thuc. VI. 21 the MSS. give εἰ ξυστῶσιν αἱ πόλεις 'if the cities combine.'

προϊοῦσι, 'for men advancing,' i.e. 'if we advance'; cf. i. 38 συνελόντι and v. 6 πειρωμένοις.

23.   εἰ δὲ—διήσουσιν, 'But if the rivers are not going to let us pass....' On the future indicative in the protasis of a conditional sentence see i. 13.

ἡμῖν γε, emphatic, 'we at any rate,' whatever may be the case with others.

Μυσούς—Πισίδας—Λυκάονας. See Map of Route. They were wild refractory peoples, kept under very imperfect control by the Great King, their nominal suzerain.

τὴν τούτων χώραν, i.e. of the Persians. The transition from the King to his people is quite a natural one.

24.   καὶ ἡμᾶς δ'—οἰκήσοντας, 'Yes, and I should have said that we ought not yet to make it clear that we have started for home, but to make preparations as if meaning to settle somewhere on the spot.' The protasis to ἂν ἔφην is virtually contained in ἀλλὰ γὰρ δέδοικα, § 25; i.e. 'I should have said, *if I had not feared.*'

αὐτοῦ που οἰκήσοντας. There are several indications in Book II. that, before this, the Persians were very nervous about the possibility of the Greeks settling in the rich garden of Babylonia. Xenophon too was well aware that the Ten Thousand were 'sufficiently numerous and well-organised to *become at once a city* wherever they might choose to settle.'

πολλοὺς δ'—ἐκπέμψειν, 'And he would give them many hostages that he would send them safe out of the country without guile, aye and he would make carriage-roads for them too.'

τοῦ—ἐκπέμψειν, genitive of the object, depending on ὁμήρους, i.e.

'securities for his intention of sending them out.' Cf. i. 18 φόβον τοῦ στρατεῦσαι.

ἄν—ἐποίει, εἰ ἑώρα, 'he would *now* be doing, if he were seeing,'— the imperfect here denoting continuous action in *present* time. Contrast ἂν δοίη above, which is quite indefinite as to time, and as to circumstances also, as no protasis is expressed.

τρισάσμενος. With this compound cf. τρίσμακαρ 'thrice-blest,' τρισκακοδαίμων 'thrice-unlucky,' τρισκατάρατος 'thrice-accursed.' So also in Latin; e.g. Plautus, *Aul.* 633 *non fur sed trifur* 'not merely a thief, but an arrant thief.'

25. ἀλλὰ γάρ, 'however.' There is no need to suppose any ellipse between ἀλλά and γάρ, as is generally done. We must remember that γάρ does not invariably mean 'for.' It is compounded of γ' ἄρ, and sometimes, especially in Homer, preserves its original meaning 'Yes, then' or 'ah, then.' So ἀλλὰ γὰρ (ἀλλά γ' ἄρ) means literally 'ah, but then,' which gives excellent sense here. 'However' is generally a satisfactory rendering. See § 26.

ἐν ἀφθόνοις, 'in luxury'; cf. IV. v. 29 ἐν πᾶσιν ἀφθόνοις ἐκοιμήθησαν 'slept in all comfort,' and *Demosth.* p. 312 ἐν ἀφθόνοις τραφείς 'bred up in luxury.'

μή, a mere repetition, for clearness' sake, of the μή after δέδοικα. Cf. § 35.

μή, ὥσπερ οἱ λωτοφάγοι, ἐπιλαθώμεθα τῆς οἴκαδε ὁδοῦ. See by all means Tennyson's *Lotos-Eaters*; and Homer *Odyssey* IX. 91—102, thus rendered by William Morris:—

> And they departing mingled with the Lotus-eaters there,
> Who indeed against our fellows devised no evil snare;
> But withal they gave unto them to taste of the Lotus meat,
> And what man of them soever did eat that sweet thing did eat
> Had no will to bear back tidings or to get him back again;
> But to bide with the Lotus-eaters for ever was he fain,
> And to eat the Lotus for ever and forget his returning day.
> So perforce these men sore weeping to the ships I dragged away.
> In the hollow ships 'neath the benches these men all bound I laid,
> And all our other fellows beloved I straitly bade
> To go up on the ships swift-sailing and haste without delay,
> Lest some should eat of the Lotus and forget their returning day.

The lotus-tree is a prickly bush. Its fruit is very sweet, like the date. It is still eaten in North Africa, the traditional home of the Lotus-Eaters; and it is called Jujuba.

26. ἐπιδεῖξαι—ὁρᾶν, 'to make it clear to the Greeks that they are poor through their own fault, seeing that it is open to them to send out hither those who are now landless citizens in Greece and see them in affluence here.'

ἑκόντες, emphatic:—'if they are poor it is their own fault.' In Greek the stress of a clause is often on the participle more than on the finite verb. Cf. i. 26.

ἐξόν, accusative absolute; cf. i. 14.

τοὺς—ἀκλήρους—πολιτεύοντας, a very expressive phrase, denoting those who have full political rights, but no property. There were many such owing to the disturbed state of the Greek world at this time.

ἀκλήρους, without a κλῆρος 'portion,' used especially of an 'allotment' of land in a colony; so the word is very applicable here where Xenophon is thinking of colonization.

ἐνθάδε κομισαμένους, 'having got them conveyed here'; such is the force of the middle. Cf. note on i. 8.

πλουσίως ὁρᾶν. Supply πολιτεύοντας.

This idea of a Greek colony in Asia seems to have been often present to the mind of Xenophon; but it did not meet with much favour among the Ten Thousand. When they were at Calpé on the Euxine, there seemed a possibility that they might actually found a city there; and this impression became so strong that the neighbouring native villages sent envoys to ask on what terms alliance with the Greeks might be obtained (VI. vi. 4). But the one prevailing wish with most of the Ten Thousand was to reach Greece with all speed.

ἀλλὰ γάρ. See § 25. The literal rendering 'yes, but then' again gives excellent sense. But the editors again suppose an awkward ellipse, which is no more necessary than in Homer *Od.* X. 201 κλαῖον δὲ λιγέως...· ἀλλ' οὐ γάρ τις πρῆξις ἐγίγνετο μυρομένοισιν 'They wept aloud.' *Aye, but then* no result came for all their lamentation.'

27. τοῦτο δὲ—ἀσφαλέστατα, 'And I must tell you this, viz. how we should travel with the greatest possible safety.'

ἵνα μὴ—στρατηγῇ, 'that our baggage animals may not regulate our march,' i.e. by making us choose routes suitable for their transit.

αὗται γὰρ αὖ—ἄγειν, 'For these wagons *in their turn* (αὖ, i.e. like the animals) are troublesome to convoy.'

28. κρατουμένων—ἀλλότρια, 'For when men are conquered you know that all their goods are alienated from them.'

κρατουμένων. For the genitive absolute with subject omitted cf. i. 40 οὕτω γ' ἐχόντων.

29. ὄντων—πειθομένων, 'as long as our commanders were alive and we obeyed them.'

31. ἦν δέ τις—κολάζειν, ' But in case any soldier is disobedient, (you must) pass a resolution that any one of you who on any such occasion happens to be on the spot must assist the officer in punishing him.'

ἀεί, 'from time to time'; cf. § 38 and Demosth. p. 585 οἱ ἀεὶ δικάζοντες 'those who are jurymen from time to time.'

ἐψευσμένοι ἔσονται, 'will find themselves deceived.'

μυρίους—Κλεάρχους. Clearchus was a very strict disciplinarian ; see the excellent description in II. vi. 8—10.

32. ἀλλὰ γὰρ—ὥρα, ' However it is now time to really (καὶ) put words into action '; cf. ἔργῳ περαίνηται below.

ἐπικυρωσάτω, 'let him ratify it,' a technical political term; cf. Thuc. III. 71 ἐπικιρῶσαι τὴν γνώμην. Xenophon is fond of employing the technicalities of the Greek assemblies at home. Cf. note on § 9.

εἰ δέ τι—διδάσκειν, 'But if any other course seems to be better than (to act) in this way, let even a private soldier have the courage to instruct us.'

ὁ ἰδιώτης, the *generic* use of the article, i.e. to denote a *class*.

33. οἷς λέγει. The relative is attracted into the case of its antecedent *τούτοις.* So in the next section ὧν προσδοκεῖ = ἐκείνων ἃ προσδοκεῖ.

καὶ αὐτίκα, 'even at once,' i.e. very soon; but first of all Xenophon's proposals must be voted on. Cf. § 35 καὶ δάκνουσιν 'actually bite,' and καὶ αὐτοί 'even themselves.'

ἀνέτειναν πάντες. Notice the *asyndeton,* i.e. the absence of a connecting particle, which is rare in Greek ; cf. § 38 ἔδοξε ταῦτα.

35. εἰ καὶ αὐτοί, merely a repetition, for clearness' sake, of εἰ οἱ πολέμιοι, on account of the parenthesis which has intervened. Cf. § 25.

πλαίσιον, 'a hollow square,' called in iv. 19 πλαίσιον ἰσόπλευρον.

36. τῶν ὅπλων, i.e. τῶν ὁπλιτῶν. The heavy infantry were to form the outside of the square; cf. iii. 7 εἴσω τῶν ὅπλων κατεκέκλειντο, VI. ii. 8 ἐπὶ τῶν τειχῶν ὅπλα ἐφαίνετο 'hoplites appeared on the walls.'

ὁ πολὺς ὄχλος, 'the great mass' of the unarmed, i.e. camp-followers, porters, etc. ; cf. iii. 6 τὸν ὄχλον ἐν μέσῳ ἔχοντες. Cf. also St Mark xii. 37 ὁ πολὺς ὄχλος ἤκουεν αὐτοῦ ἡδέως.

εἴη. This optative need cause no difficulty, though the subjunctive ᾖ might at first sight seem more natural. With ἴσως ἀσφαλέστερον we should supply, not ἐστί, but ἂν εἴη, which would harmonize better with

the modest ἴσως 'perhaps.' And after ἂν —εἴη it is quite good Greek to
have ἵνα—εἴη, the second optative being due to attraction. So in this
very section ἔλθοιεν is assimilated to ἂν—δέοι.

τὰ πρόσθεν κοσμεῖν, 'to regulate the vanguard.'

τοῖς τεταγμένοις, 'our men already in proper order.' This cannot
be neuter, 'our tactics,' as some take it.

37. εἰ δέ, elliptical. It is virtually a repetition of the condition
stated at the beginning of the previous sentence εἰ ἀποδειχθείη κ.τ.λ.
Translate 'But if (my suggestion were to be adopted).' Cf. Plato
Apology 34 D εἰ δή τις ὑμῶν οὕτως ἔχει· οὐκ ἀξιῶ μὲν γὰρ ἔγωγε· εἰ δ'
οὖν, ἐπιεικῇ ἄν μοι δοκῶ πρὸς τοῦτον λέγειν 'If any one of you is so disposed,—I don't think that he ought to be so,—*but suppose he is*, I
think I may fairly say to him...'

ἡγοῖτο—ἐπιμελοίσθην· ὀπισθοφυλακοῖμεν. These optatives, used
almost in an imperatival sense, seem very strange in an Attic Prose
writer; for note that they are used coordinately with the imperative
ἐχέτω. They seem to convey a *very modest* imperative; as we might
say, 'I venture to hope that Cheirisophus may lead.' So in VI. vi. 18
the optative is coordinated with the imperative:—μήτε πολεμεῖτε Λακεδαιμονίοις σῴζοισθέ τε ἀσφαλῶς ὅποι θέλει ἕκαστος 'Do not fight with the
Spartans and *I hope you may be brought safe*...' In the poets, especially
Homer, the optative is sometimes used exactly as in our passage; e.g.
Od. IV. 735 ἀλλά τις Δόλιον καλέσειε 'let some one call Dolius.'

ἡγοῖτο, simply 'lead the van,' not 'command the army.' See
Introduction, p. xx.

καὶ Λακεδαιμόνιος, i.e. *also* a citizen of the premier state of Greece,
in addition to his personal qualifications of courage, etc., and also the
fact of his having been a general before.

οἱ νεώτατοι, and therefore they are to fill the post of danger.

τὸ νῦν εἶναι, '*at least* for the present,' literally '*so that it be* for the
present.' εἶναι is sometimes used with this *limiting* sense. Cf. ἑκὼν
εἶναι 'at least if he can help it,' τὸ τήμερον εἶναι 'at least to-day.' See
note on i. 38.

38. πειρώμενοι. Mark the present participle, 'while we make
trial of this formation.'

ἀεί, 'from time to time'; cf. § 31 τὸν ἀεὶ ἐντυγχάνοντα.

ἔδοξε ταῦτα. Cf. § 33.

39. οὐ γάρ ἐστιν. Cf. § 13.

καὶ—δέ, 'Yes, and...' Cf. iii. I.

III.

Sir Austen Layard, who knew the ground well, has a brilliant passage on the departure of the Greeks (*Nineveh and Babylon*, p. 227); which is a striking commentary on part of this chapter :—

'Xenophon harangued the desponding Greeks and showed them how alone they could again see their homes. His eloquence and courage gave them new life. Having made their vows to the eternal gods and singing paeans, they burnt their carriages, tents and superfluous baggage; and prepared for the last great struggle. The sun must have risen in burning splendour over the parched and yellow plains of Shomamok, for it was early in the autumn. The world has rarely seen a more glorious sight than was witnessed on the banks of the Zab on that memorable morning. The Ten Thousand having eaten were permitted by the enemy, who were probably unprepared for this earnest resistance, to ford the river. Reaching the opposite bank they commenced that series of marches, directed with a skill and energy unequalled, which led them through difficulties almost insurmountable to their native shores.

'Near Abou-Sheetha, too, Darius a fugitive (after Alexander's victory at Arbela) urged his flying horses through the Zab, followed by the scattered remnants of an army which numbered in its ranks men of almost every race and clime. A few hours after, the Macedonian plunged into the ford in pursuit of the fallen monarch, at the head of those invincible legions which he was to lead to the banks of the Indus. The plains which stretch from the Zab below Abou-Sheetha have since been more than once the battle-field of Europe and Asia. I gazed with deep interest upon the scene of such great events,—a plain where nothing remains to tell of the vast armies which once moved across it, of European valour or of Eastern magnificence.' See Map, p. 78.

1. τῶν δὲ περιττῶν—ἀλλήλοις, 'And of their superfluous property they distributed to one another what each needed.'

τῶν περιττῶν—ὅτου, both partitive genitives; cf. i. 20 τῶν ἀγαθῶν τούτων οὐδενὸς ἡμῖν μετείη.

Μιθραδάτης, one of the Persians previously attached to Cyrus, to whom he had been thought 'most faithful' (II. v. 35). He had deserted the Greeks after the battle of Cunaxa. Now he comes on a mission of pretended friendship. But his purposes are treacherous, his real object being to seduce individual Greeks to desert.

2. καὶ ἐνθάδε δ'—διάγων, 'Yes, and here am I, living in great fear.'

καὶ—δ'. Cf. ii. 39 καὶ εἴ τις δέ.

εἰμὶ—διάγων. Cf. II. ii. 13 ἦν δὲ αὕτη ἡ στρατηγία οὐδὲν ἄλλο δυναμένη 'Here was this strategy, meaning nothing else.' St John i. 9 ἦν δὲ τὸ φῶς τὸ ἀληθινόν—ἐρχόμενον εἰς τὸν κόσμον, which should be translated ' There was the true light.. coming into the world' (R.V.).

καὶ—ἔχων, 'with all my attendants *too*.'

3. ἔλεγε, 'acted as spokesman.'

διαπολεμεῖν τούτῳ, 'to fight it out with him'; cf. ii. 8 διὰ παντὸς πολέμου αὐτοῖς ἰέναι. Cf. also διαμάχεσθαι, διαγωνίζεσθαι, διακινδυνεύειν.

4. ὑπόπεμπτος. For the force of the preposition, which denotes 'insidiously,' cf. II. iv. 22 τότε δὴ καὶ ἐγνώσθη ὅτι οἱ βάρβαροι τὸν ἄνθρωπον ὑποπέμψαιεν.

καὶ γάρ, 'for also,' introducing another cause for suspicion in addition to his manner and language.

πίστεως ἕνεκα, 'with a view to securing his fidelity.' Mithradates was a man of more than oriental perfidy; and he was a renegade. So he was trusted neither by Greeks nor Persians. Cf. note on § 1.

5. δόγμα—ἀκήρυκτον εἶναι, 'to pass a resolution that the war should be conducted without intercourse by heralds.' The Greeks have been deceived several times by a pretended mission of friendship from the Persians; now they are determined to have no more of it.

πόλεμον ἀκήρυκτον. Cf. Demosth. p. 314 ἄσπονδος καὶ ἀκήρυκτος πόλεμος ' truceless and heraldless war,' i.e. thoroughly implacable.

διέφθειρον—διέφθειραν. The difference of tense is instructive:— (1) 'tried to seduce' (*a series of attempts*), and (2) 'succeeded in seducing' (*one completed action*).

6. τὸν Ζαπάταν, the Great Zab River. See Map, p. 78.

' What surprises us most is that the Persians, with their very numerous force, made no attempt to hinder them from crossing so very considerable a river; for Xenophon estimates the Zab at 400 feet broad; and this seems below the statement of modern travellers, who inform us that it contains not much less water than the Tigris.... *The Persians, habitually marching in advance of the Greeks, must have reached the river first, and were therefore in possession of the crossing.*'—GROTE.

' The ford by which the Greeks crossed the Great Zab may, I think, be accurately determined. It is still the principal ford in this part of the river and must, from the nature of the bed of the stream, have been so from the earliest periods. *It is about 25 miles from the confluence of the Zab and Tigris.* The Greeks could not have crossed the Zab above the spot I have indicated, as the bed of the river is deep and confined within high rocky banks.　Mr Ainsworth (*Travels in the Track of the Ten Thousand*) would take the Greeks up to the modern ferry, where there could never have been a ford, and which would have been some miles out of their route.'—LAYARD, *Nineveh and Babylon*, p. 60.

τὸν ὄχλον.　Cf. ii. 36 ὁ πολὺς ὄχλος.

εἰς τετρακοσίους, 'up to the number of 400.'　Cf. § 20 and iv. 1.

εὐζώνους, 'well-girt,' 'active.'　οἱ εὔζωνοι is the technical name for the Greek highland troops of to-day, the *Evzones* of our newspapers.

7.　ἐγένοντο, subject 'Mithradates and his men.'

Κρῆτες, the 200 Cretans who had followed Clearchus, as Xenophon tells us in I. ii. 9.

βραχύτερα—ἐτόξευον, 'had a shorter range than the Persians,' who had larger bows; cf. iv. 17 μεγάλα δὲ καὶ τὰ τόξα τὰ Περσικά ἐστιν.

ψιλοὶ ὄντες, 'as being light-armed,' *causal* use of the participle; cf. i. 34.

εἴσω τῶν ὅπλων κατεκέκλειντο, 'had been enclosed inside the heavy-armed troops,' who formed the outside of the hollow square. For τὰ ὅπλα = οἱ ὁπλῖται cf. ii. 36; also II. iii. 3 ἐκτὸς δὲ τῶν ὅπλων μηδένα καταφανῆ εἶναι 'and that no one might be visible outside the hoplites.'　II. ii. 4 τὰ δὲ ὅπλα ἔξω 'and the hoplites marching outside.'

βραχύτερα—σφενδονητῶν, 'with shorter ranges than so as to reach the slingers.'　For the genitive after ἐξικνεῖσθαι cf. *Hellenica* VII. v. 17 ἐξικνοῦντο ἀλλήλων.　Eurip. *Electra* 612 τί δῆτα δρῶντες τοῦδ' ἂν ἐξικοίμεθα; The genitive is the usual case after verbs of *aiming at, hitting, reaching,* etc.

ὡς ἐξικνεῖσθαι.　ὡς is sometimes used by Xenophon where Attic writers generally use ὥστε.　Cf. iv. 25.

8.　τῶν ὁπλιτῶν καὶ τῶν πελταστῶν, partitive genitives after οἵ, 'those of the hoplites and peltasts who happened....'　Cf. § 8 and i. 2, 11, 35.

πελταστῶν, 'targeteers,' light-armed foot-soldiers, bearing the πέλτη or light shield of Thracian origin, crescent-shaped and covered with leather.　They formed an arm intermediate between the heavily-equipped hoplites and the sharp-shooters (γυμνῆτες, see iv. 26).　For attack they had a javelin (ἀκόντιον) and a long sword.

9.　οὔτε οἱ πεζοὶ—χωρίῳ, 'nor could their infantry overtake the infantry of the enemy, as they were fleeing with a long start and the distance was short.'

ἐκ πολλοῦ.　Cf. § 15 ἐκ τόξου ῥύματος 'with a bow-shot start.' Cf. I. x. 10 ἐκ πλείονος ἔφευγον.

10. ἅμα, with καὶ φεύγοντες, 'even while fleeing.'

εἰς τοὔπισθεν τοξεύοντες. 'Even when retiring, the Persian horseman could discharge his arrow or cast his javelin behind him with effect,—a dexterity which the Parthians exhibited afterwards still more signally, and which the Persian horsemen of the present day parallel with their carbines.'—GROTE.

ὁπόσον—ἔδει, 'And as far as the Greeks went in pursuit, so far they had to come back again, fighting all the time.'

διώξειαν, optative of frequency; cf. i. 20, 32.

11. τῆς ἡμέρας ὅλης, 'in the course of all that day.'

τὰς κώμας, the villages mentioned in ii. 34.

ἀπὸ τῆς φάλαγγος, meaning the same as § 9 ἀπὸ τοῦ ἄλλου στρατεύματος.

12. ᾐτιῶντο—μαρτυροίη. For the transition from the indicative to the optative in *oratio obliqua* cf. II. i. 3 οὗτοι ἔλεγον ὅτι Κῦρος μὲν τέθνηκεν Ἀριαῖος δὲ ἐν τῷ σταθμῷ εἴη. In our passage there is a special reason for the retention of the indicative ᾐτιῶντο. The *oratio recta* would be ὀρθῶς ᾐτιᾶσθε καὶ αὐτὸ τὸ ἔργον ὑμῖν μαρτυρεῖ. If ᾐτιᾶσθε had been turned into the optative αἰτιῷντο, the distinction between the imperfect ᾐτιᾶσθε and the present μαρτυρεῖ would have disappeared. This shows the futility of the correction αἰτιῷντο adopted by some recent editors.

14. τοῖς οὖν θεοῖς—δεόμεθα, 'Thank heaven that the enemy attacked us not with a large force but with a small detachment, so as to do us no serious harm, but rather to show us what we stand in need of.'

15. νῦν γὰρ—ἐξικνεῖσθαι, 'At present the enemy shoot and sling at such a range that our Cretan archers cannot reply, nor our hand-throwers reach so far.'

οἱ ἐκ χειρὸς βάλλοντες, i.e. the ἀκοντισταί mentioned in § 7.

πολύ, to be taken with χωρίον, 'for a great distance,'—accusative of space traversed.

ἐν ὀλίγῳ—ῥύματος, 'And over a short distance no foot-soldier, were he ever so swift, could overtake another in pursuit if he started the distance of a bow-shot in advance.'

ἐν ὀλίγῳ. Cf. § 9 ἐν ὀλίγῳ χωρίῳ.

ἐκ τόξου ῥύματος. Cf. § 9 ἐκ πολλοῦ.

16. εἰ μέλλομεν, 'if we mean to prevent the enemy from impeding our march, we want (i.e. we must get) slingers and cavalry as soon as possible.'

βλάπτειν, here in its primary sense of 'impede,' rather than 'injure.' Cf. Thuc. v. 103 ἐλπὶς κἂν βλάψῃ οὐ καθεῖλε, 'hope even though she impede them in their course does not lay them low.' This is the ordinary signification of the verb in Homer.

τὴν ταχίστην, adverbial accusative, ὁδόν being understood ; cf. iv. 17 μακράν 'a long way,' and iv. 46 τὴν λοιπήν 'the rest of the way.'

διπλάσιον—σφενδονῶν, 'double as far as the Persian slings.' For the genitive cf. i. 37, ii. 14.

17. ἐκεῖναι, 'the latter.'

διὰ τὸ—σφενδονᾶν, 'because the stones with which they slung were as large as the hand could hold.' χειροπληθέσι is a predicate.

μολυβδίσιν. Leaden bullets have been found on the plain of Marathon and elsewhere in Greece, many of them marked with thunderbolts, names of persons, and even comic inscriptions, such as ΔΕΞΑΙ 'take this,' and ΤΡΩΓΑΛΙΟΝ 'nut' or 'almond.' The Romans too used leaden bullets which they called *glandes* 'acorns,' on account of their oval shape, also stamped with thunderbolts and inscriptions, e.g. FERI POMPEIUM : MARS VLTOR : FUGITIVI PERISTIS ; and the like. During Sulla's siege of the Peiraeus we are told that two traitorous slaves gave information to the besiegers by writing on bullets.

18. αὐτῶν, partitive genitive after τίνες, 'who among them'; cf. § 8.

τούτων, 'in exchange for these slings,'—genitive of value ; cf. Homer *Il.* VI. 235 τεύχε' ἄμειβεν χρύσεα χαλκείων 'changed golden armour for bronze.'

καὶ τῷ σφενδονᾶν—εὐρίσκωμεν, 'and if for any one willing to act as slinger in the place appointed for him we find some immunity besides....'

ἄλλην, 'besides' the extra money payment; cf. iv. 21 and Soph. *Philoctetes* 38 καὶ ταῦτά γ' ἄλλα θάλπεται ῥάκη 'aye and here are rags besides drying in the sun.' Aesch. *Septem* 424 γίγας ὅδ' ἄλλος, 'here is a giant *besides*.'

ἀτέλειαν, i.e. exemption from some of the ordinary duties in camp. Aelian speaks of ἀτέλειαν φρουρᾶς 'exemption from garrison duty.'

19. τοὺς μέν τινας—σκευοφοροῦντας, 'some few with me, others belonging to Clearchus' cavalry but left behind, and many more besides captured from the enemy and now acting as baggage animals.'

τῶν Κλεάρχου. Clearchus' little body of cavalry, numbering 40 only, had deserted (II. ii. 7); but, as we see from this passage, they had left some of their horses. This is quite natural; for doubtless the troop would have had some spare horses.

ἂν οὖν—ἀνιάσουσιν, 'If then we pick out all these and substitute (regular) baggage animals for them, and adapt the horses for the use of cavalry, perhaps these too will somewhat annoy fugitives.'

σκευοφόρα, i.e. oxen, mules and asses.

εἰς ἱππέας. Cf. iv. 17 χρῆσθαι εἰς τὰς σφενδόνας.

κατασκευάσωμεν. This verb includes the ideas both of training and equipment.

ἴσως—τι—ἀνιάσουσιν. Note the refined and delicate irony which is characteristic of the Greek language. Cf. i. 37.

20. εἰς διακοσίους—εἰς πεντήκοντα. Cf. § 6 and iv. 1.

ἐγένοντο, 'amounted to'; cf. i. 33.

σπολάδες. The σπολάς was a leather cuirass or buff jerkin reaching over the hips, and fringed with strips of leather round its lower edge. It was frequently covered partly or completely with metal, especially in the form of scales.

θώρακες. The θώραξ was a metal cuirass consisting of two separate pieces, one covering the chest, the other the back, joined by means of clasps or buckles; it was also fastened by a leather belt. The front plate was sometimes extended to cover the stomach. As a protection to the hips, there was, as in the case of the σπολάς, a series of strips of leather or felt, covered with plates of metal. These resembled a kilt and were called πτέρυγες 'feathers.'

IV.

1. ταύτην τὴν ἡμέραν, 'throughout this day,' duration of time, contrasted with τῇ ἄλλῃ 'on the morrow,' point of time; cf. § 18.

χαράδραν. 'A ravine worn by winter rains may correspond with the valley mentioned by Xenophon; but I think the Ghazir (a tributary of the Great Zab) far more likely to have been the torrent-bed viewed with so much alarm by the Greek commander, and the passage of which Mithradates might have disputed with some prospect of success.'—LAYARD. See Map, p. 78.

2. λάβῃ. For the retention of the subjunctive in *oratio obliqua* to produce a graphic effect, see i. 6, 9.

καταφρονήσας ὅτι, 'since he despised them from the fact that....'

ἐνόμιζε. Mark the force of the imperfect:—'he was thinking all the time.'

3. ἔχων τὴν δύναμιν, 'with his force.' Note the use of the article as a possessive pronoun.

παρήγγελτο—δυνάμεως, 'Now orders had been passed to those of the peltasts and hoplites whose duty it was to take part in the pursuit, and the cavalry had been bidden to pursue with confidence, seeing that an adequate force would follow them close.'

πελταστῶν—ὁπλιτῶν, partitive genitives depending on ἐκείνοις understood, the antecedent of οὕς. Cf. i. 2.

4. ἐπεὶ δὲ—χαράδραν, 'And when Mithradates had overtaken them, and slings and arrows began to take effect, (the trumpeter) gave the signal to the Greeks with his trumpet, and at once those who had received instructions ran to close with the enemy and the cavalry charged. But the Persians did not withstand their onset and fled to the ravine.'

ἐξικνοῦντο. Cf. iii. 7, 15.

ἐσήμηνε. For the ellipse of the subject cf. § 36 and II. ii. 4 ἐπειδὰν σημήνῃ τῷ κέρατι.

οἷς εἴρητο, antecedent ἐκεῖνοι understood; cf. i. 21.

5. τοῖς βαρβάροις, dative of disadvantage, 'for the barbarians,' i.e. 'the barbarians lost many.' Cf. § 39.

οἱ Ἕλληνες ᾐκίσαντο, a horrible outrage for *Greeks* to commit; cf. i. 17.

6. οὕτω πράξαντες, 'having fared thus.'

7. Λάρισσα. 'That Larissa and Mespila are represented by the ruins of Nimroud and Kouyunjik no one can reasonably doubt. Xenophon's description corresponds most accurately with the ruins and with the distance between them.'—LAYARD. The ruins of Nimroud occupy a part of the great city of Nineveh. The Greeks must have given the Greek name *Larissa* to the place, as a near approach to some local name which they heard there; e.g. *Al Ashur* or *Al Rescn*.

Μῆδοι, who, with their allies, had captured Nineveh from the Assyrians about 600 B.C.

δύο παρασάγγαι, about 7 miles. 'The *parasang*, like its representative the modern *farsang* or *farsakh* of Persia, was not a measure of distance very accurately determined, but rather indicated a certain amount of time employed in traversing a given space. Travellers are well aware that the Persian *farsakh* varies considerably according to the nature of the country and the usual modes of conveyance adopted by its inhabitants. The *farsakh* and the hour are almost invariably used as expressing the same distance. That the *parasang* was the same as the modern hour we find by the distance between Larissa (Nimroud) and Mespila (Kouyunjik) being given as six parasangs, corresponding exactly with the number of hours assigned by the present inhabitants of the country, and by the authorities of the Turkish post, to the same road. The six hours in this instance are equal to about 18 English miles.'— LAYARD. See Map, p. 78.

τὸ ὕψος, accusative of respect.

εἴκοσι ποδῶν, genitive of amount; cf. § 9 τὸ μὲν εὖρος ἑνὸς πλέθρου and § 11.

8. βασιλεὺς ὁ Περσῶν, i.e. Cyrus the Great, about 550 B.C.

ἐλάμβανον, imperfect of the attempt, 'were trying to wrest.' Cf. iii. 5.

νεφέλη. Perhaps a heavy fog helped the besieging army to take the city; or, more probably, the passage refers to an eclipse of the sun, which, being a bad omen, caused the inhabitants to despair.

ἐξέλιπον, used absolutely, 'failed,' 'gave up,' i.e. abandoned the defence. Cf. Xenophon *Oeconomicus* vii. 19 τοῦ μὴ ἐκλιπεῖν ζῴων γένη 'to prevent the races of animals failing.' Eurip. *H. F.* 230 ῥώμη γὰρ ἐκλέλοιπεν 'our strength has failed.' Others less well supply τὴν πόλιν after ἐξέλιπον.

9. παρὰ ταύτην τὴν πόλιν, an unusual use of παρά with the accusative, which generally denotes *motion to* or *motion along.* Cf. v. iii. 13 στήλη ἕστηκε παρὰ τὸν ναόν 'a pillar stands by the temple.'

πυραμὶς λιθίνη, not really a pyramid. Layard, when he saw it first, made the same mistake as Xenophon. Later he writes:—'It was evident that the high conical mound, forming the N.W. corner of the ruins of Nimroud, was the remains of a square tower and not of a pyramid. The lower part, built of solid stone masonry, had withstood the wreck of ages; but the upper walls of burnt brick falling outwards, and having been subsequently covered with earth and vegetation, the ruin had taken the pyramidal form that loose materials falling in this manner would naturally assume. It is very probable that this ruin represents the tomb of Sardanapalus, which stood at the entrance of the city of Nineveh' (*Nineveh and Babylon*, p. 125).

10. σταθμὸν—ἕξ, 'one day's march consisting of six parasangs.' For the apposition cf. v. 16.

τεῖχος, 'a fort,' identified with a mound over 1000 feet long near the village of Yarumjeh. See Map, p. 78.

Μέσπιλα, now represented by the ruins at Kouyunjik, on the east bank of the Tigris opposite to the modern town of Mösul.

Layard holds that the ruins of Kouyunjik, Nimroud, Karamles and Khorsabad, which places form almost a perfect parallelogram, were all included in the area of the great city of Nineveh, whose circuit was said to be 60 miles; cf. Jonah iii. 4 'Now Nineveh was an exceeding great city of three days' journey.' See Map, p. 78.

At these four places, he says, 'were royal dwellings with their dependent buildings and parks or *paradises*, fortified like the palace-temples of Egypt, capable of standing a prolonged siege, and a place of refuge for the inhabitants in case of invasion. I will not pretend to say that the whole of this vast space was thickly inhabited or built upon. We must not judge of Eastern cities by those of Europe. In Asia gardens and orchards, containing suburbs and even distinct villages, collected round a walled city, are all included by the natives under one general name' (*Nineveh and Babylon*, p. 640).

λίθου ξεστοῦ κογχυλιάτου. Layard found 'slabs of limestone abounding in fossils, probably *the polished stone full of shells* noticed by Xenophon in the plinth of the walls of Mespila.'

11. βασιλέως, perhaps Astyages.

ὅτε ἀπώλλυσαν—Μῆδοι, 'when the Medes were losing their empire at the hands of the Persians.'

ἀπάλλυσαν, imperfect, 'were in course of losing.'

ὑπὸ Περσῶν, construction *according to the sense*, the verb virtually signifying '*they were deprived of.*' Cf. Thuc. IV. 66 ἐκπεσόντες ὑπὸ τοῦ πλήθους. Cf. also § 5 τοῖς βαρβάροις ἀπέθανον.

12. Ζεὺς δὲ βροντῇ κατέπληξε. We know nothing of any historical fact to which this legend can refer. The Prophet Nahum (i. 8) speaks thus of the fall of Nineveh:—'With an overrunning flood he will make an utter end of the place thereof, and darkness shall pursue his enemies.'

13. παρασάγγας τέτταρας. 'From Mespila the Greeks marched four parasangs and probably halted near the modern village of Batnai, an ancient site exactly four hours, by the usual caravan road, from Kouyunjik. Many ancient mounds around Batnai mark the remains of those villages, from which, after having repulsed the Persian forces under Tissaphernes and Orontas, the Greeks obtained an abundant supply of provisions.'—LAYARD. See Map, p. 78.

εἰς τοῦτον τὸν σταθμόν, a so-called *pregnant* construction, ἐπεφάνη being treated as a verb of motion :—'appeared to them on this day's march.' Cf. i. 33. *Hellenica* I. vi. 7 σῴζειν οἴκαδε 'to bring safe home.' Acts viii. 40 Φίλιππος εὑρέθη εἰς Ἄζωτον 'Philip was found at Azotus.'

ἱππέας, his 500 cavalry mentioned in I. ii. 4.

θυγατέρα. Cf. II. iv. 8. Her name was Rhodoguné.

βαρβάρους, the Asiatics commanded by Ariaeus the friend of Cyrus.

βασιλέως ἀδελφός, an illegitimate brother of Artaxerxes and Cyrus; cf. II. iv. 25.

14. τὰς μὲν—διακινδυνεύειν, 'having posted some of his troops in the rear of the Greeks, and having wheeled round others to act upon their flanks, he did not venture on a direct attack nor would he risk a decisive battle either.'

σφενδονᾶν—καὶ τοξεύειν, i.e. by continual skirmishing he hoped to provoke them to enter the *cul de sac* prepared for them by the movements just described.

15. διαταχθέντες, 'posted apart' in skirmishing order,—no longer εἴσω τῶν ὅπλων as· they were in iii. 7, and as they will be again in iv. 26.

οἱ Σκύθαι, apparently a technical term for mounted archers of the Scythian type; cf. Arrian *Tact.* ii. 13 οἱ τῶν ἱππέων τόξοις χρώμενοι ἱπποτοξόται λέγονται, ὑπ᾽ ἐνίων δὲ Σκύθαι.

οὐδὲ γάρ—ἦν, 'For it was not easy even though he were ever so anxious,' i.e. on account of the density of the enemy's host.

ἀπεχώρει—ἀπεχώρησαν. Mark the difference of tense,—'began to retire' and 'had actually retired'; cf. iii. 5 διέφθειρον—διέφθειραν.

16. οὐκέτι—ἀκροβολίσει, 'no longer did damage with their previous skirmishing,'—i.e. with their skirmishing *as they did before.* τότε not unfrequently has this meaning.

τῶν τοξοτῶν—ἐτόξευον, 'the Cretan archers shot farther than the Persian archers.'

17. ἁλίσκοιτο, optative of frequency. Cf. i. 20, 32.

ἐμελέτων—μακράν, 'they used to practise shooting a long way aiming upwards,'—so as to send the arrows further, just as we adjust the sight of a rifle according to the range.

μόλυβδος, for bullets; cf. iii. 17.

18. ταύτῃ τῇ ἡμέρᾳ—τὴν ἐπιοῦσαν ἡμέραν. Cf. § 1.

πολὺς σῖτος. We are told that fertility is the characteristic of the Plain of Nineveh at the present day.

ταῖς κώμαις, at Tel Keif, 'Mount Pleasant,' a modern town about 9 miles from Mösul. See Map, p. 78.

19—23. The general sense of this important passage is well given by Grote:—'All this march was made under unremitting annoyance from the enemy, insomuch that, though the order of the Greeks was never broken, a considerable number of their men were wounded. Experience taught them that *it was inconvenient for the whole army to march in one inflexible, undivided, hollow square;* and they accordingly constituted six *lochi* or regiments of 100 men each, subdivided into companies of 50 and *enômoties* or smaller companies of 25, each with a special officer (conformably to the Spartan practice), to move separately on each flank, and *either to fall back or fall in, as might suit the fluctuations of the central mass*, arising from impediments in the road or menaces of the enemy.'

The correct interpretation of the whole passage depends chiefly on two points:—

(1) We must understand that τὰ κέρατα (§§ 19, 20) is, as Mr Pretor points out, virtually equivalent to αἱ πλευραί (§ 22),—the only difference being this that in the case of κέρατα the flanks of the column are regarded from the *extremities*, in the case of πλευραί from the *sides*.

(2) The second sentence of § 21 must be taken as it is explained below.

19. ἀνάγκη—ἀτάκτους ὄντας, ' For if the flanks of the hollow square are compressed,—either because a road gets narrower or because hills or a bridge compel (such compression),—of necessity the hoplites are squeezed out of position and march wretchedly, partly from being crushed and partly owing to actual (καὶ) confusion, so that in such disorder they prove useless.'

στενοτέρας, the more correct form of the comparative.

ὁρέων, the uncontracted form, appears sometimes in the MSS. of Xenophon.

20. ὅταν δ' αὖ—ἐπομένων, 'And when the flanks diverge again, of necessity those who were previously squeezed out of place are now separated and the space between the flanks becomes empty of men; and those who are thus affected begin to despair when hard-pressed by the enemy.'

διασπᾶσθαι, i.e. those who were squeezed out of place do not form line again at once, and so leave a gap between the flanks.

γέφυραν—διάβασιν, 'to cross by a bridge or any other kind of crossing,' e.g. a ford or mountain-pass.

φθάσαι πρῶτος, 'to get over first,' thus breaking the ranks.

εὐεπίθετον—πολεμίοις, 'In these cases attack was easy for the enemy.' Probably εὐεπίθετον ἦν is impersonal; cf. IV. viii. 12 ᾗ ἂν εὔοδον ᾖ 'wherever there is a good road.' But possibly τὸ πλαίσιον is the subject.

21. ἀνὰ ἑκατὸν ἄνδρας, 'at the rate of a hundred men each.' For this *distributive* use of the preposition cf. IV. vi. 4 ἀνὰ πέντε παρασάγγας τῆς ἡμέρας ' at the rate of five parasangs a day.' St Luke ix. 14 κλισίας ὡσεὶ ἀνὰ πεντήκοντα ' companies at the rate of fifty each.'

ἄλλους, 'besides'; cf. note on iii. 18.

οὗτοι δὲ—κεράτων, 'And these, as they marched, (1) whenever the wings were compressed, fell behind, so as not to impede the wings; (2) at other times they marched along outside the wings.' This sentence would have been much clearer, if τότε μέν had been inserted before ὑπέμενον, to balance τότε δέ.

οὗτοι, i.e. the officers mentioned above and their men.

ὑπέμενον ὕστεροι, literally 'they waited behind in the rear.'

παρῆγον, 'marched alongside.' παράγειν is used absolutely in *Cyropaedeia* V. iv. 44. Cf. also the absolute use of ὑπάγειν in § 48 below.

22. ὁπότε δὲ—ἐξεπίμπλασαν, 'But whenever the sides of the square were parted (too far), they would fill up the gap,—if the intervening space were rather narrow, by companies; if wider, by half-companies; if very wide, by quarter-companies,—so that the gap was always filled up.'

ἂν ἐξεπίμπλασαν. The ἄν here is not *conditional*, but *frequentative*. It is so used both with the imperfect and aorist indicative. Cf. II. iii. 3 ἔπαισεν ἄν 'he *would* give a blow.' I. ix. 19 ἂν ἀφείλετο 'he *would* take away.' Soph. *Philoctetes* 295 εἶτα πῦρ ἂν οὐ παρῆν 'then I *would* have no fire.'

κατὰ λόχους—κατὰ πεντηκοστῦς—κατ' ἐνωμοτίας. The different arrangements of the 600 are described in reference to their depth :—

   (1) 100 deep or 6 abreast.
   (2) 50 deep or 12 abreast.
   (3) 25 deep or 24 abreast.

Grote inclines to the view that there were 12 λόχοι in all, 6 on each flank. But this is clearly incorrect.

23. εἴ που δέοι—οὗτοι, 'If any assistance was wanted anywhere in the main body, they came up alongside to help.' Cf. VI. v. 9 ἵν' ἄν που δέῃ οἱ ἐπιβοηθήσοντες τῇ φάλαγγι.

τῆς φάλαγγος, partitive genitive after που. Cf. v. 18 ἡνίκα τῆς ὥρας. VI. v. 22 ᾗ ἐτύγχανε τοῦ νάπους ὤν 'wherever in the woodland he happened to be'; also ποῦ γῆς; ' where in the world?' Latin *ubi gentium?* Homer *Il.* XVII. 372 νέφος δ' οὐ φαίνετο πάσης γαίης ' and a cloud appeared nowhere in all the land.'

σταθμοὺς τέτταρας. 'Instead of fording the Khabour near its

junction with the Tigris, and thus avoiding the hills, they crossed them by a precipitous pass to the site of the modern Zakhu. *They reached this range in four days, traversing it on the fifth,* probably by the modern caravan road. The distance from Batnai to Zakhu is 20 hours. This would give between four and five hours, or *parasangs,* a day for the march of the Greeks, the distance they usually performed. They were probably much retarded during the last day, *by having to fight their way over three distinct mountain ridges.*'—LAYARD.

24. τὸν πέμπτον, cognate accusative :—'when they were going the fifth day's march.' Cf. § 46 τὴν λοιπὴν πορευσόμεθα.

βασίλειόν τι—κώμας πολλάς. ' The appearance of Zakhu in the present day coincides in a remarkable manner with what it was described to be in the time of Xenophon,—*a palace amid villages,* constituting in fact a good picture of what we can imagine a baronial castle to have been in feudal times, surrounded by the cottages of serfs and retainers. As the stranger approaches, he is struck by its bold and isolated appearance. It is not like Mösul, a town in a partially civilized country; but it is an outpost of warlike Kurdistan.'—AINSWORTH.

γηλόφων ὑψηλῶν, identified with the triple range called Chá Spi by the Kurds, meaning 'White Hills.' See Map, p. 78.

τοὺς λόφους—ἱππέων, 'the Greeks saw the hills with joy, as was natural, seeing the enemy were cavalry,' and so could not pursue them any longer.

25. ὡς ἀναβαίνειν. See note on iii. 7.

ἔβαλλον, ἐσφενδόνων, ἐτόξευον. The *asyndeton* gives great vividness to the description; cf. Soph. *Ajax* 60 ὤτρυνον, εἰσέβαλλον. See note on i. 3 and cf. § 31.

ὑπὸ μαστίγων, literally 'to the accompaniment of whips,' perhaps with a half comic reference to the sound of the lash; for ὑπό is frequently used (with the genitive) of accompanying sounds; e.g. πίνειν ὑπὸ σάλπιγγος 'to drink to the sound of the trumpet,' ὑπ' αὐλητῶν χωρεῖν 'to march to the music of flute-players,' καταθάπτειν ὑπὸ κλαυθμῶν 'to bury with the accompaniment of wailing.'

For the practice of fighting under the lash cf. Herodotus' account of the Persian officers flogging their men into battle at Thermopylae (VII. 223), and a similar story told of the Egyptian army in Greece in 1827. Cf. also Herodotus VII. 21 ὤρυσσον ὑπὸ μαστίγων 'they dug to the accompaniment of whips,' of the Persian workmen at the canal through Mount Athos.

26. γυμνήτων, 'light-armed,' generic name including the different

kinds of light troops recruited from peoples specially distinguished for
the use of particular weapons, e.g. archers generally Cretans, slingers
generally Rhodians. The common characteristic of all kinds of γυμνῆτες was the absence of defensive armour.

κατέκλεισαν– εἴσω τῶν ὅπλων. See notes on ii. 36 and iii. 7.

ἐν τῷ ὄχλῳ ὄντες, 'because they became part of the crowd (of camp-
followers).' Cf. ii. 36 ὁ πολὺς ὄχλος and iii. 6 τὸν ὄχλον ἐν μέσῳ
ἔχοντες.

27. ὁπλῖται ὄντες, 'because they were heavy-armed,' *causal* use
of the participle again ; cf. i. 34, iii. 7.

28. ἀπίοιεν, 'whenever they fell back,' optative of frequency,
referring to what happened at each successive ridge.

πρὸς τὸ ὄρος, i.e. the main mountain, from which branched out the
spurs which the Greeks had to cross ; cf. § 24.

29. πολεμίων—οἱ πολέμιοι—οἱ πολέμιοι. The repetition is not
without point :—'When these slingers had got above the pursuing
enemy, the enemy no longer set upon the army as it descended, since
they were afraid they might be cut off and have *their* enemy on each
side of them.'

30. οἱ μὲν—ἐπιπαριόντες, 'the main body moving along the road
over the spurs, and the peltasts marching parallel with them along the
mountain above.'

ἐπιπαριόντες. The force of both prepositions must be given in
translation :—ἐπί 'above' and παρά 'side by side' with the main body.
The peltasts were thus able to cover the march of the main body of the
Greeks.

τὰς κώμας, those mentioned in § 24.

31. καὶ ἅμα—εἶχον. The second reason is stated independently
without the addition of ὅτι.

τῷ σατραπεύοντι, not exactly dative of the agent, but rather dative
of advantage :—'which had been collected *for* the acting satrap of the
district,' i.e. 'which *he had got* collected.' Cf. II. i. 1 ἠθροίσθη Κύρῳ τὸ
Ἑλληνικόν 'Cyrus *got* his Greek force collected.' Cf. also § 35 αὐτοῖς
δέδενται.

32. τὸ πεδίον, i.e. the valley of the Khabour. See Map, p. 78.

τῇ δυνάμει. Cf. § 3.

33. αὐτοῖς, dative after ἀκροβολίζεσθαι, on the analogy of the construction of μάχεσθαι, e.g. τοῖς πολεμίοις μάχεσθαι below.

πολὺ γὰρ—μάχεσθαι, 'For it made a great difference when they
could sally forth from a position and defend themselves, instead of

having the enemy they fought with constantly attacking them on their march.'

χώρας, 'post,' i.e. a camp; cf. Aesch. *Agam.* 78 Ἄρης οὐκ ἐνὶ χώρᾳ 'Ares is not at his post '; also the phrases κατὰ χώραν μένειν 'to remain at one's post,' χώραν λείπειν 'to desert a post,' εἰς τὴν χώραν παρεῖναι 'to be at one's post.'

34. οὔποτε γὰρ—σταδίων, 'For the barbarians never encamped at a less distance than 60 stades from the Greek force.'

ἐπιθῶνται, graphic use of the subjunctive, perhaps denoting the very real and ever-present character of the Persian fear.

35. πονηρόν, 'a wretched thing'; cf. § 19 πονηρὰ τάξις.

αὐτοῖς δέδενται, 'they have their horses tethered'; cf. § 31 τῷ σατραπεύοντι.

πεποδισμένοι, 'hobbled,' i.e. with feet fettered. The horses of Oriental cavalry are often still kept shackled at night.

εἰ λυθείησαν—ἐὰν γίγνηται. Notice the contrast between the moods :—(1) a supposed case uncertainly and vaguely stated, '*if they were to be loose*,' ὅπερ ἂν γένοιτο the apodosis being understood. (2) a supposed case stated distinctly and graphically, '*if a tumult arise.*'

δεῖ ἐπισάξαι—Πέρσῃ ἀνδρί, literally 'it is necessary to saddle his horse *for a Persian*'; *not* 'it is necessary for a Persian to saddle his horse,' which would require Πέρσην ἄνδρα. The dative is the same as that commented on above, § 31 ; i.e. the meaning is 'a Persian has to get his horse saddled,' e.g. by his servant.

δεῖ καὶ θωρακισθέντα ἀναβῆναι, 'he must also put on his armour before he mounts.' Note the emphasis on the participle; cf. i. 6, ii. 26.

θωρακισθέντα, agreeing with Πέρσην ἄνδρα understood.

36. διαγγελλομένους, 'passing the word to one another along the ranks'; cf. § 45 διακελευομένων.

ἐκήρυξε, subject κῆρυξ understood ; cf. § 4 ἐσάλπιγξε.

λύειν, 'to profit'; cf. Soph. *Electra* 1005 (with accusative as here) λύει γὰρ ἡμᾶς οὐδέν. Eurip. *Medea* 1362 λύει δ' ἄλγος (absolutely). More often with dative; e.g. Eurip. *Alcestis* 627 φημὶ τοιούτους γάμους λύειν βροτοῖς.

37. χωρίον ὑπερδέξιον, 'a commanding position on the right '; i.e. 'a spur from the main range which advances beyond the plain of Zakhu down to the banks of the Tigris and is bounded on the further side by the plain of Jezireh.'—PRETOR.

ἀκρωνυχίαν, 'nail-tip.' The range of hills is looked upon as a hand spread out; and the spur in question is represented by a nail-tip. Cf. Kinglake's comparison of the Russian army at Balaclava at first to a closed fist, and then, after Scarlett's charge, to a hand with two fingers extended.

ὑφ' ἥν. The accusative is used because of the idea of motion conveyed by κατάβασις :—'*along* the base of which.' Cf. v. 1.

38. οὐκ ἦγεν. Mark the force of the imperfect :—'did not begin to lead.'

39. ἡμῖν, dative of disadvantage, 'against us,' 'to bar our path.' Cf. § 5.

εἰ μὴ—ἀποκόψομεν. See note on i. 13.

40. πῶς τις—ἀπελᾷ, 'how one may drive away'; i.e. 'how we may...'; cf. the French *on*, and v. 8.

41. τὴν κορυφήν, 'the summit' of the mountain (called τὸ ἄκρον below) commanding the spur or 'nail-tip,' held by the Persians, which is here called ὁ λόφος.

ὑπὲρ αὐτοῦ τοῦ—στρατεύματος, '*just* above their own army.' Cf. Thuc. IV. 10 παρ' αὐτὴν τὴν ῥαχίαν '*just* at the breakers' edge.'

βούλει—ἐθέλω. Note the difference in meaning between the two verbs :—(1) 'choose'; (2) 'be ready.'

42. κελεύει—λαβεῖν, 'bids Cheirisophus despatch with him some men from the front; for it was too far to get them from the rear.'

43. τοὺς ἀπὸ τοῦ στόματος, *pregnant* construction; i.e. 'he sends *from the front* the peltasts on the front.' Cf. I. ii. 3 τοὺς ἐκ τῶν πόλεων.

ἔλαβε—πλαισίου, '(To fill their place) he took those in the centre of the square.'

τοὺς τριακοσίους—τῶν ἐπιλέκτων, 'three hundred belonging to his picked corps,' specially belonging to Cheirisophus; *not* half the 600 mentioned in § 21, as some think.

45. στρατεύματος διακελευομένων, construction *according to the sense*; cf. II. i. 6 τὸ στράτευμα—κόπτοντες τοὺς βοῦς. This syntax is not uncommon with collective nouns.

διακελευομένων, 'cheering on one another throughout their ranks.' For the preposition and the reflexive use of the middle cf. § 36 διαγγελλομένους.

46. ἀμιλλᾶσθαι. Greece and wives and children are regarded as the goal of this race.

παῖδας—γυναῖκας, the usual order in Greek; cf. Soph. *Trach.* 257 ξὺν παιδὶ καὶ γυναικί.

τὴν λοιπήν (ὁδόν), cognate accusative used adverbially ; cf. iii. 16 τὴν ταχίστην.

48. **καὶ ὅς,** 'and he,' a survival of the demonstrative use of ὅς which is common in Homer. It also survives in the Platonic expression ἦ δ' ὅς 'said he.'

ἔχων, i.e. with the shield.

θώρακα—τὸν ἱππικόν, a heavy breastplate, since the cavalry had no shields ; cf. Plutarch *Philopoemen* 9 πεζὸς ἐν ἱππικῷ θώρακι καὶ σκευῇ βαρυτέρᾳ 'a foot-soldier with a cavalry breastplate and heavier equipment.'

καὶ τοῖς μὲν—ἑπόμενος, 'And to those in front he passed the word to move on, and to those behind to pass by him as he could hardly keep up.'

ὑπάγειν, 'move on'; cf. Arist. *Clouds* 1298 ὕπαγε, τί μέλλεις; 'get on, why do you delay?'

49. **ὁ δὲ ἀναβάς,** 'But Xenophon having remounted.'

βάσιμα—ἄβατα, '*things* were (i.e. the ground was) passable...impassable,' i.e. for a horseman. Cf. note on § 20 ; also IV. vi. 17 βατὰ καὶ τοῖς ὑποζυγίοις ἔσται 'things will be passable even for baggage animals.' Thuc. I. 7 πλωϊμωτέρων ὄντων 'when things became more nautical,' i.e. 'when navigation became more general.'

V.

1. **οἱ ἀμφὶ Τισσαφέρνην καὶ 'Αριαῖον,** 'Tissaphernes and Ariaeus and their men '; cf. οἱ ἀμφὶ Χειρίσοφον below.

ἄλλην ὁδὸν ᾤχοντο, 'had gone off another way.' For the cognate accusative cf. iv. 24, 46.

πεδίῳ. 'Probably the place where the Greeks quitted the Tigris to strike into the Karduchian mountains was the neighbourhood of Jezireh ibn Omar, the ancient Bezabde. It is here that farther march up the eastern side of the Tigris is rendered impracticable by the mountains closing in. Here the modern road crosses the Tigris by a bridge from the eastern bank to the western.'—GROTE. See Map, p. 78.

παρά—ποταμόν, 'extending along the river '; cf. iv. 9, 37.

2. **καὶ γὰρ—κατελήφθησαν,** 'For indeed many herds of grazing cattle had been intercepted while being ferried across to the other bank of the river.' These words are inserted to explain καθ' ἁρπαγήν.

3. **τὰς κώμας,** the villages mentioned in § 1.

ἐννοούμενοι—λαμβάνοιεν, 'apprehending that (μή *lest*), if the enemy burnt the villages, they would not (οὐ) have any place from which to get supplies.' Cf. i. 12 ἐφοβεῖτο μὴ οὐ δύναιτο.

ἐννοούμενοι μή, 'apprehending lest...,' on the analogy of the construction after verbs of fearing ; cf. i. 5.

4. ἀπῇσαν ἐκ τῆς βοηθείας, ' were returning from the rescue,' i.e. of the Greek foraging parties mentioned in § 2.

κατέβη, 'had descended' from the hills, where the battle was fought, into the plain of Jezireh. He had stayed on the heights in order to cover the retreat of Cheirisophus.

5. ὁρᾶτε—ἀλλοτρίαν, 'Do you see, my men, that the enemy are admitting that the country is already ours? For, whereas when making the treaty, they stipulated that we should not burn the Great King's country, they are now burning it themselves, as if it belonged to strangers.'

ἃ γάρ. The beginning of the sentence is constructed, as if ποιοῦσι καίοντες were about to follow instead of καίουσιν. So we must render ἃ διεπράττοντο ' *whereas* they stipulated.'

ἐσπένδοντο. For the treaty see II. iii. 27.

διεπράττοντο μὴ καίειν. For this construction cf. i. 5.

6. οὔκουν ἔμοιγε δοκεῖ, 'For my part I think not.'

7. τὰς σκηνάς, 'their quarters ' generally, in the villages ; not their tents, which they had burnt. See iii. 1.

περὶ τὰ ἐπιτήδεια ἦσαν, 'were busy foraging'; cf. § 14.

ὄρη ὑπερύψηλα. ' The high mountains of Kurdistan, meeting the Tigris, shut out all further advance except by difficult and precipitous passes, already occupied by the Persians.'—LAYARD.

τοσοῦτος—βάθους, 'so deep that not even their spears rose above the water when they tried its depth.'

πειρωμένοις, 'to them trying,' dative of person interested ; cf. ἀπο-ρουμένοις αὐτοῖς in the next sentence. § 15 διαβάντι. i. 38 συνελόντι. ii. 22 προϊοῦσι.

τοῦ βάθους. For the genitive cf. iii. 19.

8. κατὰ τετρακισχιλίους. The κατά has a distributive force, 'four thousand at a time'; cf. iv. 21 ἀνὰ ἑκατὸν ἄνδρας.

9. πολλὰ δ' ὁρῶ ταῦτα πρόβατα, 'And I see many sheep *here*'; not '*these* many sheep,' which would require ταῦτα τὰ πολλὰ πρόβατα. The pronoun is here used δεικτικῶς, i.e. pointing to the object in question; cf. Thuc. I. 51 νῆες ἐκεῖναι ἐπιπλέουσι 'there are ships *yonder* sailing up.' Eurip. *Orestes* 380 ὅδ' εἰμ' Ὀρέστης ' *here* am I Orestes.'

ἃ ἀποδαρέντα καὶ φυσηθέντα, 'which (i.e. *the skins of which*) stripped off and inflated.'

10. τούτοις ζεύξας—ἐπιφορήσω. This sentence requires great care in translation. The meaning seems to be:—'With these I shall fasten the skins together; and then after having moored each skin, by attaching stones and dropping them like anchors into the water, I shall extend the skins across the river and secure them to each bank; then I shall put a layer of wood upon them and place earth upon that.'

11. πᾶς γὰρ ἀσκὸς—σχήσει, 'For every inflated skin will keep two men from sinking; and the wood and the earth will prevent them from slipping.'

τοῦ μὴ καταδῦναι. For the redundant μή see note on i. 13.

12. τὸ μὲν ἐνθύμημα—ποιεῖν, 'the idea seemed a charming one, but its realisation impossible; for there were many cavalry on the opposite bank ready to prevent it, and they would never have suffered the very first section to do any of the things proposed.'

χαρίεν. This adjective is often used in a playful way. So also **ἀχάριτος.** Cf. II. i. 13 λέγεις οὐκ ἀχάριτα 'you speak with charming wit.'

εὐθύς, to be taken closely with τοῖς πρώτοις, 'the first *to begin with*.'

οὐδὲν ἂν ἐπέτρεπον, literally *'would* never *have been* allowing,' continuous action in past time. The protasis, which is suppressed, would be εἰ ἐπεχείρουν 'if the others had been trying'; cf. ii. 24.

τούτων, partitive genitive depending on οὐδέν.

13. εἰς τοὔμπαλιν ἢ πρὸς Βαβυλῶνα, 'in the direction opposite to that towards Babylon.' 'That a movement in this direction should be styled a *retreat* has puzzled the commentators as a contradiction in terms. The reading, however, is unassailable, and implies nothing more than a temporary deviation from their route in contrast with the retreat (*southwards or eastwards*) which it was the object of the Persians to force on them. The latter, accordingly, are surprised at the Greeks electing to continue their course in face of the difficulties which confronted them.'—PRETOR.

ἔνθεν, i.e. (τὰς κώμας) ἐξ ὧν.

ὅμοιοι ἦσαν θαυμάζειν, a strange construction, literally 'were like to wonder.' The infinitive is on the analogy of that after ἔοικα. The normal construction after ὅμοιοι would be θαυμάζουσιν, 'like to men wondering.'

τρέψονται, graphic, 'mean to turn'; cf. i. 9.

ἐν νῷ ἔχοιεν, more vague, 'could have in mind.'

14. ἐπὶ τὰ ἐπιτήδεια ἦσαν, 'were going after provisions.' Contrast § 7 περὶ τὰ ἐπιτήδεια ἦσαν (N.B. *not* ἦσαν).

ἤλεγχον—εἴη, 'proceeded to cross-examine them about all the country round, as to what each (*district*) was.'

τὴν χώραν, anticipatory accusative ; cf. § 17.

ἑκάστη, agreeing with χώρα understood in a more limited sense.

15. τῆς ἐπὶ Βαβυλῶνα, possessive genitive; supply either (1) χώρας 'belonging to the country in the direction of Babylon'; or (2) less probably, ὁδοῦ 'on the road to Babylon.'

θερίζειν καὶ ἐαρίζειν. The Great King used to spend three spring months at Susa ; two months during the height of the summer (τὴν ἀκμὴν τοῦ θέρους) at Ecbatana ; and seven winter months at Babylon (*Cyropaedeia* VIII. vi. 22).

διαβάντι, 'to one crossing,' dative of person concerned ; see note on § 7 and cf. Thuc. I. 24 πόλις ἐν δεξιᾷ ἐσπλέοντι τὸν Ἰόνιον κόλπον.

Καρδούχους, the Kurds of modern times; but their country was only the north-western portion of the modern Kurdistan.

16. ἀνὰ τὰ ὄρη, 'up *along* the mountains,' denoting extension; cf. § 1.

στρατιὰν δώδεκα μυριάδας, 'an army consisting of 120,000.' For the apposition cf. iv. 10 σταθμὸν ἕνα παρασάγγας ἕξ.

ὁπότε μέντοι, 'However (they continued) when from time to time the Kurds made a truce with the Persian satrap in the plain, some of themselves (i.e. Persian subjects) actually (καί) had dealings with the Kurds and some of the Kurds with them.'

σφῶν—ἐκείνων, partitive genitives depending on τινάς understood.

17. τοὺς ἑκασταχόσε—εἰδέναι, 'those who professed to know (the country) in the several directions,' i.e. the directions specified in § 15.

τούτους γὰρ—ἥξειν, 'For they (i.e. the prisoners) said that, after passing through (the territory of) these people (i.e. the Carduchi), they would reach Armenia.'

18. ἐθύσαντο, 'On the strength of this information they caused sacrifice to be offered.' On this use of the middle see i. 8, ii. 26. They wished to ascertain at once the will of the gods with regard to the proposed enterprise ; and then, if the sacrifices gave favourable omens, they would be ready to start at once without more ado.

ἡνίκα καὶ δοκοίη τῆς ὥρας, 'at whatever point of time actually seemed good,' i.e. 'at the very moment they thought right.'

ἡνίκα—τῆς ὥρας, literally 'whenever of time,' partitive genitive;

cf. Aelian *N. A.* XII. 25 ἡνίκα τοῦ χρόνου and Latin *tum temporis* 'at
that point of time'; and iv. 23 ποῦ τῆς φάλαγγος.

τὴν ὑπερβολήν, anticipatory accusative again :—'with regard to
the passage of the mountains, they feared that it might be already
occupied.'

ἡνίκ' ἄν τις παραγγέλλῃ, 'whenever word should be passed along
the army.' Notice the graphic retention of the mood of the *oratio recta*,
contrasted with δειπνήσειαν just above; cf. iv. 2. And for the use of τις
cf. § 17 and iv. 40.

VOCABULARY.

ABBREVIATIONS.

*** For the principal parts of some of the compound verbs reference must be made to the simple verbs.

ἄ-βατος, ον, *impassable*, iv. 49.

ἀγαθός, ή, όν (borrowed comp. ἀμείνων, βελτίων or λῴων, superl. ἄριστος, βέλτιστος or λῷστος), *good, noble, brave;* of land, *fertile;* subst. ἀγαθά τά, *good things, advantages, provisions*, i. 22, ii. 26.

ἀγγέλλω, v. a., fut. ἀγγελῶ, aor. ἤγγειλα, pf. ἤγγελκα, *report, announce.*

ἀγείρω, v.a., fut. ἀγερῶ, aor. ἤγειρα, *collect, gather.*

ἄγκυρα ἡ, *anchor*, v. 10.

ἀγορά ἡ, *market-place, market.*

ἀγορὰν παρέχω, *provide a market*, i. 2, ii. 20.

ἄγω, v.a., fut. ἄξω, aor. ἤγαγον, *lead, bring;* absolute, of a general, *march (troops* understood), iv. 49; of a road, *lead*, v. 15. ἡσυχίαν ἄγω, *keep quiet*, i. 14.

ἀγών ὁ, -ῶνος, *contest.*

ἀγωνίζομαι, v.d. *strive, contend*, i. 16.

ἀγωνοθέτης ὁ, -ου, *judge in the games*, i. 21.

ἀδελφός ὁ, *brother.*

ἀ-διά-βατος, ον, *impassable*, i. 2.

ἀ-δόλως, adv. *guilelessly*, ii. 24.

ἀ-δύνατος, ον, (1) of persons, *unable;*
(2) of things, *impossible.*

ἀεί, adv. *always ; from time to time*, ii. 31, 38.

ἆθλον τό, *prize*, i. 21.

ἀ-θυμέω, v.n. *be discouraged.* ἀθυμητέον, verbal adj. *one must be discouraged*, ii. 23.

ἀ-θυμία ἡ, *want of spirit, despondency.*

ἄ-θυμος, ον, *without spirit.* ἀθύμως ἔχω, *be discouraged*, i. 3.

αἰδέομαι, v.d., fut. αἰδέσομαι, aor. ᾐδέσθην, *be ashamed;* with accus. *respect, reverence*, ii. 4.

αἰκίζομαι, v.d. *outrage, mutilate*, i. 18, iv. 5.

αἴξ ὁ, ἡ, αἰγός, *goat*, v. 9.

αἱρέω, v.a., fut. αἱρήσω, aor. εἷλον, pf. ᾕρηκα, *take, seize;* mid. *choose.*

αἰσθάνομαι, v.d., fut. αἰσθήσομαι, aor. ᾐσθόμην, pf. ᾔσθημαι, *perceive, be aware of.*

αἰσχρός, ά, όν, *shameful, disgraceful.* αἰσχρῶς, adv. *shamefully.*

αἰσχύνη ἡ, *shame, disgrace.*

αἰτέω, v.a. *ask; ask for;* mid. *ask for oneself.*

αἰτιάομαι, v.d. *accuse, blame*, i. 7.

αἰχμάλωτος, ον, *taken by the spear, taken captive;* subst. *captive*, iii. 19.

ἄ-καυστος, ον, *unburnt*, v. 13.

ἀ-κήρυκτος, ον, *without heralds*, iii. 5.

ἄ-κληρος, ον, *portionless, landless, poor*, ii. 26.

ἀκμάζω, v.n. *be in one's prime* (ἀκμή), *be strong*, i. 25.

ἀκοντίζω, v.n., fut. ἀκοντιῶ, aor. ἠκόντισα, *hurl a javelin.*

ἀκοντιστής ὁ, -οῦ, *javelin-man*, iii. 7.

ἀκούω, v.a., fut. ἀκούσομαι, aor. ἤκουσα, pf. ἀκήκοα, *hear; obey* (with gen. of person), v. 16.

ἀκρο-βολίζομαι, v.d. *hurl missiles from a distance, skirmish*, iv. 18.

ἀκρο-βόλισις ἡ, *skirmishing*, iv. 16.

ἄκρος, α, ον, *pointed, high ;* subst. ἄκρον τό, *summit*, iv. 1.

ἀκρ-ωνυχία ἡ, *nail-tip* (ὄνυξ); *mountain-spur*, iv. 37.

ἄκων, ουσα, ον, *unwilling.*

ἀλέξω, v.a. *ward off ;* mid. *defend oneself against* (with accus.), iv. 33.

ἄλευρον τό, *flour*, iv. 31.

ἀληθής, ές, *true.* τὸ ἀληθές, *the truth.*

ἁλίσκομαι, v.d., fut. ἁλώσομαι, aor. ἑάλων, pf. ἑάλωκα, *be captured.*

ἀλλά, conj. *but, yet ; well.* ἀλλὰ —γε, *yet at least*, ii. 3. ἀλλὰ μήν, *however*, ii. 16, iv. 40. ἀλλὰ γάρ. See notes on ii. 25, 26.

ἀλλήλω, α, ω, reciprocal pron. *one another.*

ἄλλος, η, ο, *another, other.* τῇ ἄλλῃ (sc. ἡμέρᾳ), *on the next day*, iv. 1. οἱ ἄλλοι, *the rest*, i. 46. Idiomatic use, *besides;* see notes on iii. 18, iv. 21.

ἀλλότριος, α, ον, *belonging to another, foreign*, v. 5; *alienated*, ii. 28.

ἄλλως, adv. *otherwise.*

ἅμα, (1) adv. *at the same time;* with participle, *while, as soon as*, i. 47, iii. 10.
(2) prep. *together with* (with dat.), i. 13.

ἅμαξα ἡ, *waggon*, ii. 27.

ἁμαρτάνω, v. n., fut. ἁμαρτήσομαι, aor. ἥμαρτον, pf. ἡμάρτηκα, *err; make a mistake; miss a mark* (with gen.), iv. 15.

ἀμαχεί, adv. *without fighting,* iv. 46.

ἀμείνων. See ἀγαθός.

ἄ-μετρος, ον, *immeasurable, immense,* ii. 16.

ἁμιλλάομαι, v.d. *race, contend,* iv. 44, 46.

ἀμύνω, v.a. *ward off;* with dat. *protect;* mid. *defend oneself,* i. 14, 29; *revenge oneself on, punish* (with accus.).

ἀμφί, prep. with accus. (1) *around,* ii. 2.
    (2) *about* (of time or number), i. 33.
    (3) *concerning.*

ἀμφότερος, α, ον, *both.*

ἀμφοτέρωθεν, adv. *from both sides,* v. 10; *on both sides of* (with gen.), iv. 29.

ἄν (ἄ), particle,
    (1) conditional, with indic. or opt. in the apodosis of a conditional sentence.
    (2) potential, with infin., i. 17, 38, ii. 3.
    (3) frequentative, with imp. or aor. indic., iv. 22.
    (4) indefinite, with relative or relative particle with subj.
    See notes on i. 6, 17, ii. 12.

ἄν (ἄ) = ἐάν.

ἀνά, prep. (with accus.).
    (1) *up along,* v. 16.
    (2) distributive use, iv. 21.

ἀνα-βαίνω, v. n. *go up* (esp. up country from the sea), i. 2, iv. 13; *mount* (a horse), iv. 35, 49.

ἀνάβασις ἡ, *march up country,* i. 1.

ἀνα-γιγνώσκω, v. a. *recognise; read,* i. 5.

ἀναγκάζω, v.a. *compel.*

ἀναγκαῖος, α, ον, *necessary.*

ἀνάγκη η, *necessity.*

ἀν-άγω, v.a. *lead up.*

ἀνα-ζεύγνυμι, v. a. *yoke again; break up a camp,* iv. 37.

ἀν-αιρέω, v.a. *take up;* of an oracle, *declare,* i. 6.

ἀνα-καίω, v.a. *light up.*

ἀνα-κοινόω, v.a. *communicate with, consult* (with dat.), i. 5; mid. *discuss with* (with dat.), i. 5.

ἀνα-λαμβάνω, v.a. *take up.*

ἀνα-μένω, v.a. *wait for,* i. 14, 24.

ἀνα-μιμνήσκω, v.a. *remind,* iii. 11; mid. and pass. *remember.*

ἀνα-παύω, v.a. *make to rest;* mid. *rest,* i. 3, v. 18.

ἀν-αρίθμητος, ον, *countless,* ii. 13.

ἀν-αρχία ἡ, *want of rulers, anarchy,* ii. 29.

ἀνα-σταυρόω, v.a. *impale,* i. 17.

ἀνα-τείνω, v.a. *stretch up, raise,* ii. 9.

ἀνα-τίθημι, v.a. *place upon,* i. 30; *set up;* mid. *pack up, load.*

ἀνα-χωρέω, v. n. *retreat,* iii. 13.

ἀν-εγείρω, v. a., fut. -εγερῶ, aor. -ήγειρα, *arouse;* 2 pf. (with neut. sense), -εγρήγορα, aor. pass. -ηγέρθην.

ἄνευ, prep. *without* (with gen.).

ἀνήρ ὁ, ἀνδρός, *man.*

ἄνθρωπος ὁ, *human being, man.*

ἀνιάω, v.a. *annoy,* iii. 19.

ἀν-ίστημι, v.a. *raise up;* mid. (and pf. and 2 aor. act.) *rise up, start,* i. 15, ii. 1, iii. 1.

ἀντ-επι-μελέομαι, v.d. *take care in turn,* i. 16.

ἀντί, prep. *instead of,* i. 47, ii. 31.

ἀντι-δίδωμι, v. a. *give in return,*
iii. 19.

ἀντι-καθ-ίστημι, v. a. *set up in
place of;* mid. and pass. (and pf.
and 2 aor. act.) *be set up in place
of,* i. 38.

ἀντι-λέγω, v. n. *speak against.*

ἀντίος, α, ον, *opposite, opposed,* i.
42.

ἀντι-ποιῶ, v. a. *do in return, re-
taliate,* iii. 7; mid. *lay claim
to against* (with gen. of thing).

ἀντι-τάττω, v. a. *range against,*
ii. 14.

ἀντι-τοξεύω, v. n. *shoot arrows in
return,* iii. 15.

ἄνω, adv. *upwards,* iv. 17; *inland,*
i. 8; comp. ἀνωτέρω, superl.
ἀνωτάτω.

ἄξιος, α, ον, *worthy, befitting;* with
gen. *worth.*

ἀξιο-στράτηγος, ον, *fit to be a
general,* i. 24.

ἀξιόω, v. a. *think worthy,* ii. 7;
think right, claim (with infin.),
i. 37.

ἀπ-αλλάττω, v. a. *set free, aban-
don,* ii. 28.

ἀπ-αντάω, v. n. *meet,* v. 4.

ἅπαξ, adv. *once, once for all.*

ἅπας, ασα, αν, *all together.*

ἀ-πειθέω, v. n. *be disobedient,* ii. 31.

ἄπ-ειμι, v. n. *be absent* (εἰμί).

ἄπ-ειμι, v. n. *go away* (εἶμι), often
with fut. signification; *fall back,*
iv. 28.

ἄ-πειρος, ον, *inexperienced* (with
gen.), ii. 16.

ἀπ-ελαύνω, v. a. *drive off,* i. 31, iv.
10; intrans. *ride away; march
away.*

ἀπ-έρχομαι, v. d. *go away.*

ἀπ-έχω, v. a. *keep away;* intrans.
keep away, be distant (with gen.),

i. 2, iv. 3; mid. *keep one's hands
off,* i. 22.

ἀ-πιστία ἡ, *distrust.*

ἀπό, prep. with gen.
 (1) place, *away from, from;
sprung from.*
 (2) time, *from,* ii. 14.
 (3) instrument and means.

ἀπο-δείκνυμι, v. a. *point out, direct;
appoint,* ii. 36.

ἀπο-δέρω, v. a., fut. -δερῶ, aor.
ἀπέδειρα, aor. pass. ἀπεδάρην,
flay, v. 9.

ἀπο-θνήσκω, v. n. *die, be killed.*

ἀπο-θύω, v. a. *sacrifice as a due,*
ii. 12.

ἀπο-κόπτω, v. a. *cut off, dislodge,*
iv. 39.

ἀπο-κρίνομαι, v. d. *answer.*

ἀπο-κτείνω, v. a. *kill.*

ἀπο-κωλύω, v. a. *hinder from*
(with gen.), iii. 3.

ἀπ-όλλυμι, v. a., fut. ἀπολῶ, aor.
ἀπώλεσα, pf. ἀπολώλεκα, 2 pf.
ἀπόλωλα (intrans.), aor. mid.
ἀπωλόμην, *kill, destroy; lose,* iv.
11; mid. *die, perish.*

ἀπό-μαχος, ον, *unfit for fighting,
disabled,* iv. 32.

ἀπο-νοστέω, v. n. *return,* v. 16.

ἀπο-πέμπω, v. a. *send away.*

ἀπο-πηδάω, v. n. *leap off, leap
down,* iv. 27.

ἀ-πορέω, v. n. *be in want* (with
gen.); mid. *be perplexed,* v. 8.

ἀ-πορία ἡ, *want, resourcelessness,
perplexity,* i. 2, 26.

ἄ-πορος, ον, (1) of persons, *helpless,
resourceless.*
 (2) of things, *impracticable,*
iii. 4; *impassable,* ii. 22. τὸ
ἄπορον, *difficulty.*

ἀπο-σκηνέω, v. n. *encamp apart
from* (with gen.), iv. 35.

ἀπο-στρατοπεδεύομαι, v. d. *en-camp apart from*, iv. 34.

ἀπο-τέμνω, v. a. *cut off*, iv. 29.

ἀπο-τίνω, v. a., fut. -τίσω, *repay*; mid. *punish* (with acc.), ii. 12.

ἀπο-τρέπω, v. a. *turn away, turn aside*; mid. *turn oneself away*, v. 1.

ἀπο-χωρέω, v. n. *go away, retire*.

ἄρα, particle, *then, as it seems, after all*, iv. 22.

ἆρα, interrogative particle, *then*, i. 18.

ἀργός, ον, *not working, inactive*, ii. 25.

ἀργύριον τό, *silver, money*.

ἀρετή ἡ, *virtue, bravery*.

ἀριστάω, v. n. *take the morning meal*.

ἄριστον τό, *morning meal, break-fast*.

ἀριστο-ποιέομαι, v. mid. *take the morning meal*.

ἄριστος, η, ον. See ἀγαθός.

ἄρκτος ἡ, *the Great Bear; the North*, v. 15.

ἁρπαγή ἡ, *plunder*.

ἁρτάω, v. a. *fasten*, v. 10.

ἀρχαῖος, α, ον, *ancient, old*.

ἀρχή ἡ, *beginning; command, pro-vince; empire*.

ἄρχω, v. a., fut. ἄρξω, *rule* (with gen. or absolute), v. 17; act. and mid. *begin* (with gen.), i. 24, ii. 7, 17. Subst. ὁ ἄρχων, *commander, ruler*, i. 38, ii. 29.

ἀ-σάφεια ἡ, *uncertainty*, i. 21.

ἀ-σέβεια ἡ, *impiety*.

ἀ-σινής, ες, *harmless*. ἀσινῶς, adv. *harmlessly;* superl. ἀσινέστατα, iii. 3.

ἀσκός ὁ, *skin, bag*, v. 9.

ἄσμενος, η, ον, *well-pleased, glad*; with verbs, *gladly*, iv. 24.

ἀσπίς ἡ, -ίδος, *shield*, the large oval shield of the hoplite.

ἀ-σφαλής, ές, *safe*, comp. ἀσφαλέστερος, superl. ἀσφαλέστατος. ἀσφαλῶς, adv. *safely*.

ἄ-τακτος, ον, *disorderly*.

ἀ-ταξία ἡ, *disorder*, i. 38.

ἀ-τέλεια ἡ, *exemption*, iii. 18.

αὖ, adv. *again, on the other hand*. i. 20; *in turn*, ii. 27.

αὐτίκα, adv. *immediately*.

αὐτο-κέλευστος, ον, *self-ordered, of one's own accord*, iv. 5.

αὐτός, ή, όν, demonstr. pron., *self*, i. 34, 36, 44; *in person*, ii. 4; *of one's own accord; by oneself, alone*, ii. 11; in oblique cases, *he, she, it*, etc. ὁ αὐτός, *the same*. ἐν ταὐτῷ, *in company with*, i. 27.

αὐτοῦ, adv. *at the very place, on the spot*, ii. 24, iv. 41.

ἀφ-αιρέω, v. a. *take away;* mid. *take away for oneself, for one's own interest*, i. 30, iv. 48.

ἀ-φανίζω, v. a., fut. ἀφανιῶ, pf. ἠφάνικα, *make to disappear*, iv. 8; *blot out*, ii. 11.

ἄ-φθονος, ον, *ungrudging, plentiful*, i. 19. ἐν ἀφθόνοις, *in plenty*, ii. 25.

ἀφ ίημι, v. a., fut. ἀφήσω, aor. ἀφῆκα, pf. ἀφεῖκα, *send away, let go, let down*, v. 10.

ἀφ-ικνέομαι, v. d., fut. ἀφίξομαι, aor. ἀφῖκόμην, *arrive*.

ἀφ-ίστημι, v. a. *detach, cause to revolt;* mid. (and pf. and 2 aor. act.) *withdraw, revolt, desert* (with gen.), ii. 5, 17.

ἄχθομαι, v. d., fut. ἀχθέσομαι, pf. ἤχθημαι, *be annoyed*, ii. 20.

ἄ-χρηστος, ον, *useless*.

βάθος τό, *depth*.

βαίνω, v. n., fut. βήσομαι, aor. ἔβην, pf. βέβηκα, *go, march.* See note on ii. 19.

βάλλω, v. a., fut. βαλῶ, aor. ἔβαλον, pf. βέβληκα, *throw, shoot; pelt* (with accus. or absolute), iv. 25, 49.

βάρβαρος, ον, *barbarous, foreign, not Greek.*

βασιλεία ἡ, *kingdom, royalty.*

βασίλειος, a, ον, *royal;* subst. βασίλειον τό, *castle,* iv. 24.

βασιλεύς ὁ, *king.* Without article, *the Great King,* i.e. the King of Persia.

βασιλικός, ή, όν, *royal.*

βίσιμος, ον, *passable,* iv. 49.

βέλος τό, *missile, dart.*

βελτίων, βέλτιστος. See ἀγαθός.

βία ἡ, *strength, force.*

βιοτεύω, v. n. *live,* ii. 25.

βλάπτω, v. a. *impede,* iii. 16; *injure.*

βοήθεια ἡ, *help, reinforcements.*

βοηθέω, v. n. *come to the rescue* (with dat.); *make a sally,* v. 6.

βοιωτιάζω, v. n. *talk the Boeotian dialect,* i. 26.

βόσκημα τό, *fattened animal;* plur. *cattle,* v. 2.

βουλεύω, v. a. *plan, devise;* mid. *deliberate (with oneself),* iii. 3.

βούλομαι, v. d. *wish, be willing.*

βοῦς ὁ, ἡ, βοός, *ox, cow.*

βραχύς, εῖα, ύ, *short.* ἐπὶ βραχύ, *for a short distance,* iii. 17. βραχύτερα, comp. adv. *with a shorter range,* iii. 7.

βρέχω, v. a. *wet,* ii. 22.

βροντή ἡ, *thunder.*

γάρ, conj. *for.* ἀλλὰ γάρ, see notes on ii. 25, 26. καὶ γάρ, *for indeed, for also.*

γε, particle enclitic, *at least, at*

any rate; sometimes need not be translated except by an emphasis on the word to which it is attached, ii. 23. καὶ—γε, *yes and.* δέ γε, *yes and.* γε μήν, *however.*

γείτων ὁ, -ονος, *neighbour.*

γεύομαι, v. mid. *taste.*

γέφυρα ἡ, *bridge,* iv. 20.

γῆ ἡ, *earth, land; soil,* v. 10.

γήλοφος ὁ, *hill,* iv. 24.

γῆρας τό, -ως, *old age.*

γίγνομαι, v. d., fut. γενήσομαι, aor. ἐγενόμην, pf. γέγονα and γεγένημαι, *become, come about; be born,* ii. 13; *be made, be done,* ii. 18; *amount to,* i. 33, iii. 20.

γιγνώσκω, v. a., fut. γνώσομαι, aor. ἔγνων, pf. ἔγνωκα, *observe, know; determine, decide,* i. 43, ii. 22.

γνώμη ἡ, *opinion, judgment; mind,* i. 41.

γονεύς ὁ, -έως, *parent.*

γόνυ τό, -ατος, *knee.*

γοῦν (γε οὖν), particle, *at least, at any rate,* ii. 17.

γυμνής ὁ, -ῆτος, *light-armed soldier,* iv. 26.

γυνή ἡ, -αικός, *woman, wife.*

δάκνω, v. a., fut. δήξομαι, aor. ἔδακον, *bite.*

δέ, conj. *but, and, now; on the other hand* (answering to μέν). In apodosis, i. 43. δέ γε, *yes and,* i. 35. καὶ—δέ, *yes and,* i. 25, ii. 24, 25.

δέδοικα, v. n., perf. with pres. signification, *fear.*

δεῖ, v. impers., fut. δεήσει, *it is necessary;* with gen. *there is need of;* partic. δέον. τὰ δέοντα, *things necessary,* i. 46.

δείκνυμι, v.a., fut. δείξω, *show, point out.*

δείλη ἡ, *afternoon,* iii. 11.

δειλός, ή, όν, *cowardly,* ii. 35.

δεινός, ή, όν, *terrible, strange.* τὰ δεινά, *dangers,* ii. 10.

δειπνέω, v.n. *dine, sup.*

δεῖπνον τό, *evening meal, dinner, supper.*

δεξιός, ά, όν, *right, on the right hand.* Subst. ἡ δεξιά (χείρ), *the right hand,* iii. 3. Hence *pledge,* clasped right hands being pledges of friendship, ii. 4.

δέομαι, v. mid. *want* (with gen.), v. 8, 9; absolute, i. 46; *request* (with gen. of person).

δέον. See δεῖ.

δεσμός, -οῦ, *fetter, strap.*

δεσπότης ὁ, -ου, *master, owner.*

δεύτερος, α, ον, *second.*

δέχομαι, v.d., fut. δέξομαι, pf. δέδεγμαι, *receive; await the attack of,* i. 42, ii. 16.

δέω, v.a. *bind, tether,* iv. 35.

δή, particle, *indeed, now;* emphasises, i. 2; *forsooth,* i. 29; *in particular,* i. 38.

δῆλος, η, ον, *clear, evident.* δῆλον ὅτι, *clearly* (parenthetical), i. 16, ii. 26.

δηλόω, v.a. *show, explain.*

δή-που, particle, *I suppose,* ii. 15.

διά, prep.

  (1) with accus. *owing to, because of,* i. 10, 22, iv. 16.

  (2) with gen. *through* (of place or time), iv. 18; *through, by means of; by way of, in* (manner), ii. 8.

δια-βαίνω, v.a. *go across, traverse.*

διά-βασις ἡ, *crossing, passage, ford,* iv. 20, 23.

δια-βατός, ή, όν, *that can be crossed, passable,* ii. 22.

δια-βιβάζω, v.a., fut. -βιβάσω, *make to cross, convey across,* v. 2.

δι-αγγέλλω, v.a. *send word through;* mid. *pass the word down the ranks,* iv. 36.

δι-άγω, v.a. *bring through, bring across,* v. 10; absolute (βίον or χρόνον understood), *spend time, live,* i. 43.

δια-θεάομαι, v.d. *survey,* i. 19.

διά-κειμαι, v.d. *be disposed, be in a certain state,* i. 3.

δια-κελεύομαι, v. mid. *cheer on one another,* iv. 45.

δια-κινδυνεύω, v.a. *run a risk to the end,* iv. 14.

διακόσιοι, αι, α, *two hundred.*

δια-νοέομαι, v.mid. *have in mind, purpose.*

δια-πολεμέω, v.n. *fight out to the end* (with dat.), iii. 3.

δια-πορεύω, v.a. *convey over, let pass through;* mid. and pass. *go through, traverse.*

δια-πράττω, v.a. *arrange, settle;* mid. *arrange for oneself, effect, gain,* v. 5.

δια-σπάω, v.a. *draw asunder, disperse,* iv. 20.

δια-τάττω, v.a. *post apart,* iv. 15.

δια-τελέω, v.a. *accomplish;* absolute, *continue* (with partic.), iv. 17.

δια-φέρω, v. n. *differ from; excel* (with gen.), i. 37; absolute, *it makes a difference,* iv. 33.

δια-φθείρω, v.a. *destroy utterly; corrupt,* iii. 5.

διδάσκω, v.a., fut. διδάξω, *teach.*

δίδωμι, v.a., fut. δώσω, aor. ἔδωκα, pf. δέδωκα, *give, give up.*

δι-είργω, v.a. *separate,* i. 2.

86 VOCABULARY.

δι-έρχομαι, v.d. *pass through.*
δι-έχω, (1) v.a. *divide.*
　(2) v.n. *stand apart,* iv. 20.
τὸ διέχον, *the gap,* iv. 22.
δι-ίημι, v.a. *send through, let pass,*
　ii. 23.
δίκαιος, a, ον, *just.*
δίκη ἡ, *justice; penalty,* ii. 8.
Διός. See Ζεύς.
διπλάσιος, a, ον, *double.* διπλάσιον, adv. *twice as much.*
δισ-χίλιοι, αι, a, *two thousand.*
διώκω, v.a. *pursue.* διωκτέος,
　verbal adj. *to be pursued,* iii. 8.
δίωξις ἡ, *pursuit.*
δόγμα τό, *resolution,* iii. 5.
δοκέω, (1) v.a., fut. δόξω, *think.*
　(2) intrans. *seem,* i. 5; impers. δοκεῖ, *it seems good, it is
resolved.* See note on i. 11. τὰ
δεδογμένα, *resolutions,* ii. 39.
δοκιμάζω, v.a. *test, approve,* iii.
20.
δόρυ τό, -ατος, *spear.*
δοῦλος ὁ, *slave; vassal,* i. 17.
δύναμαι, v.d., fut. δυνήσομαι, aor.
ἠδυνήθην, *be able.*
δύναμις ἡ, *power; military force,*
iv. 3, 13, 32.
δύο, *two.*
δύσ-χρηστος, ον, *hard to use,* iv.
19.
δυσ-χωρία ἡ, *difficulties of the
ground,* v. 16.
δώδεκα, indecl. *twelve.*

ἑάλωκα, ἑάλων. See ἁλίσκομαι.
ἐάν, *if* (with subj.).
ἐαρίζω, v.n. *spend the spring,* v.
15.
ἑαυτόν, ήν, ό, reflexive pron. *himself.*
ἐάω, v.a., fut. ἐάσω, aor. εἴασα, *let,
allow.*

ἐγγύς, comp. ἐγγυτέρω, superl. ἐγ-
γυτάτω and ἐγγύτατα.
　(1) prep. *near* (with gen.).
　(2) adv. *near, nearly.*
ἐγ-χειρέω, v.a. *attempt,* ii. 8.
ἐγ-χειρίζω, v.a. *put into the hands
of, deliver to* (with accus. and
dat.), ii. 18.
ἐγώ, pers. pron., ἐμοῦ or μου, *I.*
ἔγωγε, *I for my part.*
ἐθέλω or θέλω, v.n., fut. ἐθελήσω,
aor. ἠθέλησα, *will, be willing,
be ready.*
ἔθνος τό, *tribe, nation.*
εἰ, conj. *if* (with indic. and opt.);
idiomatic use, ii. 17; *whether,*
ii. 22. εἰ μή, *unless, except.* εἰ
δὲ μή, *but if not, failing that,*
ii. 3. εἰ δέ, see note on ii. 37.
εἶδον. See ὁράω.
εἰκός τό, -ότος, neut. partic. of
ἔοικα, *likely, reasonable,* i. 13,
ii. 26.
εἴκοσι, indecl. *twenty.*
εἰμί, v.subst., fut. ἔσομαι, *be, exist.*
Impers. ἔστι, *it is possible,* ii.
13, 39.
εἶμι, v.n. *go; will go.*
εἶπον, used as 2 aor. of φημί.
εἴργω, *cut off; shut in,* i. 12; *prevent,* iii. 16.
εἴρηκα, used as perf. of φημί.
εἴρητο, plup. pass. impers. *instructions had been given,* iv. 3.
εἰρήνη ἡ, *peace.*
εἰς, prep. with accus.
　(1) motion, *to, into; against,*
ii. 16.
　(2) time, *into, for, towards,*
i. 3; *up to.*
　(3) idiomatic uses, ii. 27, iii.
6, 19, iv. 13, 17.
εἷς, μία, ἕν, *one.*
εἴσομαι. See οἶδα.

εἴσω, (1) adv. *within*.

   (2) prep. *within* (with gen.),
iii. 7.

εἴτε—εἴτε, *whether—or*, i. 40.

ἐκ (ἐξ), prep. with gen.

   (1) *out of*, ii. 11 ; *from ;* idiomatic, i. 43.

   (2) *starting from*, ii. 3, iii. 7,
9, iv. 47 ; *after*, i. 15, 35, ii. 9.

   (3) *because of*, ii. 11.

ἑκασταχοσε, adv. *in each direction*,
iv. 17.

ἕκαστος, η, ον, *each*.

ἑκάτερος, α, ον, *each of two*.

ἑκατόν, indecl. *hundred*.

ἔκ-γονος, ον, *sprung from ;* subst.
descendant.

ἐκεῖ, adv. *there*.

ἐκεῖνος, η, ο, demonstr. pron. *that,
yonder; the latter*, iii. 17 ; *he,
she, it*.

ἐκ-θλίβω, v. a. *squeeze out*, iv.
19.

ἐκ-λέγω, v.a. *pick out*, iii. 19; mid.
pick out for oneself.

ἐκ-λείπω, v.a. *leave, desert;* absolute, *give up, fail*, iv. 8.

ἐκ-πέμπω, v.a. *send out*.

ἐκ-πίμπλημι, v.a., fut. -πλήσω, *fill
up*.

ἐκ-πλέω, v.n. *sail out*.

ἔκ-πλεως, ων, *filled up*, iv. 22.

ἐκ φαίνω, v.a. *make clear, show
openly*, i. 10.

ἐκ-φέρω, v.a. *carry out ; carry on
openly*, ii. 29.

ἑκών, οῦσα, όν, *willing*, ii. 26.

ἐλάττων, ον, used as comp. of
μικρός.

ἐλαύνω, v.a., fut. ἐλῶ, aor. ἤλασα,
pf. ἐλήλακα, *drive ;* intrans. *ride,
drive ; march*.

ἐλαφρός, ά, όν, *light* (of troops),
iii. 6.

ἐλάχιστος, η, ον, used as superl. of
μικρός.

ἐλέγχω, v.a., fut. ἐλέγξω, *examine*,
v. 14.

ἐλευθερία ἡ, *freedom*.

ἐλπίς ἡ, *hope, expectation*.

ἐμαυτόν, ἥν, reflexive pron. *myself*.

ἐμ-βάλλω, v.a. *throw upon ;* intrans. *attack*, v. 16.

ἐμός, ή, όν, possessive pron. *my,
mine*.

ἔμ-παλιν, adv. *backwards*, v. 13.

ἐμ-πεδόω, v.a. *make firm, ratify*.

ἐμ-πίπτω, v.n. *fall upon* (with
dat.) ; *occur to*, i. 13.

ἐμ-ποδών, adv. *in the way of*, i. 13.

ἔμ-προσθεν, adv. *before ; earlier*.

ἐν, prep. with dat.

   (1) place, *in, on, at, among*.

   (2) time, *in, during*, i. 1.

ἐν-αντίος, α, ον, *opposite, opposed*.

ἕνεκα and ἕνεκεν, prep. *on account
of* (with gen.), ii. 28.

ἔνθα, adv. *there; where*, v. 15 ;
thither; whither; thereupon, then.

ἐνθάδε, adv. *here, hither*.

ἔνθεν, adv. *thence ; whence*, v. 13.

ἐν-θυμέομαι, v.d. *think of, feel*,
i. 43, ii. 18.

ἐν-θύμημα τό, *thought, idea, device*,
v. 12.

ἐνιαυτός ὁ, *year*.

ἐνίοτε, adv. *sometimes*, i. 20.

ἐν-νοέω, v.a. *think of, perceive, apprehend ;* also mid., v. 3.

ἔν-νοια ἡ, *thought, idea*, i. 13.

ἐν-οχλέω, v.n. *disturb, annoy* (with
dat.), iv. 21.

ἐνταῦθα, adv. *there, then, thereupon*.

ἐντεῦθεν, adv. *thence, from that
time, then, therefore*.

ἐν-τυγχάνω, v.n. *light upon* (with
dat.); *be present*, ii. 31.

ἐν-ωμοτ-άρχης ὁ, *commander of a section*, iv. 21.

ἐν-ωμοτία ἡ, literally, *band of sworn troops; quarter of a λόχος, section*, iv. 22.

ἐξ. See ἐκ.

ἐξ-απατάω, v.a. *deceive utterly.*

ἐξ-απίνης, adv. *suddenly.*

ἔξ-ειμι, v.n. *go forth* (εἶμι), v. 13.

ἐξ-έρχομαι, v.d. *go out, come out.*

ἔξ ἐστι, v. impers. *it is allowed, it is possible.* ἐξόν, accus. absolute, *it being possible*, i. 2, 21.

ἐξήκοντα, indecl. *sixty.*

ἐξ-ικνέομαι, v.d. *arrive at; reach, hit* (with gen.), iii. 7, 15, iv. 4.

ἐξόν. See ἔξεστι.

ἐξ-οπλίζομαι, v. mid. *arm oneself completely*, i. 28.

ἐξ-ορμάω, v.a. *urge on*, i. 24; mid. *start.*

ἔξω, (1) adv. *outside.*
    (2) prep. *outside* (with gen.), iv. 15.

ἔξωθεν, adv. *outside*, iv. 21.

ἔοικα, v.n. *seem like, seem.*

ἐπ-αινέω, v.a., fut. ἐπαινέσω, aor. ἐπῄνεσα, *praise.*

ἐπ-αίρω, v.a. *raise up.*

ἐπ-ακολουθέω, v.n. *follow closely on* (with dat.).

ἐπ-ανα-χωρέω, v.n. *retreat*, iii. 10.

ἐπεί, conj. *when, since.*

ἐπειδάν, conj. *whenever, as soon as* (with subj.).

ἐπειδή, conj. *when, since.*

ἔπ-ειμι, v.n. *be upon* (εἰμί).

ἔπ-ειμι, v.n. *come upon* (εἶμι). ἡ ἐπιοῦσα (sc. ἡμέρα), *the next day*, iv. 18.

ἔπειτα, adv. *then, next.*

ἐπ-έρομαι, v.d., fut. -ερήσομαι, aor. -ηρόμην, *ask besides*, i. 6.

ἐπ-έχω, v.a. *hold back;* intrans.

stop, cease from (with gen.), iv. 36.

ἐπ-ήκοος, ον, *within hearing*, iii. 1.

ἐπί, prep.
    (1) with accus. *to, against; after; with a view to*, ii. 7.
    (2) with gen. *upon*, ii. 19, iv. 28, 47; *towards.*
    (3) with dat. *upon*, i. 45, ii. 4; *in charge of*, iv. 41; *in the power of*, i. 13, 17, 35; *at*, i. 2; *after*, ii. 4; *in confirmation of*, ii. 4.

ἐπι-βάλλω, v.a. *throw upon.*

ἐπι-βουλεύω, v.n. *plot against* (with dat.), i. 35.

ἐπι-γίγνομαι, v.d. *come upon*, iv. 25.

ἐπι-δείκνυμι, v.a. *show off*, ii. 26; mid. *show off oneself.*

ἐπι-δίδωμι, v.a. *give in addition, contribute.*

ἐπι-θυμέω, v.n. *desire* (with gen. or infin.), ii. 39.

ἐπι-κυρόω, v.a. *confirm*, ii. 32.

ἐπι-λανθάνομαι, v.mid. *forget* (with gen.), ii. 25.

ἐπί-λεκτος, ον, *chosen, picked*, iv. 43.

ἐπι-μελέομαι, v.d. *take care of*, ii. 37; *make it one's business*, i. 14.

ἐπι-μελής, ές, *anxious, careful*, ii. 30.

ἐπι-μίγνυμι, v.n. *mingle with*, v. 16.

ἐπι-νοέω, v.a. *think of, purpose.*

ἐπι-ορκέω, (1) v.a. *swear falsely by*, i. 22.
    (2) v.n. *break an oath*, ii. 10.

ἐπι-ορκία ἡ, *perjury*, ii. 4.

ἐπι-πάρ-ειμι (εἰμί), v.n. *be present besides.*

ἐπι-πάρ-ειμι (εἶμι), v.n.
    (1) *march along side of*, iv. 30.
    (2) *come up to the help of*, iv. 23.

ἐπι-σάττω, v. a., fut. -σάξω, *saddle,*
iv. 35.
ἐπι-σιτίζομαι, v. mid. *get provisions,*
iv. 28.
ἐπι-σκέπτομαι, v. d. *inspect, exa-mine,* iii. 18.
ἐπίσταμαι, v.d. *know;* with infin.,
iii. 16.
ἐπι-στολή ἡ, *message, command;
letter,* i. 5.
ἐπι-τάττω, v. a. *order* (with dat.).
ἐπιτήδειος, α, ον, *fitting, proper,
necessary.* τὰ ἐπιτήδεια, *pro-visions,* i. 28.
ἐπι-τίθημι, v. a. *put upon, inflict,*
ii. 8; mid. *attack* (with dat.), iv.
3, 16, 29.
ἐπι-τρέπω, v. a. *entrust, give up;
allow,* ii. 31, v. 12.
ἐπι-τυγχάνω, v. n. *light upon* (with
dat.), iv. 18.
ἐπι-φαίνομαι, v. mid. *appear,* iii. 6.
ἐπι-φορέω, v. a. *pile upon,* v. 10.
ἐπι-χειρέω, v. a. *attempt,* iv. 27, 33.
ἐπ-οικοδομέω, v. a. *build upon.*
ἔπομαι, v. d., impf. εἱπόμην, aor.
ἑσπόμην, *follow* (with dat.).
ἐράω, v. n. *love, desire* (with gen.),
i. 29.
ἔργον τό, *work, deed ; execution,* v.
12; *result,* iii. 12. ἔργῳ, *in
action,* ii. 32.
ἔρημος, ον, *deserted, abandoned.*
ἔρομαι, v. d. *ask,* i. 7.
ἐρρωμένος, η, ον, perf. partic. of
ῥώννυμι, *strong, vigorous,* i. 42 ;
comp. ἐρρωμενέστερος, superl.
ἐρρωμενέστατος.
ἐρύκω, v. a. *ward off,* i. 25.
ἔρυμα τό, *defence.*
ἐρυμνός, ή, όν, *strong.* τὰ ἐρυμνά,
forts, ii. 23.
ἔρχομαι, v. d., fut. ἐλεύσομαι, aor.
ἦλθον, pf. ἐλήλυθα, *come, go.*

ἐρῶ, v. a. used as fut. of φημί, *say.*
ἐρωτάω, v. a. *ask.*
ἐσθής ἡ, -ῆτος, *clothing.*
ἑσπέρα ἡ, *evening ; the west,* v. 15.
ἔστε, conj. *while,* i. 19 ; *until,* i.
28.
ἔσχατος, η, ον, *last; extreme,* i. 18.
ἔτι, adv. *still ; further,* ii. 28; with
negative, *any longer,* i. 2, 3, 14.
εὖ, adv. *well.*
εὐ-δαίμων, ον, *prosperous ; fertile,*
ii. 23, iv. 17.
εὔ-δηλος, ον, *clear, plain.*
εὐ-επίθετος, ον, *easy to attack,* iv. 20.
εὔ-ζωνος, ον, *well-girt, active,* iii. 6.
εὔ-θυμος, ον, *cheerful.*
εὐθύς, adv. *immediately ; to begin
with,* v. 12.
εὔ-νους, ουν, *well-disposed.*
εὐ-πετῶς, adv. *easily* (εὖ, πίπτω),
ii. 10.
εὔ-πορος, ον, *easy to pass,* v. 17.
εὑρίσκω, v. a., fut. εὑρήσω, aor.
εὗρον, pf. εὕρηκα, *find;* mid.
find for oneself, obtain.
εὖρος τό, *breadth.*
εὔ-τακτος, ον, *orderly, well-disci-plined,* ii. 30.
εὐ-ταξία ἡ, *good order,* i. 38.
εὔχομαι, v. d. *pray ; vow,* ii. 9, 12.
ἐφ-έπομαι, v. d. *follow after, pursue.*
ἐφ-ίστημι, v. a. *set over ; make to
halt ;* mid. (and 2 aor. and pf.
act.) *stand on ; halt ; be set over,*
iii. 20.
ἔφ-οδος ἡ, *approach,* iv. 41; *ad-vance, attack.*
ἐφ-οράω, v. a. *look upon, live to
see,* i. 13.
ἐχθρός, ά, όν, *hateful, hostile,* comp.
ἐχθίων, superl. ἔχθιστος. Subst
ἐχθρός ὁ, *enemy.*
ἔχω, v. a., fut. ἕξω or σχήσω, aor.
ἔσχον, pf. ἔσχηκα, *hold, have;*

*have in one's power, be able,
have to wife,* iv. 13 ; *keep, prevent,* v. 11 ; *hold oneself, be,* esp.
with adverbs, i. 31, 40, ii. 9, 37.
ἕως ἡ, ἕω, *dawn, morning; the
east,* v. 15.
ἕως, conj. *while* (with indic.); *until* (with opt.).

ζάω, v.n., infin. ζῆν, fut. ζήσω, *live.*
ζεύγνυμι, v. a., fut. ζεύξω, *join,
bridge over.*
ζεῦγος τό, *pair of beasts,* plur. *baggage-animals,* ii. 27.
ζωός, ἡ, όν, *alive.*

ἤ, conj. *either, or; than.*
ᾗ (sc. ὁδῷ), *by which way, where.*
ἡγεμών ὁ, -όνος, *guide, leader.*
ἡγέομαι, v.d. *lead, guide* (absol.
or with dat.), ii. 20, 37.
ᾔδειν. See οἶδα.
ἤδη, adv. *now, already; at once,
from the first; ere now,* i. 38.
ἥκω, v.n. *have come, have arrived.*
ἡλικία ἡ, *age; maturity,* i. 14;
prime, i. 25.
ἥλιος ὁ, *sun.*
ἡμεῖς, nom. plur. of ἐγώ.
ἡμέρα ἡ, *day.* ἅμα τῇ ἡμέρᾳ, *at
daybreak,* i. 13.
ἡμέτερος, α, ον, possessive pron.
our.
ἤν, contr. for ἐάν, i. 22.
ἡνίκα, conj. *when,* v. 4, 18.
ἤν-περ, conj. *if indeed.*
ἡσυχία ἡ, *quietness.*
ἡττάομαι, v.d., fut. ἡττήσομαι, *be
inferior, be worsted,* i. 2, ii. 39.
ἧττον, comp. adv. *less.*

θάλαττα ἡ, *sea.*
θάλπος τό, *heat;* plur., i. 23.
θάνατος ὁ, *death.*

θαρραλέος, α, ον, *brave, confident.*
θαρρέω, v.n. *have courage,* iv. 3;
with accus., ii. 20.
θάττων, ον, comp. of ταχύς.
θαυμάζω, (1) v.n. *wonder.*
　　　　(2) v.a. *wonder at.*
θαυμάσιος, α, ον, *wonderful.*
θεάομαι, v.d. *be a spectator,* v. 13.
θέλω. See ἐθέλω.
θεός ὁ, *god.*
θεράπων ὁ, -οντος, *servant.*
θερίζω, v.n. *spend the summer,* v.
15.
θέω, v.n. *run.*
θνήσκω, v.n., fut. θανοῦμαι, aor.
ἔθανον, pf. τέθνηκα, *die, be killed.*
θνητός, ἡ, όν, *liable to death ; easily
killed,* i. 23.
θόρυβος ὁ, *disorder, tumult.*
θυγάτηρ η, -τρός, *daughter.*
θυμόομαι, v.mid. *be angry.*
θύρα ἡ, *door.* αἱ θύραι, *the doors*
of the Great King's palace, i. 2.
θύω, v.a. *sacrifice;* mid. *have a
sacrifice offered,* i. 8, v. 18.
θωρακίζομαι, v. mid. *put on a
breastplate,* iv. 35.
θώραξ ὁ, *breastplate, cuirass,* iii. 20,
iv. 48.

ἰατρός ὁ, *physician.*
ἰδιώτης ὁ, -ου, *private person ; layman ; private soldier,* ii. 32.
ἵημι, v.a., fut. ἥσω, aor. ἧκα, pf.
εἷκα, *send ; shoot,* iv. 17 ; mid.
attack, iv. 41.
ἱκανός, ἡ, όν, *sufficient; competent,
able,* i. 23, iii. 18.
ἵνα, conj. *in order that* (with subj.
and opt.).
ἵππ-αρχος ὁ, *commander of cavalry,*
iii. 20.
ἱππεύς ὁ, *horseman;* plur. ἱππεῖς,
cavalry.

ἱππικός, ή, όν, *belonging to cavalry*, iv. 48.

ἵππος ὁ, *horse.*

ἰσόπλευρος, ον, *with equal sides*, iv. 19.

ἴσος, η, ον, *equal.* ἐξ ἴσου, *on equal terms*, iv. 47. ἴσως, adv. *equally, fairly; perhaps*, i. 24, 37.

ἵστημι, v. a., fut. στήσω, 1 aor. ἔστησα, *make to stand, make to halt, set up, place;* mid. (and 2 aor. ἔστην and pf. ἔστηκα), *stand, halt.*

ἰσχυρός, ά, όν, *strong.* ἰσχυρῶς, adv. *strongly, exceedingly.*

ἰσχύς ἡ, -ύος, *strength, force.*

ἰτέον, verbal adj. from εἶμι, *one must go*, i. 7.

καθ-ίζομαι, v.d., fut. -εδοῦμαι, *sit down.*

καθ-εύδω, v.n. *sleep.*

καθ-ήκω, v.n. *reach down*, iv. 24.

καθ-ίζω, v.a., fut. καθιῶ, *seat, place*, iv. 17.

καθ-ίστημι, v.a. *place, appoint*, ii. 5, iv. 30; of troops, *draw up;* mid. (and 2 aor. and pf. act.), *place oneself.*

καί, conj. *and; also, too*, i. 24, 34, ii. 37, iii. 1; *even, actually*, i. 17, ii. 22, 33, 35. καὶ—καί or τε—καί, *both—and.* καὶ—γε, *yes and*, ii. 24, iii. 5. καὶ—δέ, *yes and*, i. 25, ii. 24, 25. καὶ—γάρ, *for indeed, for also*, iii. 4, v. 2. καὶ μήν, *moreover*, i. 17.

καί-περ, conj. *although* (with participle).

καιρός ὁ, *opportunity, right time.* ἐν καιρῷ, *opportunely*, i. 39.

καίω, v.a., fut. καύσω, *burn.*

κακός, ή, όν, comp. κακίων, superl. κάκιστος, *bad, wicked, cowardly.*

κακόν τό, *misfortune, evil.* κακῶς, adv. *ill, wickedly.*

καλέω, v.a., fut. καλέσω or καλῶ, aor. ἐκάλεσα, pf. κέκληκα, *call, summon;* mid. *call for myself*, iii. 1.

καλός, ή, όν, comp. καλλίων, superl. κάλλιστος, *beautiful, noble, honourable; excellent*, ii. 34. καλῶς, adv., comp. κάλλιον, superl. κάλλιστα, *well, nobly.*

κάμνω, v.n., fut. καμοῦμαι, aor. ἔκαμον, pf. κέκμηκα, *be weary, toil.*

καρπόομαι, v.mid. *reap the fruit of, enjoy; plunder*, ii. 23.

καρπός ὁ, *fruit.*

κατά, prep.
 (1) with accus. *down, over, along*, iv. 30; *over against; at*, iv. 43; *according to*, idiomatic uses, ii. 9, 12, 13, iv. 22, v. 2, v. 8.
 (2) with gen. *down from, down over.*

κατα-βαίνω, v.n. *go down, descend*, v. 4.

κατά-βασις ἡ, *going down, descent*, iv. 37.

κατ-άγω, v.a. *bring down, bring home;* mid. *return home*, iv. 36.

κατα-δύω, v.n., fut. -δύσομαι, *sink*, v. 11.

κατα-θύω, v.a. *sacrifice*, ii. 12.

κατ-αισχύνω, v.a. *disgrace*, i. 30.

κατα-καίνω, v.a. *slay*, i. 2, ii. 12, 39.

κατα-καίω, v.a. *burn down.*

κατα-κεῖμαι, v.d. *lie down.*

κατα-κλείω, v.a. *shut up*, iii. 7.

κατα-κόπτω, v.a. *cut down*, v. 2.

κατα-λαμβάνω, v.a. *seize*, iv. 37; *overtake*, ii. 17, iv. 4, 32; *find*, i. 8.

κατα λείπω, v.a. *leave behind.*
κατα-μανθάνω, v.a. *understand thoroughly, observe,* i. 44.
κατα-πηδάω, v.n. *leap down.*
κατα-πίπτω, v.n. *fall down, be thrown down,* ii. 19.
κατα-πλήττω, v. a. *strike down,* iv. 12.
κατα-σκευάζω, v.n. *train, equip,* iii. 19; mid. *equip oneself, prepare,* ii. 24.
κατα-σκηνέω, v.n. *encamp,* iv. 32.
κατα-στρατοπεδεύομαι, v. mid. *form a camp,* iv. 18.
κατα-φρονέω, v.a. *despise,* i. 27.
κατ-έχω, v.a. *hold down, restrain.*
κεῖμαι, v.d., fut. κείσομαι, *lie; be laid, be set,* i. 21.
κελεύω, v.a. *order, command.*
κενός, ή, όν, *empty, groundless.*
κεντέω, v.a. *goad,* i. 29.
κεραμεοῦς, ᾶ, οῦν, *made of clay,* iv. 7.
κέρας τό, κέρατος, κέρως, *horn; wing* (of an army), iv. 19.
κεφαλή ή, *head.*
κηδεμών ό, -όνος, *protector,* i. 17.
κήρυξ ό, -υκος, *herald,* i. 46.
κηρύττω, v.a., fut. κηρύξω, *proclaim,* iv. 26.
κινδυνεύω, v. n. *be in danger,* iii. 11.
κίνδυνος ό, *danger.*
κινέω, v.a. *move.*
κογχυλιάτης ό, -ου, *shelly limestone,* iv. 10.
κοινός, ή, όν, *common.* κοινῇ, adv. *in common,* iii. 2.
κολάζω, v.a., fut. κολάσω, *punish.*
κομίζω, v.a., fut. κομιῶ, *carry, convey.*
κορυφή ή, *head, top, crest,* iv. 41.
κοσμέω, v.a. *arrange, marshal,* ii. 36.

κόσμος ό, *order, arrangement; dress,* ii. 7.
κρατέω, v.n. *be powerful, be conqueror;* with gen. *be master of, overcome.*
κράτιστος, η, ον (superl. of κρατερός), *strongest, chief; best,* iv. 41. κράτιστα, adv. *most stoutly,* ii. 6.
κραυγή ή, *shout, noise.*
κρείττων, ον (comp. of κρατερός), *stronger; better,* i. 4, ii. 17.
κρέμαμαι, v.d. *hang,* ii. 19.
κρηπίς ή, -ῖδος, *foundation, base,* iv. 7.
κριθή ή, *barley;* plur., iv. 31.
κρίνω, v.a., fut. κρινῶ, aor. ἔκρινα, pf. κέκρικα, *choose, decide.*
κτείνω, v.a., fut. κτενῶ, aor. ἔκτεινα, pf. ἔκτονα, *kill.*
κτῆνος τό, *possession;* plur. *cattle,* i. 19.
κύκλος ό, *circle.* κύκλῳ, *round about,* i. 2, 12, v. 14.
κύων ό, ή, κυνός, *dog.*
κωλύω, v. a. *hinder, prevent.*
κώμη ή, *village.*

λαγχάνω, v.a., fut. λήξομαι, aor. ἔλαχον, pf. εἴληχα, *obtain by lot, get* (with gen.), i. 11.
λακτίζω, v. a. *kick.*
λαμβάνω, v.a., fut. λήψομαι, aor. ἔλαβον, pf. εἴληφα, *take, seize, catch.*
λάμπω, v.n. and λάμπομαι, v. mid. *shine; blaze,* ii. 11.
λέγω, v.a., fut. λέξω, *say, speak; mean.*
λείπω, v. a., fut. λείψω, aor. ἔλιπον, pf. λέλοιπα, *leave.*
λήγω, v. n. *cease,* i. 9.
λίθινος, η, ον, *composed of stone,* iv. 7.

VOCABULARY.

λογίζομαι, v.d. *reckon, calculate.*

λόγος ὁ, *word, speech; narrative,* i. 1. **εἰς λόγους ἐλθεῖν,** *come to a conference,* i. 29.

λοιδορέω, v.a. *abuse, revile,* iv. 49.

λοιπός, ή, όν, *remaining.* λοιπόν (ἐστι), *it remains,* ii. 29. τὸ λοιπόν, *for the future,* ii. 8, 38; *during the rest (of the day),* iv. 6, 30. τὴν λοιπήν (sc. ὁδόν), *for the rest of the way,* iv. 46.

λόφος ὁ, *ridge, crest.*

λοχαγία ἡ, *captaincy,* i. 30.

λοχᾱγός ὁ, *captain* of a λόχος, i. 2, iv. 21.

λόχος ὁ, *company* of 100 foot-soldiers, iv. 22.

λυπέω, v.a. *hurt, annoy.*

λύπη ἡ, *pain, grief.*

λύω, v.a., fut. λύσω, *loose,* iv. 35; *break,* ii. 10; *be expedient,* iv. 36.

λωτο-φάγοι, *Lotus-eaters,* ii. 25.

λώων, λῷστος. See ἀγαθός.

μακαρίζω, v.a. *count happy, congratulate,* i. 19.

μακρός, ά, όν, *long.* μακράν (sc. ὁδόν) *for a long way,* iv. 17. μακρότερον, comp. adv. *with a longer range,* iv. 16.

μάλα, adv. *much, very;* comp. μᾶλλον, *more, rather;* superl. μάλιστα, *most, especially.*

μανθάνω, v.a., fut. μαθήσομαι, aor. ἔμαθον, pf. μεμάθηκα, *learn, find out.*

μαντεία ἡ, *prophecy, oracle,* i. 6.

μαρτυρέω, v.n. *bear witness* (with dat.), iii. 12.

μαστεύω, v.a. *seek after, desire,* i. 43.

μάστιξ ἡ, -ιγος, *whip.*

μάχη ἡ, *battle.*

μάχομαι, v.d., fut. μαχοῦμαι, *fight.*

μέγας, μεγάλη, μέγα, *great, important,* comp. μείζων, superl. μέγιστος. μεγάλως, adv. *greatly.* μείων, used as comp. of ὀλίγος, *fewer, less.* μεῖον ἔχειν, *have the disadvantage,* ii. 17, iv. 18.

μελετάω, v.a. *practise;* with infin., iv. 17.

μέλλω, (1) v.n. *be likely, be about to, intend,* i. 8, iii. 16, v. 17. (2) v.a. *intend, delay,* i. 46, 47.

μέν, particle, *indeed, on the one hand,* answered by δέ. In apodosis, i. 43. μὲν δή, see note on i. 10.

μέντοι, *however.*

μένω, (1) v.n. *remain, stay; remain in force.* (2) v.a. *wait for.*

μέρος τό, *part, share.* ἐν τῷ μέρει, *in their turn,* iv. 23.

μεσ-ημβρία ἡ, *mid-day; the South,* v. 15.

μέσος, η, ον, *middle.* ἐν μέσῳ, *in the middle,* i. 21; *between,* i. 2.

μεστός, ή, όν, *full* (with gen.), v. 1.

μετά, prep. (1) with accus. *after, next to,* i. 13, 45. (2) with gen. *with.*

μετα-δίδωμι, v.a. *give a share,* iii. 1.

μεταξύ, (1) adv. *in the middle,* i. 26; *meanwhile.* (2) prep. (with gen.), *between,* iv. 37.

μετα-πέμπω, v.a. *send after;* mid. *send for,* i. 14.

μέτ-εστι, v.impers. *there is a share* (with dat. of person and gen. of thing), i. 20.

μέτρον τό, *measure.*

μέχρι, (1) conj. *until* (with indic.), iv. 8.
(2) prep. *as far as* (with gen.), i. 1.

μή, neg. particle, *not; do not; lest,* after verbs of fearing, etc. See also notes on i. 5, ii. 25, v. 3, 11. μὴ οὐ, see notes on i. 12, 13.

μηδέ, conj. *nor, not even.*

μηδείς, μηδεμία, μηδέν, *not one, none.*

μηδέ-ποτε, adv. *never.*

μήν, particle, *verily, indeed.* ἀλλὰ μήν, *however.*

μή-ποτε, adv. *never.*

μή-πω, adv. *not yet.*

μή-τε, conj. *neither, nor.*

μικρός, ά, όν, *small, little.* μικρόν, adverbial neut. accus. *a little,* i. 11.

μιμέομαι, v.d. *imitate.*

μιμνήσκω, v.a., fut. μνήσω, *remind;* mid. *remember,* pf. μέμνημαι, i. 27.

μισθός ό, *reward, pay.*

μνημεῖον τό, *memorial,* ii. 13.

μόλις, adv. *scarcely, with difficulty.*

μολυβδίς ή, -ίδος, *leaden bullet,* iii. 17.

μόλυβδος ό, *lead,* iv. 17.

μόνος, η, ον, *alone, only.* μόνον, adv. *only.*

μυριάς ή, -άδος, *the number of ten thousand,* v. 16.

μύριοι, αι, α, *ten thousand.*

μῶρος, α, ον, *foolish.*

νέος, α, ον, *young, new.*

νεῦρον τό, *sinew; cord,* iii. 4.

νεφέλη ή, *cloud.*

νικάω, v.a. *conquer; be conqueror,* i. 2, ii. 13.

νίκη ή. *victory.*

νομή ή, *pasture; herd,* v. 2.

νομίζω, v.a., fut. νομιῶ, *think, consider.*

νοῦς ό, *mind, sense, attention.*

νύκτωρ, adv. *by night,* iv. 35.

νῦν, adv. *now.* νῦν δέ, *but as it is.* τὸ νῦν εἶναι, see note on ii. 37.

νύξ ή, νυκτός, *night ;* plur. νύκτες, *night watches,* i. 33.

ξένιος, α, ον, *hospitable.* Ζεὺς ξένιος, *Zeus god of strangers,* ii. 4.

ξένος ό, *stranger ; guest-friend,* i. 4.

ξεστός, ή, όν, *polished,* iv. 10.

ὁ, ή, τό, article, *the ;* also used as demonstr. pron., e.g. οἱ μὲν—οἱ δέ, *the one—and the other,* iv. 16. τῇ μὲν—τῇ δέ, *partly—partly,* i. 12. ὅδε, ἥδε, τόδε, demonstr. pron., *this, this one here.*

ὁδο-ποιέω, v.a. *make a road,* ii. 24.

ὁδός ή, *way, road, march.*

οἱ, dat. (enclitic) of reflexive pron. ἕ, gen. οὗ, *himself,* iv. 42.

οἶδα, perf. with pres. meaning, *know,* plup. ᾔδειν, fut. εἴσομαι.

οἴκαδε, adv. *homewards.*

οἰκεῖος, α, ον, *belonging to the house, related, intimate,* ii. 26.

οἰκέω, (1) v.a. *inhabit,* ii. 23.
(2) v.n. *dwell,* ii. 24, v. 15.

οἰκία ή, *house.*

οἰκο-δομέω, v.a. *build.*

οἴκοθεν, adv. *from home.*

οἶκος ό, *house, home.*

οἰκτείρω, v.a. *pity.*

οἶνος ό, *wine.*

οἴομαι, contr. οἶμαι, v.d. *think.*

VOCABULARY.

95

οἷος, α, ον, *what kind of; such as.*
οἷός τε, *able; possible,* iii. 9, 15.
οἴχομαι, v. d. *be gone, be off,* iii.
5; *be lost,* i. 32.
οἰωνός ὁ, *bird; omen,* ii. 9.
ὀκτώ, indecl. *eight.*
ὀκτω-καί-δεκα, indecl. *eighteen.*
ὀλίγος, η, ον, *small;* plur. *few.*
ὀλισθάνω, v. n. *slip,* v. 11.
ὅλος, η, ον, *whole.*
ὅμηρος ὁ, *hostage,* ii. 24.
ὁμιλέω, v. n. *associate with* (with dat.).
ὄμνυμι, v. a., fut. ὀμοῦμαι, aor. ὤμοσα, pf. ὀμώμοκα, *swear.*
ὁμοῖος α, ον, *like;* with infin. v. 13.
ὁμο-μήτριος ον, *born of the same mother,* i. 17.
ὁμόσε, adv. *to one place, together,* iv. 4.
ὁμο-τράπεζος ον, *sitting at the same table,* ii. 4.
ὅμως, conj. *nevertheless.*
ὄναρ τό, *dream,* i. 11.
ὄνομα τό, -ατος, *name.*
ὄνος ὁ, ἡ, *ass.*
ὅπῃ, adv. *in whatever way, how; where.*
ὄπισθεν, adv. *behind.*
   (1) of place, *in the rear.* τοὔπισθεν, *the rear,* iii. 10.
   (2) of time, *after.*
ὀπισθο-φυλακέω, v. a. *guard the rear, bring up the rear,* ii. 36.
ὀπισθο-φύλαξ ὁ, -ακος, *one who guards the rear,* iii. 7.
ὁπλίτης ὁ, -ου, *heavy-armed soldier.*
ὅπλον τό, *weapon;* gen. in plur. ὅπλα, *arms; the place where the arms were piled,* i. 3, 33; *hoplites, heavy-armed troops,* ii. 36, iii. 7, iv. 26.
ὁπόθεν, adv. *whence,* i. 32.

ὁποῖος, α, ον, *of what sort, whatever.*
ὁπόσος, η, ον, *how great, as much as;* plur. *as many as.*
ὁπόταν, conj. *whenever* (with subj.).
ὁπότε, conj. *whenever* (with ind. and opt.) ; *now that, since,* ii. 2, 15, 16.
ὁπότερος, α, ον, *which of two,* i. 21.
ὅπου, adv. *where.*
ὅπως, (1) adv. *as; how,* i. 14, ii. 27.
   (2) conj. *that, in order that* (with subj. and opt.).
ὁράω, v. a., fut. ὄψομαι, aor. εἶδον, pf. ἑώρακα, *see, perceive.*
ὀρθῶς, adv. *rightly.*
ὅρκος ὁ, *oath.*
ὁρμάω, act. *set in motion;* neut. *start,* i. 8, iv. 33, 44; pass. and mid. *start, set out, hasten,* ii. 24.
ὁρμή ἡ, *impulse,* ii. 9 ; *attack,* i. 10.
ὁρμίζω, v. a. *anchor,* v. 10.
ὄρος τό, *mountain;* gen. plur. uncontr. ὀρέων, iv. 19, v. 15.
ὅς, ἥ, ὅ, (1) relative pron. *who, which.* See note on i. 17.
   (2) demonstr. pron. (rare), *he.* See note on iv. 48.
ὅσος, η, ον, *how great, as great as;* plur. *how many, as many as.* ὅσον, adv. *as much as, about* (with numerals), iv. 37.
ὅσ-περ, ἥπερ, ὅπερ, relative pron. *who, which.*
ὅσ-τις, ἥτις, ὅ τι, *who, whosoever; he who, in as much as he,* ii. 4.
ὅ τι, sometimes *why* (indirect).
ὅταν, conj. *whenever* (with subj.).
ὅτε, conj. *when.*
ὅτι, conj. *that; because.* ὅτι

πλεῖστοι, as many as possible, i. 45.

ὅτου, ὅτῳ, gen., dat. (contr.) of ὅστις.

οὐ (οὐκ, οὐχ), neg. particle, *not*.

οὗ, adv. *where*.

οὐδαμοῦ, adv. *nowhere*.

οὐδέ, conj. *nor; nor yet*, i. 15, 27; *not even*, ii. 4.

οὐδ-είς, οὐδεμία, οὐδέν, *no one, none*. οὐδέν, also adv. *not at all*.

οὐκ-έτι, adv. *no longer*.

οὖκ-ουν, adv. *not therefore*, v. 6.

οὖν, particle, *therefore, then*.

οὔ-ποτε, adv. *never*.

οὔ-πω, adv. *not yet*.

οὐρά ή, *tail; rear* (of an army), iv. 38.

οὖς τό, ὠτός, *ear*.

οὔτε, conj. *neither, nor*.

οὗτος, αὕτη, τοῦτο, demonstr. pron. *this*. On its 'deictic' force see note on v. 9.

οὕτω (οὕτως), adv. *thus, so*.

ὀχέω, v. a. *carry;* pass. *be carried, ride*, iv. 47.

ὄχημα τό, *carriage, conveyance*, ii. 19.

ὄχλος ὁ, *throng*, esp. of camp-followers, ii. 36, iii. 6, iv. 26; *annoyance, trouble*, ii. 27.

ὀψέ, adv. *late*.

ὄψομαι. See ὁράω.

παιανίζω, v. n. *sing a paean or war-song*, ii. 9.

παῖς ὁ, ἡ, παιδός, *child, boy*.

παίω, v. a. *strike, wound*.

παλαιός, ά, όν, *ancient, old*. τὸ παλαιόν, adverbial, *in old times*, iv. 7.

πάλιν, adv. *back*, i. 6; *again*.

παμ-πληθής, ές, *very numerous*, ii. 11.

πάμ-πολυς, -πόλλη, -πολυ, *very much, very many*, iv. 13.

παντάπασι, adv. *wholly, altogether*, i. 38, iv. 26. οὐ παντάπασι, *not at all*, i. 31.

πάντῃ, adv. *on every side*.

πάντοθεν, adv. *from every side*.

πάνυ, adv. *altogether, very*.

πάομαι, v.d., fut. πάσομαι, *acquire;* pf. πέπαμαι, *possess*, iii. 18.

παρά, prep.
   (1) with accus. *to the side of, to; alongside of*, i. 32, iv. 8, v. 1; *beyond, contrary to*, ii. 10.
   (2) with gen. *from the side of, from*, iv. 8.
   (3) with dat. *at the side of, near, with*, iii. 19.

παρ-αγγέλλω, v.a. *pass orders along* (the line), iv. 3, 14, v. 18.

παρα-γίγνομαι, v.d. *come up to, come to help*, iv. 38.

παρ-άγω, v. a. *lead along-side, wheel round*, iv. 14; absolute, *march along-side*, iv. 21.

παρα-δίδωμι, v.a. *deliver up*.

παρα-θαρρύνω, v.a. *encourage*, i. 39.

παρα-καλέω, v.a. *summon*, i. 32; *exhort*, i. 38; Attic fut. παρακαλῶ, i. 24.

παρα-κελεύω, v.a. and mid. *encourage*, iv. 46.

παρ-ακολουθέω, v.n. *accompany*.

παρασάγγης ὁ, *parasang*, a Persian measure; N.B. not a fixed unit of measurement, but varying according to the character of the country traversed. See note on iv. 7.

παρα-σκευάζω, v.a. *prepare, provide*.

παρα-σκηνέω, v.n. *encamp beside*, i. 28.

πάρ-ειμι, v.n. *be present, be at one's side* (εἰμί).

πάρ-ειμι, v.n. *pass by, advance* (εἶμι), ii. 35, iv. 48.

παρ-ελαύνω, v.a. *drive past;* absolute, *drive* or *ride past,* iv. 46, v. 4.

παρ-έρχομαι, v.d. *pass.*

παρ-έχω, v.a. *provide, offer,* v. 9; *render, cause,* i. 18, ii. 27.

παρθένος ἡ, *maiden.*

παρ-ίημι, v.a. *send past, let pass.*

πᾶς, πᾶσα, πᾶν, *all, every.* ἐπὶ πᾶν, *to extremities,* i. 18.

πάσχω, v.a., fut. πείσομαι, aor. ἔπαθον, pf. πέπονθα, *experience, suffer; be treated,* i. 41, ii. 3.

πάτριος, α, ον, *ancestral,* ii. 16.

πατρίς ἡ, -ίδος, *fatherland.*

πατρῷος, α, ον, *hereditary,* i. 11.

παύω, v.a. *stop, make to cease;* mid. *cease,* i. 19.

πεδίον τό, *plain.*

πεζός, ἡ, όν, *on foot.* οἱ πεζοί, *infantry.* πεζῇ, adv. *on foot,* iv. 49.

πείθω, v.a., fut. πείσω, aor. ἔπεισα, pf. πέπεικα, *persuade;* 2 pf. πέποιθα, and mid. *obey, trust* (with dat.).

πεῖρα ἡ, *attempt, trial.*

πειράω and πειράομαι, *attempt, make trial of,* ii. 38, v. 7.

πείσομαι. See πάσχω.

πελταστής ὁ, -οῦ, *peltast, targeteer,* armed with the πέλτη, iii. 8.

πέμπτος, η, ον, *fifth.*

πέμπω, v.a., fut. πέμψω, aor. ἔπεμψα, pf. πέπομφα, *send.*

πένομαι, v.d. *be poor,* ii. 26.

πεντακόσιοι, αι, α, *five hundred.*

πέντε, indecl. *five.*

πεντήκοντα, indecl. *fifty.*

πεντηκοντήρ ὁ, -ῆρος, *commander of fifty,* iv. 21.

πεντηκοστύς ἡ, -ύος, *band of fifty, half-company,* iv. 22.

περαίνω, v.a. *accomplish,* i. 47, ii. 32.

πέραν, (1) adv. *on the other side,* v. 12.
(2) prep. *beyond* (with gen.), v. 2.

περί, prep.
(1) with accus. *around,* v. 7; *concerning,* ii. 20; *about* (of time and number).
(2) with gen. *about, concerning,* ii. 15. περὶ πλείστου, *at a very high rate,* ii. 4.

περι-γίγνομαι, v.d. *overcome,* ii. 29.

περί-ειμι, *be superior, get the best of it,* iv. 33.

περί-οδος ἡ, *circuit,* iv. 7.

περιττός, ἡ, όν, *excessive, superfluous,* ii. 28, iii. 1.

περί-φοβος, ον, *very frightened,* i. 12.

πηγή ἡ, *spring, source,* ii. 22.

πιέζω, v.a. *press, press hard,* iv. 48.

πίπτω, v.n., fut. πεσοῦμαι, aor. ἔπεσον, pf. πέπτωκα, *fall.*

πιστεύω, v.n. *trust* (with dat.).

πίστις ἡ, *trust; loyalty,* iii. 4.

πιστός, ἡ, όν, *faithful.* τὰ πιστά, *pledges,* ii. 5.

πλάγιος, α, ον, *sideways.* τὰ πλάγια, *flanks,* iv. 14.

πλαίσιον τό, *oblong, rectangle,* ii. 36, iv. 19.

πλατύς, εῖα, ύ, *broad.*

πλέθρον τό, *plethrum,* Greek measure of length, one sixth of a stade, 100 Greek feet = 101 English.

πλεῖστος, η, ον ⎫
πλείων, ον   ⎬ See πολύς.
πλέκω, v.a., fut. πλέξω, *plait*, iii. 18.
πλεονεκτέω, v.n. *have an advantage* (with gen.), i. 37.
πλευρά ἡ, *side, flank*, ii. 36, iv. 22.
πλευρόν τό, *side, flank*.
πλῆθος τό, *multitude*.
πλήν, (1) prep. *except* (with gen.), i. 10.
(2) adv. *except*.
(3) conj. *except that*, i. 26.
πλήρης, ες, *full* (with gen.), v. 1.
πλησίον, adv. *near*. ὁ πλησίον, *the neighbouring*, iv. 9.
πλίνθινος, η, ον, *made of brick*, iv. 11.
πλίνθος ἡ, *brick*, iv. 7.
πλούσιος, α, ον, *rich*.
ποδίζω, v.a. *fasten, hobble*, iv. 35.
πόθος ὁ, *yearning, regret*, i. 3.
ποιέω, v.a. *make, render, do;* mid. *make for one's self ; consider*, ii. 4. κακῶς ποιεῖν, *injure*, ii. 5.
ποιητέος, α, ον, verbal adj. *to be done*.
ποῖος, α, ον, *of what kind?*
πολεμικός, ή, όν, *belonging to war, apt for war*, v. 16. τὰ πολεμικά, *warlike matters*, i. 38.
πολέμιος, α, ον, *hostile* , subst. *enemy*. ἡ πολεμία (sc. χώρα), *the enemy's country*, iii. 5.
πόλεμος ὁ, *war*.
πολιορκέω, v.a. *besiege*.
πόλις ἡ, *city, state*.
πολιτεύω, v.n. *live as a citizen, be a citizen*, ii. 26.
πολλάκις, adv. *often*.
πολλαπλάσιος, α, ον, *many times as great*, ii. 16; with gen. ii. 14.
πολυάνθρωπος, ον, *populous*.

πολύς, πολλή, πολύ, comp. πλείων, v. 17; superl. πλεῖστος, *much; great*, see note on ii. 36 ; plur. *many*. οἱ πολλοί, *the many, the majority*. πολύ, *far, considerably*, ii. 15, ii. 30. ἐκ πολλοῦ, *with a long start*, iii. 9. περὶ πλείστου, *of the greatest importance*, ii. 4. ὡς ἐπὶ τὸ πολύ, *for the most part*, i. 42.
πονέω, v.n. *toil, suffer*.
πονηρός, ά, όν, *wicked, bad, wretched*, iv. 35. πονηρῶς, adv. *badly*.
πόνος ὁ, *toil*.
πορεία ἡ, *journey, march*, i. 5, iv. 36.
πορεύω, v.a. *convey;* mid. and pass. *go, march*.
πορίζω, v.a., fut. πορίω, *provide, supply;* mid. *provide for one's self*, i. 20.
πόρρω or πρόσω, adv. *forwards; far*, ii. 22, iv. 35.
ποταμός ὁ, *river*.
πότε, adv. *when?*
ποτε, enclitic, *at some time, ever*.
πότερος, α, ον, interrogative, *which of two*. πότερον and πότερα, conj. *whether* (answered by ἤ, or), i. 7.
ποτόν τό, *drink*.
ποῦ, adv. *where?*
που, enclitic, *somewhere*, ii. 24; *somehow*.
πούς ὁ, ποδός, *foot*.
πρᾶγμα τό, -ατος, *thing, matter*.
πρανής, ές, *downhill*, iv. 25.
πράττω, v.a., fut. πράξω, aor. ἔπραξα, pf. πέπραχα, *do, perform;* intrans. *fare* (2 pf. πέπραγα), i. 6, iv. 6.
πρέπω, v.n. *be conspicuous; be fitting* (with dat.), ii. 7.

πρεσβεύω, v. n. *go as envoy.*

πρέσβυς ὁ, *old man;* plur. πρέσβεις, *ambassadors;* comp. πρεσβύτερος, superl. πρεσβύτατος.

πρίαμαι, v. d. *buy,* i. 20.

πρίν, (1) adv. *before, formerly.*
　(2) conj. *before that, until,* i. 16.

πρό, prep. *before, in front of* (with gen.).

προ βαίνω, v. n. *go forward, advance.*

πρόβατον τό, *sheep.*

προ-βουλεύω, *plan beforehand; plan better than* (with gen.), i. 37.

πρό-γονος ὁ, *ancestor.*

προ-δίδωμι, v. a. *betray, forsake.*

πρό-ειμι, v. n. *go forward* (εἶμι).

προ-έρχομαι, v. d. *go forward.*

προ-έχω, (1) v. a. *hold before.*
　(2) v. n. *have the advantage of* (with gen. or absolute), ii. 19.

προ-θυμέομαι, v. d. *be eager; urge,* i. 9.

πρό-θυμος, ον, *eager.* προθύμως, adv. *eagerly.*

προ-ίημι, v. a. *send before, send forward.*

προ-καλύπτω, v. a. *cover in front.*

προ-κατα-λαμβάνω, v. a. *seize beforehand,* v. 18.

προ-πονέω, v. n. *toil for; work harder than,* i. 37.

πρός, (1) prep.
　(1) with accus. *to, towards; against; with a view to.*
　(2) with gen. *from; on the side of,* i. 5; *by* (in adjurations), i. 24.
　(3) with dat. *close to; at; in addition to,* ii. 33, iv. 13.
　(II) adv. *besides,* ii. 2.

προσ-δοκάω, v. n. *expect.*

προσ-δοκέω, v. n. *seem good besides,* ii. 34.

πρόσ-ειμι, v. n. *approach, attack* (εἶμι).

προσ-ελάυνω, v. a. *drive up to;* absolute, *ride up,* iv. 39, v. 13.

προσ-έρχομαι, v. d. *come to.*

προσ-ήκει, v. impers. *it belongs to* (with dat. of person and gen. of thing), i. 31, ii. 11.

πρόσθεν, (1) adv. *before* (both of time and place). ὁ πρόσθεν, *previous; that which is in front,* ii. 36.
　(2) prep. (both of time and place) *before.*

προσ-ίημι, v. a. *send to; admit;* mid. *admit to one's company,* i. 30.

προσ-κυνέω, v. a. *do obeisance to, worship,* ii. 9, 13.

πρόσω. See πόρρω.

πρότερος, α, ον, *before, earlier, former.*

προφασίζομαι, v. d. *plead as an excuse,* i. 23.

προ-φυλακή ἡ, *outpost.*

προ-φύλαξ ὁ, *advanced guard.*

πρωΐ or πρῴ, adv. *early,* comp. πρωΐαίτερον or πρῳαίτερον, iv. i.

πρῶτος, η, ον, *first; foremost.* πρῶτον, adv. *first, in the first place.*

πτάρνυμαι, v. d. *sneeze,* ii. 9.

πυνθάνομαι, v. d., fut. πεύσομαι, aor. ἐπυθόμην, pf. πέπυσμαι, *learn, hear of.*

πῦρ τό, πυρός, *fire.*

πυραμίς ἡ, -ίδος, *pyramid,* iv. 9.

πω, enclitic, *some time, yet.* πώποτε, adv. *even yet.*

πῶς, adv. *how?*

πως, enclitic, *in any way; somehow,* i. 26.

ῥᾴδιος, α, ον, *easy;* comp. ῥᾴων,
   superl. ῥᾷστος. ῥᾳδίως, adv.
   easily.
ῥᾷστος, η, ον. See ῥᾴδιος.
ῥίπτω or ῥιπτέω, v. a., fut. ῥίψω,
   throw, hurl, iii. 1.
ῥῦμα τό, *drawing* (of a bow), *bow-
   shot,* iii. 15.
ῥώμη ἡ, *strength; military force,*
   iii. 14.

σάλπιγξ ἡ, -ιγγος, *trumpet.*
σατραπεύω, v. n. *act as satrap*
   (with gen.), iv. 31.
σατράπης ὁ, -ου, *satrap,* Persian
   viceroy, v. 16.
σαφής, ές, *clear, sure.*
σαφῶς, adv. *clearly.*
σημαίνω, v. a., fut. σημανῶ, aor.
   ἐσήμηνα, *signify; give a signal,*
   iv. 4.
σίνομαι, v. d. *damage,* iv. 16.
σῖτος ὁ, *corn; food;* plur. σῖτα
   τά, *provisions.*
σκεδάννυμι, v. a., fut. σκεδῶ, aor.
   ἐσκέδασα, *scatter,* v. 2.
σκευή ἡ, *equipment.*
σκεῦος τό, *vessel;* plur. *baggage,*
   i. 30.
σκευο-φορέω, v. n. *carry baggage,*
   ii. 28.
σκευο-φόρος, ον, *carrying baggage.*
   οἱ σκευοφόροι, *porters,* ii. 28.
   τὰ σκευοφόρα, *baggage animals,*
   iii. 19.
σκηνή ἡ, *tent, hut.* σκηναί,
   quarters generally, v. 7.
σκηπτός ὁ, *squall; thunderbolt,*
   i. 11.
σκοπέω, v. a., fut. σκέψομαι, aor.
   ἐσκεψάμην, pf. ἔσκεμμαι, *view,
   consider;* intrans. *watch, spy.*
σπένδομαι, v. mid., fut. σπείσομαι,
   make a treaty (lit. *pour a libation*

for oneself; cf. σπονδή), v. 5,
   16.
σπεύδω, (1) v. a. *urge on.*
   (2) v. n. *hasten,* iv. 49.
σπολάς ἡ, *leather cuirass, buff
   jerkin,* iii. 20.
σπονδή ἡ, *libation;* plur. σπονδαί,
   truce, treaty.
στάδιον τό (plur. στάδιοι οἱ), *stade*
   =600 Greek feet or 606 English
   (lit. *race-course*), i. 2.
σταθμός ὁ, *halting-place, encamp-
   ment; stage, day's march,* iv.
   10.
στέλλω, v. a., fut. στελῶ, aor.
   ἔστειλα, *send; arrange; equip,*
   ii. 7.
στενός, ή, όν, *narrow,* comp.
   στενότερος, superl. στενότατος,
   iv. 19, 22.
στέρομαι, v. d. *be deprived of, lack*
   (with gen. of thing), ii. 2.
στερρῶς, adv. *stiffly, sternly,* i. 22.
στόλος ὁ, *armament; march,* i. 9.
στόμα τό, -ατος, *mouth; front,
   van* (of an army), iv. 22.
στρατεία ἡ, *expedition.*
στράτευμα τό, -ατος, *army.*
στρατεύω, v. n. and στρατεύομαι,
   v. mid. *serve as a soldier, march,
   go on an expedition,* i. 10, 17.
στρατηγέω, v. n. *be a general, command* (with gen., or absolute);
   metaphorical, *regulate,* ii. 27.
στρατηγός ὁ, *general.*
στρατιά ἡ, *army.*
στρατιώτης ὁ, -ου, *soldier.*
στρατοπεδεύομαι, v. d. *encamp.*
στρατόπεδον τό, *camp; army.*
στρέφω, v. a., fut. στρέψω, *turn.*
σύ, personal pron. *thou, you.* σύ-
   γε, *you at least.*
συγ-καλέω, v. a. *call together.* Attic
   fut. συγκαλῶ, i. 46.

συγ-κατα-καίω, v.a. *burn down at the same time,* ii. 27.

συγ-κύπτω, v.n. *bend together,* iv. 19.

συλ-λαμβάνω, v.a. *seize,* i. 35.

συλ-λέγω, v.a. *collect.*

συμ-βαίνω, v.n. *come together, agree; happen,* i. 13.

συμ-βάλλω, v.a. *throw together, collect,* iv. 35.

συμ-βουλεύω, v.a. *give advice, counsel,* i. 5; mid. *ask advice, consult.*

σύμ-μαχος, ον, *allied.* σύμμαχος ὁ, *ally.*

συμ-πολεμέω, v.n. *fight along with.*

συμ-προ-θυμέομαι, v.d. *be eager together with; join in urging,* i. 9.

συμ-φέρω, (1) v.a. *bring together,* iv. 31.
 (2) v.n. *be expedient* (with dat.), ii. 27.

σύν, prep. with dat.
 (1) *together with,* i. 2, iii. 1, iv. 32.
 (2) *with the aid of,* i. 23, 42, ii. 8, 16 (rare in Attic Prose except in Xen.).

συν-άγω, v.a. *bring together, collect.*

συν-αιρέω, v.a. *seize together; make short,* i. 38.

συν-ακολουθέω, v.n. *follow along with.*

σύν-ειμι, v.n. *come together* (εἰμι), v. 7.

συν-επ-εύχομαι, v.d. *join in prayer with, join in a vow with,* ii. 9.

συν-έπομαι, v.d. *follow along with.*

συν-έρχομαι, v.d. *come together, meet.*

συν-εφ-έπομαι, v.d. *follow up along with.*

συν-ίστημι, v.a. *place together, bring together, introduce,* i. 8.

συν-ωφελέω, v.a. *join in helping.*

συ-σκευάζω, v.a. and συσκευάζομαι, v.mid. *pack up,* iv. 36, v. 18.

σφενδονάω, v.n. *sling,* iii. 15, 16.

σφενδόνη ἡ, *sling,* iii. 18.

σφενδονήτης ὁ, -ου, *slinger,* iii. 6.

σχεδόν, adv. *near; nearly.*

σχολή ἡ, *leisure.* σχολῇ, *leisurely; scarcely,* iv. 27.

σῴζω, v.a., fut. σώσω, pf. σέσωκα, *save; bring in safety,* i. 6, ii. 4.

σῶμα τό, -ατος, *body.*

σῶος contr. σῶς, σώα, σῶον contr. σῶν, *safe.*

σωτήρ ὁ, *saviour, preserver.*

σωτηρία ἡ, *safety.*

σωτήριος, ον, *saving,* iii. 2. Subst. τὰ σωτήρια, *thank-offerings for safety,* ii. 9.

τάλαντον τό, *talent,* a sum of money = 60 minae = about £230, v. 8.

ταξίαρχος ὁ, *taxiarch, commander of a τάξις,* i. 37.

τάξις ἡ, *rank, line of battle, array.*

ταράττω, v.a., fut. ταράξω, *confuse.*

τάττω, v.a., fut. τάξω, aor. ἔταξα, pf. τέταχα, aor. pass. ἐτάχθην, *draw up, arrange,* ii. 36, iii. 18; *order,* i. 25.

ταύτῃ, adv. *in this way,* ii. 33.

ταχύς, εῖα, ύ, *quick,* comp. θάττων, superl. τάχιστος. Adverbial neut. accus. ταχύ, *quickly.* ταχέως, adv. *quickly.*

τε, conj. enclitic, *both, and.*

τέθριππον τό, *four-horse chariot,* ii. 24.

τεῖχος τό, *wall; fort,* iv. 10.

τεκμήριον τό, *sign, proof.*
τελέθω, v. n. *become, be,* ii. 3.
τελευτάω, v. a. *end; absolute, come to an end, die,* i. 1, ii. 7.
τελευτή ἡ, *end, death,* ii. 7.
τελέω, v. a., fut. τελῶ, aor. ἐτέλεσα, *finish; pay,* iii. 8.
τέταρτος, η, ον, *fourth.*
τετρακ.σ.χίλιοι, αι, α, *four thousand.*
τετρα-κόσιοι, αι, α, *four hundred.*
τέτταρες, α, *four.*
τῇ. See ὁ.
τήμερον, adv. *to-day.*
τί, interrogative particle, *why?*
τίθημι, v. a., fut. θήσω, aor. ἔθηκα, pf. τέθεικα, *place;* mid. *place for oneself.*
τιμάω, v. a. *honour.*
τιμή ἡ, *honour; value.*
τις, τι, indefinite pron. enclitic, *some one, some, a.* τι, *in some way,* i. 5, 37.
τίς, τί, interrogative pron. *who? what?* τί, *why?*
τιτρώσκω, v. a., fut. τρώσω, aor. ἔτρωσα, pf. τέτρωκα, *wound.*
τλήμων, ον, *miserable.*
τοι, particle enclitic, *you know, truly, indeed,* i. 18, 37.
τοίνυν, particle, *therefore, then,* i. 36.
τοιοῦτος, -αύτη, -οῦτο, *such.*
τολμάω, v. a. *dare.*
τ.ξευμα τό, -ατος, *arrow.*
τοξεύω, v. a. *shoot with a bow.*
τόξον τό, *bow.*
τοξότης ὁ, -ου, *archer.*
τοσοῦτος, -αύτη, -οῦτο(ν), *so great, so much;* plur. *so many.*
τότε, adv. *then, at that time; on the previous occasion,* iv. 20.
τοὔμπαλιν. See ἔμπαλιν.
τοὔπισθεν. See ὄπισθεν.

τρεῖς, τρία, *three.*
τρέπω, v.a., fut. τρέψω, aor. ἔτρεψα, *turn; put to flight;* mid. *turn oneself,* v. 13; *flee;* pf. partic. pass. τετραμμένος, *facing,* v. 15.
τρέφω, v.a., fut. θρέψω, pf. τέτροφα, pf. pass. τέθραμμαι, *nourish, rear.*
τριάκοντα, indecl. *thirty.*
τρισ-άσμενος, η, ον, *thrice-glad,* ii. 24.
τρίτος, η, ον, *third.*
τρόπαιον, τό, *trophy,* ii. 13.
τρόπος ὁ, *way, manner; character.*
τρυπάω, v. a. *bore, pierce,* i. 31.
τρωτός, ή, όν, verbal adj. from τιτρώσκω, *vulnerable, easy to wound,* i. 23.
τυγχάνω, v. n., fut. τεύξομαι, aor. ἔτυχον, pf. τετύχηκα, *hit, meet with, obtain* (with gen.), i. 26, ii. 19; *happen; happen to be,* i. 3. τυγχάνω λέγων, *happen to be saying,* ii. 10.
τῷ = τινί. See τις.

ὑβρίζω, fut. ὑβριῶ.
 (1) v. a. *insult, outrage,* i. 13.
 (2) v. n. *be insolent.*
ὕβρις ἡ, -εως, *insolence, outrage,* i. 13.
ὕδωρ τό, -ατος, *water; rain.*
ὕλη ἡ, *wood, timber.*
ὑμεῖς, plur. of σύ.
ὑπ-άγω, v. a. *lead on;* absolute, *advance,* iv. 48.
ὑπ-αίτιος, ον, *liable to accusation,* i. 5.
ὑπ-ανα-χωρέω, v. n. *retire gently,* v. 13.
ὕπ-ειμι, v. n. *be under,* iv. 7.
ὑπέρ, prep.
 (1) with accus. *beyond, over.*

VOCABULARY. 103

(2) with gen. *above*, iv. 29; *on behalf of*, v. 6.

ὑπερ-βολή ἡ, (1) *superiority, excess*. (2) *crossing over, passage*, v. 18.

ὑπερ-δέξιος, ον, *above on the right*, iv. 37.

ὑπερ-έχω, (1) v. a. *hold above*. (2) v. n. *be above, rise above*, v. 7.

ὑπερ-ύψηλος, ον, *exceedingly high*, v. 7.

ὑπ-ηρετέω, (1) v. n. *serve* (with dat.). (2) v. a. *supply*, v. 8.

ὑπ-ηρέτης ὁ, -ου, *servant, helper*, lit. *under-rower* (ἐρέτης).

ὑπ-ισχνέομαι, v. d., fut. ὑποσχήσομαι, aor. ὑπεσχόμην, pf. ὑπέσχημαι, *promise*.

ὕπνος ὁ, *sleep*.

ὑπό, prep. (1) with accus. *under* (motion to); *under* (extension along), iv. 37. (2) with gen. *from under; by* (agent); *from* (cause), i. 3; accompaniment, iv. 25. (3) with dat. *under* (rest under), iv. 24.

ὑπο-ζύγιον τό, *beast of burden*, lit. *animal under the yoke* (ζυγόν), iii. 6.

ὑπο-λαμβάνω, v. a. *catch up, interrupt*, i. 26.

ὑπο-μένω, (1) v. n. *stay behind*, iv. 21. (2) v. a. *wait for*.

ὑπό-πεμπτος, ον, *sent secretly*, iii. 4.

ὑπ-οπτεύω, v. a. *suspect;* with accus. of the thing, *view with suspicion*.

ὑπο-στράτηγος ὁ, *lieutenant-general*, I. 32.

ὑπο-φαίνω, v. a. *show under, show slightly;* intrans. *shine slightly, break* (of the day), ii. 1.

ὑπο-χείριος, ον, *under the hand, subject*, ii. 3.

ὑστεραῖος, α, ον, *belonging to the next day.* ἡ ὑστεραία (sc. ἡμέρα), *the next day*, iii. 20.

ὕστερον, adv. *after, afterwards*.

ὕστερος, α, ον, *later; behind, in the rear*, iv. 21. Superl. ὕστατος.

ὑφ-ίημι, v. a. *give up*, v. 5; mid. *yield on self*, i. 17, ii. 3.

ὑφ-ίστημι, v. a. *place under;* mid. (and 2 aor. and pf. act.) *undertake; resist*, ii. 11.

ὑψηλός, ή, όν, *high*. τὸ ὑψηλόν, *the high ground*, iv. 25.

ὕψος τό, *height*.

φαίνω, v. a., fut. φανῶ, aor. ἔφηνα, 2 pf. πέφηνα (intrans.), aor. pass. ἐφάνην, *show;* intrans. *give light;* mid. and pass. *be shown, appear*.

φάλαγξ ἡ, -γγος, *line of battle* (to be distinguished from the Macedonian plalanx); *main body*, iii. 11, iv. 23.

φανερός, ά, όν, *visible, manifest;* with partic., ii. 24. φανερῶς, adv. *clearly*.

φάσκω, v. a. *say*.

φέρω, v. a., fut. οἴσω, aor. ἤνεγκον, pf. ἐνήνοχα, *bear, bring;* intrans. of roads, *lead*, v. 15.

φεύγω, v. a. and n., fut. φεύξομαι or φευξοῦμαι, aor. ἔφυγον, pf. πέφευγα.

φημί, v. a., fut. φήσω, *say*.

φθάνω, v. a., fut. φθάσω or φθήσομαι, aor. ἔφθασα or ἔφθην, pf. ἔφθακα, *anticipate, be beforehand*, iv. 20, 49.

φιλία ἡ, *friendship.*
φίλος, η, ον, *beloved, dear;* subst.
  φίλος ὁ, *friend.*
φλυαρέω, v.n. *talk nonsense,* i. 26.
φοβερός, ά, όν, *fearful, terrible.*
φοβέω, v.a. *frighten;* mid. and
  pass. *fear, be afraid.*
φόβος ὁ, *fear.*
φρόνημα τό, *high spirit, confidence,*
  i. 22.
φυγή ἡ, *flight.*
φυλακή ἡ, *guard, watch, outpost,*
  i. 40.
φύλαξ ὁ, -ακος, *guard.*
φυσάω, v.a. *inflate,* v. 9.
φωνή ἡ, *voice.*
φῶς τό, *light.*

χαλεπός, ή, όν, *hard, severe, cruel,*
  i. 13.
χαλεπῶς, adv. *hardly, cruelly.*
χαλινόω, v.a. *bridle,* iv. 35.
χαράδρα ἡ, *mountain torrent, ra-*
  vine, iv. 1.
χαρίεις, εσσα, εν, *graceful, charm-*
  ing, v. 12.
χάρις ἡ, -ιτος, *favour, thanks,*
  gratitude, iii. 14.
χείρ ἡ, χειρός, *hand.*
χειρο-πληθής, ές, *filling the hand,*
  iii. 17.
χίλιοι, αι, α, *a thousand.*
χίμαιρα ἡ, *she-goat,* ii. 12.
χράομαι, v.d., pres. inf. χρῆσθαι,
  fut. χρήσομαι, *use, enjoy* (with
  dat.).
χρή, v. impers., imp. ἐχρῆν, inf.
  χρῆναι, *it is necessary, it behoves,*
  one ought.
χρῄζω, v.n. *desire.*
χρῆμα τό, -ατος, *thing;* plur. *goods,*
  property, money.

χρήσιμος, η, ον, *useful.*
χρόνος ὁ, *time.*
χρυσός ὁ, *gold.*
χώρα ἡ, *country, district; position,*
  iv. 33.
χωρίον τό, *place, position.*
χωρίς, adv. *separately, apart.*

ψεύδω, v.a., fut. ψεύσω, *deceive;*
  mid. *speak falsely, lie;* pass. *be*
  deceived, ii. 31.
ψηφίζομαι, v.mid. *vote.*
ψιλός, ή, όν, *bare.* οἱ ψιλοί, *light-*
  armed troops, iii. 7.
ψυχή ἡ, *soul, life.*
ψῦχος τό, *cold;* plur., i. 23.

ὦ, interj. *oh!*
ὧδε, adv. *thus, as follows.*
ὠθέω, v.a., fut. ὤσω, *push;* mid.
  push out of one's way, iv. 48.
ὠνέομαι, v.d. *buy.*
ὥρα ἡ, *season, proper time; time,*
  v. 18.
ὡς, (1) adv. *how; as; as if;* with
  numerals, *about,* iii. 1, 5.
  (2) conj. *when, since; that*
  (introducing statements); *in or-*
  der that (with subj. and opt.);
  so that (with infin. =ὥστε), iii. 7,
  iv. 25. ὡς εἰπεῖν, *so to speak,*
  i. 38.
  (3) prep. *to* (with accus., of
  persons only).
ὥς, adv. *thus.* οὐδ' ὥς, *not even*
  thus, ii. 23.
ὡσ-αύτως, adv. *in like manner.*
ὥσ-περ, adv. *just as.*
ὥστε, conj. *so that* (with indic.
  or infin.), iii. 14, iv. 13, 21, 48.
ὠφελέω, v.a. *help, benefit.*

LIST OF UN-ATTIC WORDS.

The following words which occur in the Third Book of the Anabasis are not found in any other Attic Prose writer:—

ἀλέξω, iv. 33.
ἀξιοστράτηγος, i. 24.
ἐρύκω, i. 25.
κατακαίνω, i. 2, ii. 12, 39.
λύω, in sense of 'profit,' iv. 36.
μαστεύω, i. 43.
πάομαι, iii. 18.
τελέθω, ii. 3.
τρισάσμενος, ii. 24.
χειροπληθής, iii. 17.

INDEX OF PROPER NAMES.

the modern Kurdistan. v. 15, 17. See Map of Route.
Κιλικία ἡ, *Cilicia*, district in the south-east of Asia Minor. i. 10. See Map of Route.
Κλεάνωρ, *Cleanor*, of Orchomenus; one of the Greek Generals. i. 47, ii. 4, 8.
Κλέαρχος, *Clearchus*, of Sparta; chief of the Greek Generals till his seizure by Tissaphernes. i. 10, 47, ii. 4, 31. See Introduction, §§ 2, 4, 5.
Κρής, Κρητός, *Cretan*, i.e. belonging to Crete, island at the south of the Aegean. iii. 7, 15, iv. 16
Κῦρος, *Cyrus*, son of Darius, i. 1, etc. See Introduction, §§ 2—4.

Λακεδαιμόνιος, *Lacedaemonian*, belonging to Lacedaemon or Sparta. ii. 1, 37.
Λάρισσα, *Larissa*, the modern Nimroud. iv. 7. See Map of Route.
Λυδία, *Lydia*, district on the west coast of Asia Minor. v. 15. See Map of Route. **Λυδός**, *Lydian*. i. 31.
Λυκάων, -ονος, *Lycaonian*, i.e. belonging to Lycaonia, district in the middle of Asia Minor. ii. 23. See Map of Route.
Λύκιος, *Lycius*, native of Athens; cavalry officer in the Greek army. iii. 20.

Μένων, *Menon*, of Pharsalus in Thessaly; one of the Greek Generals. i. 47.
Μέσπιλα, *Mespila*, the modern Kouyunjik. iv. 10. See Map of Route.
Μήδεια, *Medeia*, a Median Queen. iv. 11.
Μηδία, *Media*. v. 15. See Map of Route.
Μῆδος, *Mede*, i.e. belonging to Media. ii. 25, iv. 7.

Μιθραδάτης, *Mithradates*, satrap of Cappadocia and Lycaonia; formerly a friend of Cyrus. iii. 1, 6, iv. 2.
Μυσοί, *Mysians*, inhabitants of Mysia, the north-western district of Asia Minor. ii. 23. See Map of Route.

Νίκαρχος, *Nicarchus*, of Arcadia; captain in the Greek army. iii. 5.

Ξανθικλῆς, έους, *Xanthicles*, of Achaia; one of the Greek Generals. i. 47.
Ξενοφῶν, *Xenophon*. i. 4, etc. See Introduction (throughout).
Ξέρξης, *Xerxes*, King of Persia, who invaded Greece. ii. 13, iii. 6.

Ὀρόντας, *Orontas*, son-in-law of King Artaxerxes; satrap of Eastern Armenia. iv. 13, v. 17.
Ὀρχομένιος, *of Orchomenus*, town in Arcadia. ii. 4.

Πέρσης, -ου, *a Persian*. ii. 11, 25, etc.
Περσικός, *belonging to the Persians*. iii. 16, iv. 17, 35.
Πισίδαι, *Pisidians*, a mountain people between Cilicia and Lycia. i. 9, ii. 23. See Map of Route.
Πρόξενος, *Proxenus*, of Thebes; one of the Greek Generals. i. 4, sqq., i. 47. See Introduction, § 3.

Ῥόδιος, *Rhodian*, i.e. belonging to Rhodes, island off the coast of Caria. iii. 16, iv. 15, v. 8. See Map of Route.

Σάρδεις αἱ, *Sardis*, capital of Lydia. i. 8. See Map of Route.

Σικνώνιος, *Sicyonian*, i.e. belonging to Sicyon. iv. 47.

Σκύθης, -ου, *Scythian*, i.e. belonging to Scythia. iv. 15.

Σοῦσα τά, *Susa*, winter and spring residence of the Great King, on the east of the river Choaspes. v. 15.

Σοφαίνετος, *Sophaenetus*, of Stymphalus, a Greek General. v. 37.

Στυμφάλιος, *Stymphalian*, native of Stymphalus, town in Arcadia. i. 31.

Σωκράτης, *Socrates*, (1) an Athenian; the celebrated philosopher. i. 5. See Introduction, § 1. (2) an Achaean, one of the Greek Generals. i. 47.

Σωτηρίδας, *Soteridas*, of Sicyon;

a soldier in the Greek army. iv. 47.

Τίγρης, *the Tigris*. iv. 7, v. 1. See Map of Route.

Τιμασίων, *Timasion*, of Dardanus; one of the Greek Generals. i. 47, ii. 37.

Τισσαφέρνης, *Tissaphernes*, satrap of Caria. i. 1, etc. See Introduction, §§ 2, 4, 5.

Τολμίδης, *Tolmides*, of Elis; a herald. i. 46.

Φιλήσιος, *Philesius*, of Achaia; one of the Greek Generals. i.47.

Χειρίσοφος. *Cheirisophus*, of Sparta; one of the Greek Generals. i. 45, ii. 1, 33, 37, etc.

GRAMMATICAL INDEX.

asyndeton, i. 3, ii. 33, 38, iv. 25.
  elliptical, ii. 2, 4, v. 12.
  mixed, i. 11.
  pregnant, iv. 11, 45.
INFINITIVE:
  after γιγνώσκω, i. 43.
  after ὁμοῖος, v. 13.
  after ὡς, iii. 7, iv. 25.
  limitative, i. 38, ii. 17.
  with ἄν, i. 17, 38, ii. 3.
MIDDLE VOICE:
  causal use, i. 8, ii. 26, v. 18.
  reflexive use, iv. 36, 45.
MOODS:
  Optative:
    attracted, ii. 36.
    conditional, iv. 35.
    frequentative, i. 20, 32, iii. 10, iv. 17, 28.
    pure, ii. 3.
    quasi-imperatival, ii. 37.
  Subjunctive:
    after εἰ(?), ii. 22.
    conditional, iv. 35.
    deliberative, i. 14.
    vivid use, iv. 34.
NEGATIVES:
  See *Vocabulary* under οὐ and μή.
  accumulation of, i. 10, 38.
ORATIO OBLIQUA:
  ἄν with optative in, ii. 12.
  imperf. indic. in, i. 2, iii. 12.
  indicative and optative combined, iii. 12.
  transition in, iii. 12.
  vivid constructions, i. 6, 9, iv. 2, v. 13, 18.
PARTICIPLE:
  denotes concession, i. 10, 22, ii. 5.
  denotes condition, i. 2.

denotes manner, i. 13.
denotes reason, i. 34, iii. 7, iv. 26, 27.
future, denotes purpose, i. 17, 24.
imperfect, ii. 4, 5.
stress of sentence on, i. 6, ii. 26, iv. 35.
with εἰμί, iii. 1.
PARTICLES:
  See *Vocabulary* under various Particles.
  omission of connecting particle, ii. 33, 38.
PREPOSITIONS:
  See *Vocabulary* under various Prepositions.
PRONOUNS:
  demonstrative, in 'deictic' sense, v. 9.
  relative, attracted, i. 6, ii. 21, 33.
  „ antecedent omitted, i. 21, iv. 5.
  „ irregular relative sentences, i. 17, ii. 5.
SUBJECT:
  omission of, iv. 4, 36.
TENSES:
  Aorist:
    force of, i. 12, iii. 5, iv. 15.
    infinitive with ἄν, ii. 17.
  Future:
    i. 13, ii. 23, iv. 39.
  Imperfect:
    i. 12, ii. 4, 17, iii. 5, iv. 2, 8, 11, 15, 38.
    with ἄν, ii. 23, iv. 22.
  Perfect:
    force of, i. 21, ii. 19.
  Present:
    infinitive, denoting *attempt*, i. 29.